The Sporting News PRESENTS

The Ballpark Book

By Ron Smith ◆ Illustrations by Kevin Belford

Photo Credits

T = Top   B = Bottom   L = Left   R = Right   M = Middle

TSN Archives—Cover, 10, 14, 15(2), 16(3), 17(2), 25(2), 32(2), 35, 36, 40, 41(2), 42, 43, 44(2), 45T, 50, 51, 63, 64, 75(2), 95, 96, 97B, 100(2), 101(2), 102T, 113T, 114-115, 120, 121(3), 122, 150, 189(2),199, 200, 201, 205(2), 208, 209, 210, 211, 213, 216, 217(2), 218(4), 219, 222(2), 223, 224, 225(3), 232, 233, 234, 235L, 235R, 238(2), 239(3), 241(2), 242L, 246(4), 249, 252(2), 256, 257(3), 258(2), 259, 260, 261, 264, 265, 266, 267(3), 272, 273, 274(2), 278, 279, 280L, 280R, 281T, 281B.

Albert Dickson/The Sporting News—26, 27B, 28(2), 29, 44R, 45B, 94(2), 97T, 112, 113(2), 153, 158(2), 165L, 165R, 168, 169, 170, 171(3), 195, 239T, 240(3), 242-243.

Robert Seale/The Sporting News—37, 90, 102(2), 103, 140, 141, 142(2), 143(2), 151, 152, 159, 193B, 194TL, 194R, 247, 248.

Bob Leverone/The Sporting News—65, 68B, 70, 146, 147, 162L, 162R, 163, 284, 285(2).

Dilip Vishwanat/The Sporting News—33.

Corbis Bettmann/UPI—56, 57, 62, 63, 69, 88L, 89, 107, 123, 132, 134, 135, 275, 298, 300B.

AP/Wide World—18, 19(2), 38, 58R, 68T, 75M, 164, 178T, 183T, 193T, 299, 300T, 301.

Library of Congress—11, 12, 13, 268, 269.

Cleveland Press Collection of Cleveland State University—228.

John Cordes—51, 52, 53.

Fred Vuich—106R, 108, 109, 133.

John Dunn—25TR, 27T.

Elsa Hasch/Allsport—58L.

Mike Powell/Allsport—59.

John Ferry/Allsport—82TR, 82B.

Otto Greule Jr./Allsport—74, 76, 77.

Jonathan Daniel/Allsport—88R, 156.

Jed Jacobsohn/Allsport—82TL.

Ezra Shaw/Allsport—71.

Brian Bahr/Allsport—175.

Scott Halleran/Allsport—182.

Peter Taylor/Allsport—182B.

Vincent Laforet/Allsport—9, 80, 178, 179.

Zoran Milich/Allsport—174.

Phillip Norton/Montreal Gazette—127, 128.

Dave Sidaway/Montreal Gazette—129B.

Andre Pichette/Montreal Gazette—129T.

Peter Newcomb—32L.

Scott Rovak—106, 126.

Ken Kerr/Toronto Sun—294.

Paul Henry/Toronto Sun—295.

Paul Tepley—24.

Louis DeLuca—194BL.

Frank Bryan—102

Jason Wise—83.

Jay Crihfield—34.

All photos used on top of ballpark illustrations are TSN Archives except as noted.

AP/Wide World—54 (Hershiser), 55 (Gibson)

Corbis Bettmann/UPI—214 (Riot)

Janice Rettaliata—190 (Horner)

ISBN: 0-89204-633-3

10 9 8 7 6 5 4 3 2

Acknowledgements

Any book-creation process is a team effort, filled with important contributions from knowledgeable research sources and those people who plan, edit, proofread, gather, process, design and assist in ways too countless to list. Many dedicated people, both inside and outside the office of *The Sporting News*, participated in preparation of *The Ballpark Book*, often providing valuable insight and assistance in addition to their regular weekly obligations.

The book's direction and concept reflect in large part the vision of executive editor Steve Meyerhoff, who oversaw the project, assisted with the editing, compiled information boxes and provided much-needed understanding and encouragement. The special photographs that give the book depth and relevance reflect the determination and hard work of TSN chief photographer Albert Dickson and the quality reproduction of those photos reflect the abilities of prepress specialist Steve Romer.

The book's design, a collaborative effort by prepress director Bob Parajon and creative director Bill Wilson, was executed by a talented team that included Becky Carr, Michael Behrens, Angie Pillman, Christen Webster, Matt Kindt, Beth Carter and Amy Beadle. Romer received assistance from prepress specialists David Brickey, Jack Kruyne and Vern Kasal.

Many contributions were made to the editorial process, starting with the insights of senior editor Joe Hoppel, a longtime student of ballparks and the games people play there, and the proofreading efforts of associate editor Dave Sloan. The book would have suffered without the knowledge of specific parks offered by staffers Carl Moritz, Bob Hille, Sean Deveney, Steve Gietschier, Mike Nahrstedt and Steve Siegel. Many TSN baseball correspondents also contributed, including Luciana Chavez (Kauffman Stadium), Marc Topkin (Tropicana Field), Mike Berardino (Pro Player Stadium), Stephanie Myles (Olympic Stadium), Henry Schulman (Candlestick Park), Tom Maloney (SkyDome), Susan Slusser (the Oakland Coliseum), Mike DiGiovanna (Anaheim Stadium), Larry LaRue (the Kingdome), John Mehno (Three Rivers Stadium), Chris Edwards (Veterans Stadium) and Tom Krasovic (Jack Murphy Stadium).

A special thanks to TSN executives Kathy Kinkeade and John Rawlings, who provided physical and emotional support for the project, and to everyone at *The Sporting News*, who exemplified the essence of the word "team" by picking up the workload of others to allow this project to move forward. Thanks, also, to Stew Thornley, who shared memories about Minnesota's Metropolitan Stadium and the Metrodome, Rodney Johnson, who helped with Bank One Ballpark in Phoenix, and TSN librarian Jim Meier, who was always ready, willing and able to assist with critical research needs.

◆ ◆ ◆

As you read this book, there no doubt will be questions about the way we refer to particular ballparks, most notably those that in recent years have sold corporate naming rights. Our rule of thumb was simple, albeit subjective: We refer to ballparks by their most commonly known name over the course of their history. So in this book, Cincinnati's park remains Riverfront Stadium, even though it now is officially known as Cinergy Field.

Table of Contents

Ballparks
Now, yesterday and forever

Of course you remember. The crack of the bat and the snap of ball hitting glove are as vivid today as they were 20 years ago when you attended your first major league game. Or 5 years ago. Or 40. Maybe you sat in the bleachers at Fenway Park, the outfield grandstand at old Ebbets Field, next to the center field clubhouse at the Polo Grounds or in the Jury Box at Braves Field. Of course you remember.

You remember the smells, of the hot dogs that always taste better here than anywhere else, roasted peanuts with shells you can throw right on the floor, food-stained concourses, beer, factories and railroad yards beyond the fences, grass—the real, honest-to-goodness natural stuff, like what you have in your front yard. You remember the excited chatter of fans and the sounds of vendors, distinctive public address announcers, umpires making their calls, wild cheers and frustrated, heartfelt boos from people who obviously care.

You remember your heroes, larger than life in victory, painfully human in defeat, and the anticipation you feel before the game and the sadness you feel when it's over. You remember the explosion of green when you spot the field and the comforting sense of camaraderie, pride, fun, excitement and exultation after you sit down. You remember yelling and screaming, as loud as you want, and crying, without fear of ridicule or painful embarrassment.

Of course you remember. A ballpark is personal, it's sensual and it's filled with soul-stirring magic. It's a special place, a special time in your life, a feeling you may never recapture, a bond that can never be broken. A ballpark defines the timeless fascination we have for a game and fills voids in our lives. It's now, it's yesterday and it's forever.

◆ ◆ ◆

Life in late 19th-century America was not about feelings, emotions and soul-stirring magic. It was about an agrarian, working-class society with little leisure time and only a moderate appetite for sporting diversions. Baseball was growing in popularity, but it also was waging a difficult battle against its own reputation as a rowdy, pugilistic sport played by unsavory characters and watched by unciv-ilized fans who often behaved violently. The gentility that might normally have been attracted to the sport was repulsed.

The baseball venues in this context were little more than open fields with hastily erected wooden stands—maybe dugouts, but seldom a clubhouse and few amenities beyond the joy of watching the local nine in action. Fields, like the teams that played there, were transient and fragile. A team could disappear in the blink of an eye; a field could disappear in a puff of smoke.

Such was the evolution of baseball that the stage upon which it was played

Ballparks like Messer Field in Providence, R.I. (circa 1878) featured wooden grandstands and view-obstructing pillars. In the early 1900s, wood gave way to steel.

seemed inconsequential and fleeting. That would change. As baseball turned the corner on the 20th century and the nation took important steps toward industrialization, the sport began cleaning up its act and became more deeply rooted in neighborhood and community life. So did the ballpark, which became a place to congregate, socialize and get away from the daily grind.

The profile of an early 20th-century major league ballpark focused on the basics: wood based with small grandstands; located on the edge of big-city development; strategically placed on a trolley or subway line, opening up access beyond the immediate neighborhood; usually single-decked; sometimes enclosed, but often an open outfield roped off to viewers; little or no ornamentation; small seating capacities often expanded with temporary bleachers when needed.

Into this profile fit such early parks as Philadelphia's Baker Bowl and Columbia Park, New York's Polo Grounds and Hilltop Park, Pittsburgh's Exposition Park, Brooklyn's Washington Park, Chicago West Side Grounds and South Side Park, Boston's Huntington Avenue Grounds and South End Grounds, Cincinnati's Palace of the Fans, Detroit's Bennett Park, Washington's American League Park and St. Louis' Sportsman's Park.

The Baker Bowl, which served as home for the Phillies from 1887-1938, was an early architectural example of cantilever construction and its home plate grandstand was made of steel and concrete. The early Polo Grounds featured an unusually aggressive double-deck grandstand with prominent Y-shaped support posts spaced about 15 feet apart. The first World Series, with Boston fans ringing the outfield, was decided at Huntington Avenue Grounds in 1903. The entire 1906 fall classic, the Cubs vs. the White Sox, was played in Chicago.

Baseball's formative years were filled with stories of ballparks burning to the ground and being resurrected in short order. That certainly was a factor in the

great ballpark building boom that started in 1909 and set the standard by which future facilities would be judged. But there also were other forces at work. A healthier, wealthier society was interested in expanding its sports horizons and wide-eyed major league owners were only too willing to offer their help.

The result was an explosion of large, fireproof, multi-decked ballparks that could help fuel baseball's rising popularity while providing a regional identity for the teams and their fans. Not only were they constructed entirely out of steel and concrete, they were attractive, inviting, amenity-filled arenas that gave new meaning to watching baseball. And new meaning to the profitable way baseball could be packaged.

Detroit fans ring the open outfield during Game 5 action between the Tigers and Cubs in the 1907 World Series.

Philadelphia's Shibe Park, home of the Athletics, was hailed as the crown jewel of baseball when it opened its gates for the first time on April 12, 1909. Its dignified French Renaissance dome, which towered over the intersection of 21st and Lehigh, was flanked by arched windows and entryways that led fans into a marvelously clean ballpark with folding-chair seats, underground garages and restrooms manned by attendants and matrons. This Ben Shibe-Connie Mack production was first class.

So was Forbes Field, which opened 11 weeks later in Pittsburgh and featured baseball's first luxury boxes—a covered row of seats that stretched from one end of its double-deck grandstand roof to the other. It didn't take long for other owners to take heed. Charles A. Comiskey opened sparkling new Comiskey Park for his Chicago White Sox in 1910, Boston's Fenway Park, Cincinnati's Redland Field (later Crosley) and Detroit's Navin Field (later Tiger Stadium) opened in 1912, Brooklyn's Ebbets Field made its debut in 1913, Boston's Braves Field opened in 1915 and Chicago's Wrigley Field, a former Federal League stronghold built in 1914, played host to its first National League game in 1916.

Joining the parade were the Polo Grounds and Washington's Griffith Stadium, both of which were rebuilt into steel-and-concrete facilities in 1911 after destructive fires. Cleveland's League Park was converted to Shibe-like building standards in 1910.

The profile of these classic-era ballparks is familiar to the 21st-century fan: entirely steel and concrete; baseball-only facilities; often double-decked behind the plate, from first base to third, with single decks down both lines; seats close to the field; some sight-obstructing posts; larger seating capacities with room to expand; large scoreboards, occasionally electric but mostly manual; attractive and fan-friendly—charming.

Charm and charisma were not goals of early century ballpark builders, who were looking for form, function and more fans to stream through their turnstiles. But their idiosyncratic originals would become ballpark masterpieces, wonderful accidents of creation that would transcend time in the hearts and memories of their fans. For many, a Shibe Park or Wrigley Field would be the only ballpark

they would know in their lifetime. For most, that would be just fine.

Nothing defined that charm more than the ballpark's relationship with the community, and city, of which it was a part. These were urban centers tucked into a neighborhood like a hand into a glove—in some cases, a very tight one. Invariably, team owners bought their land and drew up ballpark blueprints to correspond to the irregular contours of streets, homes, businesses and railroad yards that might surround it. No two were alike and fans became accustomed to such quirky nuances as angled and concave outfield fences, unexpected inclines, 33-foot screens and fair-territory bullpens.

Because the left field at Fenway Park backed up to Lansdowne Street only 300-plus feet from home plate, a huge wall would be needed to compensate for the short home run distance. Because the Polo Grounds was built between an existing ballpark and a bluff in 1891, it took on an elongated shape that resulted in the biggest center field in baseball. Because the owner of five Washington D.C. duplexes refused to sell, Griffith Stadium was constructed with a center field wall that indented around the obstacles. Oddly shaped Crosley Field was a product of the strangely angled streets that circled its perimeter. And all were subject to the local whims of Mother Nature.

Schoolboy Rowe, an outstanding pitcher who worked in most of the major league parks that existed in the 1930s and '40s, offered this thought in an interview published in 1948.

"Ballparks are individuals to me, not just so much stone, concrete and steel,"

The Miracle Braves, not the Red Sox, were a World Series attraction for Boston fans at Fenway Park in 1914 (above). Note how fans were crammed into temporary bleachers in front of what would become the left field Green Monster. Giants and Phillies players inspect rubble from the Polo Grounds fire of 1911 (left), from which ashes rose the modern-day Polo Grounds.

the former Tigers, Dodgers and Phillies star said. "They are like a lot of old ladies with varying temperaments. You have to study them, go along with their whims on certain days. They are all built differently, dressed differently, react differently to rain, sunshine, fog, wind."

They also were cozy and intimate—and all promoted a special relationship between players and fans.

Players often lived near the ballpark and became family extensions of the community. Fans would see them shopping at the store, eating in a local restaurant. Gil Hodges married a Brooklyn woman and became a fulltime resident of Flatbush, and many of his Dodgers teammates also lived there. Baseball became an intricate part of the Brooklyn fabric, much like it did in other major league cities.

"Brooklyn was a town that lived and died with the Dodgers," said Phil Rizzuto, a Brooklyn native who went on to baseball fame with the New York Yankees. "When the Dodgers were playing, you could walk up and down the streets of Brooklyn and never miss a pitch. Everybody had the game on the radio. It meant so much to them."

Contact also was possible at the ballpark, where a player's path from clubhouse to field often would lead right through the stands—or maybe even the concourse where fans would gather to greet and encourage him. Fans could hear the field chatter of players and coaches during games; players, like it or not, could hear the opinions and ravings of nearby fans. It was a personal experience, equal parts uplifting and humbling.

The 1909 ballpark boom would carry Americans through the deadball era, the Roaring '20s, the Great Depression and two World Wars—a long, memorable period of growth and stability in baseball. For half a century beginning in 1903, the major league franchise alignment remained frozen in time. And for much of that period, those franchises remained committed to the ballparks they called home. Changes, renovations and improvements kept them modern and fan-

Yesterday: Ballparks, like Hilltop Park in New York, weren't the grand edifices of today.

friendly, but nobody was foolish enough to mess with the quirks and personalities that made them special.

After Braves Field opened in 1915, ballpark construction virtually stopped for the next four decades—with two notable exceptions. The first, in 1923, would affect the very essence of the game.

Through the deadball era of Ty Cobb, Walter Johnson, Christy Mathewson, Eddie Collins and Tris Speaker, ballpark dimensions were irrelevant. Most outfields were expansive, set up to encourage gap hitters. That changed with the rise to prominence of a round-faced, pitcher-turned outfielder who demonstrated an amazing ability to hit the ball farther and more frequently than anybody who had played before him. When Babe Ruth, a former Baltimore orphan with a flair for the dramatic, was sold by the Boston Red Sox to New York Yankees in 1920, major league ballparks entered the first stage of what would become a serious identity crisis.

Ruth's arrival helped the game survive the stain of a 1919 World Series scandal and ushered in a new era of prosperity. He pounded 54 home runs in 1920, almost double his previous single-season record, 59 in 1921, 35 in 1922—inconceivable numbers that would draw new waves of fans through the turnstiles. Suddenly, there wasn't a ballpark big enough to hold his towering blasts and opposing teams rushed to find big, powerful hitters who could match his feats. The Yankees, who had been forced to play in the shadow of the Giants at the Polo Grounds since 1913, decided it was time to build their own showcase ballpark, tailored to fit their young star, in the South Bronx, just across the Harlem River from the Polo Grounds. The House That Ruth Built was bigger, grander and more spectacular than anything fans had ever seen.

Yankee Stadium was exactly that—a stadium, massive, imposing and able to seat more than 70,000 fans. New Yorkers marveled at its architecture and attention to ornamental detail. Early visitors called it a cathedral and, with Ruth and Lou Gehrig leading the charge, it would become the greatest of all baseball shrines and the home of more championship teams than any park before or after.

The only other newcomer to the major league scene in the first half century was another monster—Cleveland's huge, hulking Municipal Stadium, which played host to its first game in 1932. It, too, was large and imposing, able to seat 75,000-plus, but it couldn't match Yankee Stadium's class and charisma. Municipal was barren and hollow, so large that Cleveland officials played their weekday schedules at tiny League Park, which was much less expensive to operate. Municipal was limited to weekend and holiday games for more than 15 years.

It was only three years after the debut of Municipal Stadium, in the shadow of the Great Depression, that ballpark evolution took another giant leap for-

Forever: Ebbets Field, (above) opened to much fanfare in 1913 and remains a special memory for Brooklyn fans; Crosley Field (left) hosted baseball's first night game.

Time was when the ballpark experience was about community, where parks, like Crosley Field, were cut into neighborhoods, and where fans, like those in 1920 Brooklyn (right), dined in the streets and in Boston (below), contributed gifts to players.

ward. When Cincinnati general manager Lee MacPhail installed lights at Crosley Field and staged the first night game in major league history in 1935, he, like Ruth more than a decade earlier, changed the course of history. Night games increased attendance and helped baseball regain its footing after the depression and World War II. Soon it would be expanding its horizons beyond anyone's wildest dreams.

With more efficient automobiles carrying fans to the suburbs, improved air travel triggering a population shift west and the power of television turning the national pastime into a bottom line-oriented

When baseball went West, temporary parks with less-than-ideal playing conditions were used, like the Los Angeles Memorial Coliseum, with its short left field screen.

enterprise, the first chink in baseball's long stability appeared in 1953 when the Boston Braves moved operations to Milwaukee and County Stadium, a longtime minor league facility. The St. Louis Browns became the Baltimore Orioles a year later and moved into Memorial Stadium and the Philadelphia A's took refuge in Kansas City's Municipal Stadium in 1955. Owners suddenly were searching for more fertile markets—fertile as in big. The ballpark business really exploded in 1957 when the Dodgers and Giants, New York staples since the beginning of baseball time, announced their shocking plans to move to Los Angeles and San Francisco.

The Giants spent their first two California seasons at tiny Seals Stadium, another minor league facility, and the Dodgers suffered through four years at the Los Angeles Memorial Coliseum—a 93,000-seat football stadium that had been converted (awkwardly) for baseball. When the Giants moved into new Candlestick Park in 1960, they introduced the first of 20 parks that would become permanent major league home bases over an expansion-filled 18-year period.

One was beautiful Dodger Stadium, a baseball-only gem that opened in 1962 in the hills overlooking Los Angeles. But it was merely a mirage. Most of the newcomers were big, round, sterile, symmetrical, concrete structures that focused on amenities and comfort at the expense of intimacy and atmosphere. With population centers shifting to the suburbs, so did the new ballparks. Most were located in open areas, often surrounded by massive parking lots. Without neighborhood contours to dictate shape, they often were devoid of personality.

By the late 1950s, old favorites Braves Field, League Park and Ebbets Field were gone. By the early 1960s, Griffith Stadium and the Polo Grounds had been cast aside. Sportsman's Park, Shibe Park, Forbes Field and Crosley Field soon would be thrown out like memorabilia from the attic. In their place were the new-wave ballparks, dedicated to technology and comfort and the almighty bottom line. The new buzzword was multi-purpose, as in multiple sports and events that provided year-round revenue streams.

Candlestick Park was a stadium pioneer, the first to be built entirely with reinforced concrete and unobstructed sightlines. It was at first a baseball-only facility located on scenic Candlestick Point overlooking the San Francisco Bay, but it would eventually become a prime example of multi-purpose. Like such followers as the Oakland Coliseum, Anaheim Stadium and Jack Murphy Stadium in San Diego, it would succumb to the lure of the National Football League, substantially increase its seating capacity to accommodate a team and eventually enclose

Seattle's ballpark experience spans the generations, from the departed Kingdome and the Dome Era, to Safeco Field (above) and the New Wave Era.

its once-open outfield, creating a sterile, concrete bowl.

Houston's Astrodome, which was introduced as the Eighth Wonder of the World in 1965, took the multi-purpose concept a step further. Fans marveled at the thought of baseball indoors and they weren't disappointed. They were amazed at its luxury, its size, its state-of-the-art scoreboard and that green carpet it introduced to the world—labeled, appropriately, AstroTurf. They also were shocked at the advanced technology and climate control it introduced to the game. While traditionalists winced, many fans embraced the idea of symmetrical baseball without interference from wind, heat, cold, fog or any other whim of Mother Nature.

The next domed stadium would not appear for another dozen years (Seattle's Kingdome in 1977), but many of the Astrodome's innovations were embraced by outdoor facilities. Technology and luxury were two, but artificial turf was the most important.

When St. Louis' Busch Stadium opened in 1966, nobody entertained any baseball-only illusions—this was absolutely, unequivocally, a multi-purpose stadium. Round, fully enclosed and multiple-decked with retractable seats for football,

Busch provided the mold for what would eventually be known as the cookie-cutter stadiums—bowl-like, concrete, artificial turf-covered look-alikes that sprang up in Atlanta, Cincinnati, Pittsburgh and Philadelphia.

Because those parks were designed to accommodate both football and baseball, they lacked the intimacy of their predecessors and never allowed a close relationship between players and fans. Seats were free of obstructions, but they often were far away from the action and not angled toward home plate, another football concession. While football might draw 60,000-plus crowds, baseball attendance often averaged only a third of capacity, giving the stadium a hollow, empty feel. Owners relied on technology, gimmicks and promotions to freshen up a sterile atmosphere.

Ambience was not a consideration during this booming expansion, when the major league roster increased from 16 teams (1960) to 26 (1977) and introduced baseball to fans in such cities as Montreal, Toronto, Houston, Dallas-Fort Worth, Minneapolis, San Diego, Anaheim, Oakland, Seattle and Atlanta. Small ballparks like Colt Stadium (Houston), Jarry Park (Montreal) and Wrigley Field (Los Angeles) often served as warmups while bigger, fancier stadiums were being constructed.

When Toronto's SkyDome, a veritable indoor baseball city, opened in 1989, that signaled the end of another era. With player salaries spiraling out of sight and teams searching frantically for new sources of revenue, they began aligning with corporate sponsors and appealing to the nostalgia craze sweeping the nation. Jack Murphy changed its name to Qualcomm Stadium, Anaheim became Edison International Field, Riverfront changed to Cinergy Field and a new retractable-roof facility in Phoenix was introduced as Bank One Ballpark. But change was not limited to names.

New Comiskey Park opened in 1991, right across the street from old Comiskey and with many of the same features and nuances of its venerable predecessor. A year later, Baltimore took the budding "retro park" concept to new levels when it replaced Memorial Stadium with Oriole Park at Camden Yards—a beautiful throwback facility with all the quirks and oddities of old, but all the amenities and comforts fans have come to expect. In short order, Cleveland unveiled Jacobs Field, Texas opened The Ballpark in Arlington and the Rockies introduced us to mountain ball in Coors Field.

The ballpark-building craze continued into the new century with every city trying to outquirk and outquaint the other. Several of the parks were nestled into downtown areas, like the parks of old, but others were positioned away from the city, within the walls of self-contained neighborhoods that offered fans every amenity known to man and many never before imagined.

As the building spree continues—Safeco Field replaced the Kingdome, Pacific Bell Park replaced Candlestick, Comerica Park replaced Tiger Stadium and Enron Field replaced the Astrodome—and the corporate sponsors line up, it's easy to get a feeling of deja vu. But in reality, the modern appeal to old-time ballparks is nothing more than an illusion.

The old ballpark sounds have been shut off by nonstop recorded music, scoreboards go into pyrotechnic convulsions and tell fans when to "chaaaarge!", life-size mascots romp around the field and through the stands, cartoon characters and advertisements bombard our senses on huge video boards, giveaways dominate the P.A. system, clam chowder, mountain oysters and tacos compete with hot dogs for fan affection and we fall victim to such corporate gimmicks as dot races and Mexican hat dances.

This is cutting-edge, 21st-century baseball. It's now, it's yesterday and it's forever.

Pacific Bell Park was still under construction in February 2000 when Giants star Barry Bonds took batting practice (left) and hit his first balls into the San Francisco Bay. Houston's Enron Field (above) was taking shape at the same time.

The Classics

They are the elders of baseball society, ballparks that have endured for more than 75 years; ballparks that have withstood the pressures and urgings to change with the times; ballparks that are comfortable and cozy, charming in their presentation and stories of days gone by.

With the 1999 passing of Tiger Stadium, only three Classics remain—Boston's Fenway Park, Chicago's Wrigley Field and New York's Yankee Stadium.

These, too, will someday pass, but here's hoping the lessons they have learned will be passed to succeeding generations, that their legacies will live long after the wrecking ball has buried them in the earth.

Fenway Park

The former site of Duffy's cliff—an incline at the base of left field wall

Former home of Tris Speaker, one of the great center fielders in baseball history

Where Carlton Fisk hit dramatic 12th-inning homer, winning Game 6 of '75 World Series

Williams and Yaz, both left fielders, had a special rapport with Fenway's Green Monster

Former stomping ground of Joe Cronin and current home of Nomar Garciaparra

Site of Williams' big All-Star show: 4-for-4, 2 home runs in 1946

TED WILLIAMS:
The Splendid Splinter batted .344, hit 521 homers, won 2 Triple Crowns and earned 2 MVPs

Lou Boudreau's two home runs lift Indians past Red Sox in playoff to decide 1948 N.L. pennant

The red-brick facade, which camouflages the entryway to heaven on the corner of Brookline and Yawkey Way, stands frozen in time—like a picture of Dorian Gray. It's no illusion. Fenway Park appears to a first-time visitor much the way it must have looked to Babe Ruth, to Lefty Grove, to Ted Williams and to Carl Yastrzemski during the prime of their long-ended careers. It's a Boston relic and landmark—an artifact etched into a city's psyche like its name was carved into the concrete exterior almost nine decades ago.

This is a love affair that won't go away. Boston fans have renewed their

Roger Clemens strikes out record 20 Mariners en route to 24-4 record and MVP-Cy Young double in 1986

22

What Harry Frazee tore down in 1920 . . . Tom Yawkey built back up as long-time owner

Cardinals slugger Mark McGwire lights up Fenway with incredible power display during All-Star Game home run contest, July 12, 1999

World Series bridesmaids, 1975 and '86

Jim Lonborg beats Twins to win "Dream" pennant, Oct. 1, 1967

Where Williams homered in final big-league at-bat, Sept. 28, 1960

The Triangle

Yaz collects 3,000th career hit, Sept. 12, 1979

Wade Boggs: 7 straight 200-hit seasons, 5 batting titles 1983-89

Where Fred Merkle and Chief Meyers let Speaker's pop foul drop—the critical play of 1912 World Series

Triple play heaven: Twins pull off two in one game, July 17, 1990, and Red Sox shortstop John Valentin goes unassisted, July 8, 1994

The mound Babe Ruth worked from in his early Red Sox years

Pedro Martinez rose to Cy Young heights here in 1999

CARL YASTRZEMSKI won Triple Crown and MVP in Red Sox's "Impossible Dream" season of 1967

Where Tony Conigliaro was beaned, Aug. 18, 1967

Red Sox swamp Browns in consecutive games, 20-4 and 29-4 (June 7, 8, 1950) and score modern-record 17 runs in one inning vs. Tigers (June 18, 1953)

Bucky Dent goes deep, Red Sox go home after loss to Yankees in one-game East Division playoff, Oct. 2, 1978

The Yankees, always a great Fenway draw, were especially attractive during an August 1949 contest when the teams were battling for first place. Excited fans (left) line up along Lansdowne Street to get their precious tickets.

vows with Fenway every game day since 1912, a ritual of exciting sights, sounds and smells that fill the packed subway cars, trolleys and buses transporting rooters to the Fenway area and eventually come together in a festive mania on the crowded streets around the park. Pregame activity on Yawkey Way is a wonderful blend of fans, vendors, baseball banter, scalpers, hot dogs, sausages, roasted peanuts—and a deep-rooted, single-minded passion for the beloved Red Sox.

With these people, it's personal, much like it was decades ago for Brooklyn fans at Ebbets Field. The fervor is reflected in their eyes, their dress and the intensity with which they discuss the Red Sox and bat around their strong opinions, like a Dodger Stadium beach ball. To the 21st century fan, Fenway is a shrine. To a Red Sox fan, Fenway is an important piece of Boston's fabric and an extension of community—a corner supermarket where he can get a basic necessity of life.

Dressed on the outside like one of the city's finest, red-brick institutions, Fenway opens into an incongruous Norman Rockwell-like portrait of our national pastime. Concourses are narrow and dingy, aisles are difficult to navigate, seats are cramped and uncomfortable, pillars block some views and your eyes

FENWAY PARK (1912-)

There have been but two homes in the history of the Boston Red Sox (also known as the Pilgrims, Puritans and Somersets in earlier days). First there was the Huntington Avenue Grounds (1901-1911), site of the first game of the first World Series, in 1903.

In 1911, construction began on a new ballpark, one at the corner of Lansdowne and Jersey, in a marshy area of the city known as the Fens. After three games were rained out, Fenway Park, named for the area in which it was built, finally opened for business in 1912.

Almost any ballgame in Fenway can be a surreal experience, but if you want a truly extraordinary experience, take in the traditional Patriots Day game. It's played every year on a Monday in April, the same Monday as the annual running of the historic Boston Marathon. The marathon course passes just north of the park at Kenmore Square, which marks just one mile to go on the course. The game's 11 a.m. start usually means that the game ends just in time for fans to head to Kenmore and catch the race leaders in their final steps to the finish line.

First game: April 20, 1912. Perhaps a precursor of the great Red Sox-Yankees rivalry, Boston beat New York in the Fenway debut, 7-6, in 11 innings.

■ Site of seven World Series (1912, '14 '18, '46, '67, '75 and '86)
■ Site of three All-Star Games (1946, '61 and '99)

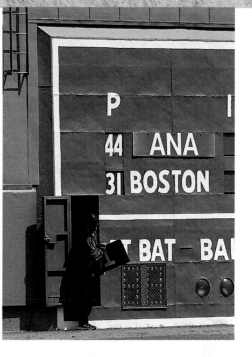

The Green Monster (above) comes complete with manual scoreboard, ladder and a doorway (above right) to its inner thoughts. The right field corner (right) is more like a loop that quickly expands home run distance from 302 feet at the pole to 380 at the bullpen marker.

have trouble coming to terms with one of the most absurd ballpark configurations ever conceived. When they do, you fall head-over-heels in love.

"I don't know anything about classical music," said former Yankees manager Buck Showalter, "but if there's a baseball symphony, this is it."

A symphony of cheers, boos, insults, shrieks and agonizing epithets, accompanied by the drumbeat of balls bouncing off a 37-foot left field wall nicknamed, appropriately, the Green Monster. The wall, by baseball standards, is intimidating—a mere 310 feet (or so they say) from home plate—and mesmerizing. No single ballpark feature has influenced games more consistently and dictated more thoroughly the personality of a franchise.

On one hand, it can eat up scorching line drives that would sail out of most other ballparks and shoot them back onto the field like a pinball machine. On the other, it can coax lazy fly balls into its 23-foot home run screen, like a spider enticing a fly into its web. Many casual baserunners have been cut down at second base by a Williams, Yaz or Jim Rice throw off a friendly carom. Championships, subtly and obviously, have been decided by not-so-routine fly balls.

This is a monster that has wrecked the careers of horrified lefthanded pitch-

Expectant kids, gloves at the ready, are bleacher regulars during batting practice before any game at Fenway Park. Not far below their center field perch is the Triangle.

ers, ruined the stroke of power-hitting wannabes and shattered the defensive confidence of bewildered left fielders. This is a house of offense and it's no coincidence that the Red Sox hold the major league records for runs in a game (29 in 1950) and an inning (17 in 1953).

If you can wrest your eyes away from the Green Monster, you'll discover a green-tinted baseball world full of interesting quirks. Aside from the Wall, there's the Ladder, the Scoreboard, the Door, the Triangle, the Yellow Line and the Jimmy Fund sign, to capture attention within the park. Beyond the walls are more sizeable landmarks like the Citgo sign (located several blocks away in Kenmore Square) in left and the Prudential building in right. The newest scene stealer, a slap in the face for Boston traditionalists, is the three-Coca Cola bottles advertisement perched atop the light standard in left field.

Most of the quirks are part of a zigging and zagging outfield fence that has more angles than a 500-piece jigsaw puzzle. The vertical yellow line rises from the point where the center field fence angles into the Green Monster, a visual reference for umpires to call a home run. The triangle marks another fence angle in right-center where the bullpens jut forward—the deepest point of the park at 420 feet. The large manual scoreboard is a fixture on the left field wall, as is the ladder that allows workers a scenic climb to remove balls from the screen.

It's easy to become entranced with the left field visuals and miss one of the park's most interesting features. There is no right field corner, thanks to a cozy 302-foot foul pole atop a right field fence that rolls quickly backward and levels off at 380 feet. Beyond the right field bullpens, high in the bleachers that back the right and center field fences, is a single red seat that marks the spot where Williams hit the longest measured home run in Fenway's history—a 1946 blast that traveled 502 feet.

Contrary to popular belief, this was not a ballpark designed by out-of-work architects in one of Boston's friendly corner pubs. Like most parks of its era, Fenway was built to conform to a crazy, patchwork neighborhood of strangely angled streets and railroad lines in a marshy area of Boston known as the Fens. Lansdowne Street, only 300-plus feet on the left field side of the park from where home plate would be located, was banked by the Boston & Albany Railroad, meaning there wasn't room for stands and the fence could not be moved out.

That was not a problem in the dead-ball era to which Fenway Park was introduced in 1912—with a brick facade patterned after Philadelphia's Shibe Park. There was no monster in left, but there was a 10-foot incline that rolled up to the

Seats near the left field corner are coveted (top photo), as are seats near the first base dugout where 1999 All-Star Game attendees got good looks at Derek Jeter (2), a dreaded Yankee, and home-town favorite Nomar Garciaparra (right).

The Fenway corner of Brookline Avenue and Yawkey Way is a beehive of activity before Red Sox games—a throwback to the excitement that has been gripping ballpark neighborhoods for decades.

The left field screen appeared in 1936, a concession to businessmen and home owners on Lansdowne who tired of broken windows. In 1940, the bullpens were added in front of the right field wall, shortening the home run distance by 23 feet for second-year man Williams. Lights came in 1947, the same year advertising was removed from the Green Monster, the Citgo sign went up in 1965 and in 1970 the flagpole, a fixture on the left-center field warning track for more than half a century, was moved out of play.

The final serious additions were an electronic scoreboard atop the right-center field scoreboard in 1976, padding for the outfield walls after star rookie Fred Lynn crashed into the center field fence in

fence, a warning for outfielders to put on the brakes. Red Sox left fielder Duffy Lewis became so adept at playing the hill that it became known as Duffy's Cliff, a nickname that lasted until the major 1934 renovation under new owner Thomas A. Yawkey. That's when the cliff was removed, the wall was built to 37 feet, the scoreboard was installed and the single-deck park, destroyed by a major fire, was virtually rebuilt, yielding the basic configuration we know today.

the 1975 World Series, luxury boxes in 1982 and the 600 Club boxes behind home plate in 1989, a reconstruction that forced relocation of the press box. Through all of its makeovers, Fenway has always been charming, intimate, charismatic and a perfectly tinted backdrop for baseball's whitest uniforms and the most colorful fans this side of Brooklyn.

Former Red Sox stars, who have felt the tenderness of their affection and the sting of their wrath, might call them fanatics. They don't watch the game, they participate. Fenway allows them that luxury and refrains from the frills and distractions that entertain fans at other parks. Red Sox rooters are interested only in the game and anything beyond the background organ will not be tolerated. Everybody at Fenway keeps score, everybody knows the team's roster and everybody offers their verbal opinions, knowing full well they probably will be heard. Woe to any fan of the hated Yankees who dares enter Fenway's gates and shame on anybody who might leave early, an obvious character flaw. Baseball is serious business here—and disappointment an annual rite.

The Red Sox of Tris Speaker, Ruth, Harry Hooper, Smoky Joe Wood and Dutch

Leonard won World Series in 1912, 1915, 1916 and 1918—but no Boston team has won one since. A Williams, Johnny Pesky and Bobby Doerr-led team won the A.L. pennant in 1946 and three other pennant-winners have been cut down in the World Series. The 1986 Red Sox, featuring Rice, Dwight Evans and Wade Boggs, put a dagger into the heart of their fans when they came within one out of the elusive championship, only to lose on a 10th-inning error.

Disappointment is a relative term at Fenway Park. It's hard to go there and feel any emotion other than exhilaration. Many exclusive nuances only enhance the feeling.

This is the only ballpark where you can get Fenway Franks and clam chowder.

It's the home of baseball's worst sun field—"The sun rises in the east and sets in right field at Fenway"— unpredictable breezes, occasional fogs, pesky pigeons and the smallest foul territory in baseball, which means more souvenirs—and more scrapes and bruises—for the fans. Did you ever notice the vertical morse code inscription on the right side of the scoreboard (the initials of Yawkey and his wife)? And how can anybody forget the distinctive public address announcements of (6-second hesitation) the late Sherm (14-second hesitation) Feller ... Feller?

It's crazy and intense, fun and serious, happy and sometimes sad. It's Fenway Park, where baseball is still the king.

A mural on the Lansdowne Street side of the Green Monster pays tribute to some of baseball's greatest stars.

Wrigley Field

Also known as Cubs Park (1916-1926)

Y ou can't escape its allure, that tantalizing aura that wafts through the residential neighborhoods on Chicago's North Side. Wrigley Field sneaks up on you, pulls you into its embrace and hugs you until your baseball senses are squeezed dry. Resist if you want, but prepare to be coddled, charmed and enchanted when you enter the friendly confines of the most affectionate little ballpark in North America.

Wrigley has been coddling, charming and enchanting baseball fans since 1914, when it opened as a

Wrigley finally saw the light on Aug. 9, 1988, when it played host to its first official night game

Where Stan Hack's hit skipped over Hank Greenberg's shoulder, winning Game 6 of 1945 World Series

Where Banks hit 500th homer, May 12, 19[...]

Where Cardinals star Stan Musial lined a double for career hit No. 3,000, May 13, 1958

Where Gabby Hartnett hit his "Home in the Gloamin' " in 1938

Rookie Kerry Wood strikes out record-tying 20 batters in one-hitter vs. Astros, May 6, 1998

Gary Gaetti homer keys 5-3 win over Giants in one-game playoff to decide wild-card berth, Sept. 28, 1998

Site of Fred Toney (Reds) and Hippo Vaughn (Cubs) double no-hitter, May 2, 1917

Second baseman RYNE SANDBERG posted a record 123-game errorless streak, 1989-90

Billy Williams ends his playing streak at 1,117 games, Sept. 3, 1970

Mark Grace:
11-for-17,
8 RBIs in NLCS
loss to
Giants, 1989

Wrigley traditions: Ivy-covered walls, flags that
fly after every game—white flag with "W" after
win, blue flag with "L" after loss

Where broadcaster Harry Caray
stayed out of tune from 1982-97,
much to the delight of raucous
Wrigley bleacher bums. Holy Cow!

Where Babe Ruth's "called shot"
landed in 1932 World Series

The wind's blowing out and Mike Schmidt
goes deep four times in Philadelphia's 10-
inning, 18-16 win, April 17, 1976

Fergie Jenkins
(left) and Andre
Dawson (right):
1971 Cy Young
winner and
1987 MVP

Sammy Sosa: 66 homers and
MVP in 1998, 63 homers in '99—
but no home run title

Cubs beat Phillies 26-23 as teams combine
for record 49 runs, Aug. 25, 1922

Pete Rose ties baseball's all-time hits record with
two singles in game vs. Cubs, Sept. 8, 1985

Pirates' Rennie Stennett goes
7-for-7 in 22-0 victory over
Cubs, Sept. 16, 1975

Home of Hack Wilson, who
drove in big-league-record
191 runs in 1930

Mr. Cub ERNIE BANKS holds
franchise records for games
(2,528), home runs (512) and total
bases (4,706). "Let's play two!"

No pennant has flown at Wrigley since 1945, when Cubs lost their last World Series to Tigers

14,000-seat Federal League base under the alias of Weeghman Park. It stands today, almost nine decades later, as a stately 39,056-seat baseball time machine, one of the few places you can go to experience the game as it was presented a half century ago. Billed nonchalantly as "Home of the Cubs," Wrigley more accurately is a sanctuary for the entire baseball world and one of the last bastions for many of the game's fading traditions.

That's a perception Chicago's North Siders take seriously. This is neighborhood ball, the kind where venue, team and surroundings live in perfect harmony with each other and with the city of which all are an intricate part. Wrigleyville is all about the Cubs; the Cubs are all about the mystique fans associate with baseball through their childhood memories. Lovable, affable, colorful, entertaining and frustrating underachievers, they light up a com-

You know you've reached Wrigley Field when you see the colorful red sign (left) at the main entrance. Life is fine, friendly and fun in the outfield bleachers (below, above left) at any Cubs game.

munity and are rewarded with a shower of loyal, undying affection.

Wrigleyville buzzes on game day—a tunnel-vision baseball experience that includes corner taverns, an old-fashioned red-brick fire station, narrow residential streets, the rumble of nearby elevated trains, noisy bleacherites lining up for tickets, expectant fans waiting on Waveland Avenue for batting-practice home runs, vendors hawking their wares, a lifesize statue of Harry Caray and voices from the rooftops of brownstone apartments, some of which provide free views into the ballpark below.

For a first-time visitor, a pregame refresher at Murphy's Bleachers or the Cubby Bear Lounge might be needed to prepare for the unexplainable shiver that's sure to come with a first sighting of the giant red "Wrigley Field: Home of Chicago Cubs" sign that has marked the corner of Clark and Addison streets for generations of fans. Everything around the park's white, blue-trimmed exterior cries out baseball, from the corner hot dog and ice cream stands to the team flags that blow in the breezes along the stadium's outer rim.

The outside of Wrigley is nostalgia; the inside is pure, unadulterated ambience. The open, green-grass field spreads out before you like a Norman Rockwell painting—pure Americana, not as quirky as Boston's Fenway Park or as cozy as Detroit's Tiger Stadium, but intimate and refreshing in ways neither can match. In a burst of Ernie Banks-like enthusiasm, you have an immediate yearning to "play two." No matter where you sit, you're part of the game—you can almost reach out and touch someone in a white, blue-striped uniform.

If Wrigley's not the most visual ballpark in the major leagues, it's close. From ivy-covered walls and distinctive wooden bleachers to the largest manual score-board still in use, baseball is played with old-time flavor and the kind of charisma today's retro parks aspire to, but somehow never quite attain.

Nothing in baseball can compare to the thick, green ivy that covers the red-brick outfield wall, a brainstorm of young Bill Veeck during a 1937 ballpark renovation. Patches of brick peek out from ivy cutouts, revealing big yellow numbers that mark the outfield distances. The wall, uncovered in foul territory, circles the rest of the perimeter, providing a distinctive brick divider for player and fan.

Big yellow numbers on the red-brick wall, telling the distance down the left field line, offer a striking contrast to Wrigley's thick green ivy.

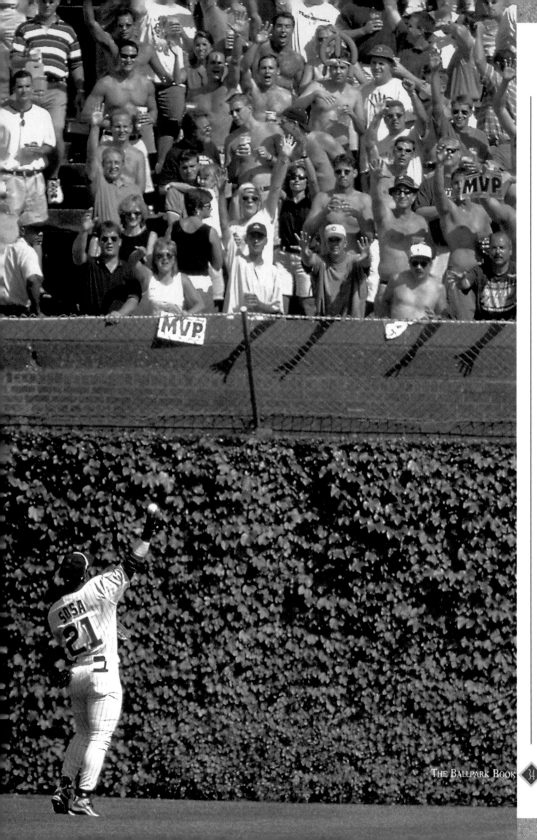

Above the outfield wall, rising before you in all their rowdy glory, are the most famous bleachers in the game, another product of the 1937 makeover. The boomerang-shaped bleachers begin at a narrow point in both corners, widen symmetrically as you move through the outfield and then crest dramatically in center field—a melting pot for partiers, shirtless sun worshipers and the park's most boisterous rooters.

Perched atop the bleacher crest is a 27-foot manual scoreboard, slightly off-kilter with home plate and topped by a round clock that brings the board's height above the field to 85 feet. Inside that hollow structure toil Wrigley's most anonymous statisticians and the rear of the board marks the outside corner of Sheffield and Waveland—with a photo of a pennant and the words "Chicago Cubs."

Amazingly, no one has ever driven a ball off the face of the scoreboard—even with the infamous home run-aiding wind gusting over the fence toward nearby Lake Michigan. Pittsburgh's Roberto Clemente and former Cub Bill Nicholson came close, but prodigious home runs are measured here by their landing points on Waveland and Sheffield—streets frequently visited by such power hitters as Banks, Billy Williams, Nicholson, Ron Santo, Dave Kingman, Ryne Sandberg and, of course, current record chaser Sammy Sosa.

It was during the bleacher construction that the park gained its most unusual feature—an inward jog of both the left and right field fences, resulting in an odd situation in which home runs hit 30 or 40 feet inside the foul poles have to travel shorter distances than those hit down the lines. Those lines measure a hefty 355 to left and 353 to right, not too much different than friendly power alleys of 368. But dimensions are irrelevant when the wind blows out—or the ill, cold winds off the lake turn Wrigley into a pitcher's paradise.

The Cubs have always been vulnerable to the unpredictable whims of Lake Michigan. After being acquired by Charles H. Weeghman in 1916, they moved into his lakeside ballpark and began a long North Side association that would blossom under the eventual ownership of chewing gum magnate William Wrigley. Cubs Park was renamed Wrigley Field in 1926, the same year the facility's first important makeover took place—a second deck was added to the

Wrigley's wild-and-crazy bleacher fans have formed an understandably close relationship with Cubs right fielder Sammy Sosa.

WRIGLEY FIELD (1916-)

Also known as Cubs Park (1916-1926)

For a park long identified by a single name — it has been Wrigley Field since 1926 — the history of baseball at Clark and Addison has not been so simple.

Baseball at the North Side corner predated even the Cubs. Ground was broken for the site in 1914 for Charlie Weeghman's Federal League team. It originally was named North Side Ball Park and during the 1914 season changed to Weeghman Park. In 1915, it was renamed again, to Whales Park, Whales being the name of the Federal League team.

In 1916, Weeghman headed a group that included William Wrigley Jr. and purchased the Cubs. In 1916, Weeghman's Cubs played their first game in what was now known as Cubs Park.

In 1918, Weeghman sold controlling interest in the team to Wrigley and in the middle of the 1926 season, it was renamed Wrigley Field.

Wrigley is such a special place, the game itself can get lost, especially for first-timers who see, in person, the ivy, the scoreboard, the brick wall, the flags ... and it's well worth the experience.

First game: April 20, 1916. Cubs Win! ... Cubs Win! ... 7-6 in 11 innings over the Cincinnati Reds.

■ Site of six World Series (1918, '29, '32, '35, '38, '45)
■ Site of three All-Star Games (1947, '62 and '90)

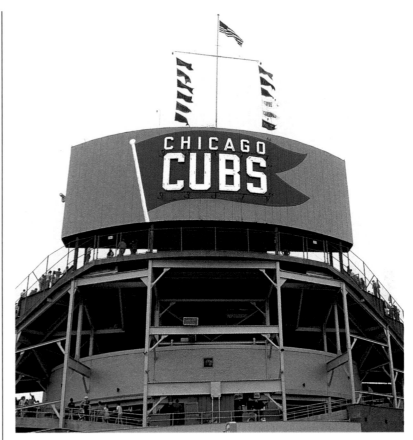

The back of Wrigley is notable for its 'Chicago Cubs' pennant and flags that blow in the Lake Michigan breezes atop the scoreboard.

entire foul-territory grandstand, almost doubling the park's capacity.

That soon paid dividends. The 1929 Cubs won a National League pennant and began a run that would net five more pennants through 1945. Players like Hack Wilson, Nicholson, Gabby Hartnett, Charlie Grimm, Charlie Root, Claude Passeau, Bill Lee and Stan Hack passed through the friendly confines, as did any Cubs' championship hopes. The team would never win another pennant, much less a World Series title.

The big renovation of 1937 came under the direction of Philip K. Wrigley, William's son. He added the bleachers, installed a new scoreboard on its current center field perch and created many of the physical nuances that have become so much a part of the ballpark's lore. Wrigley, home of baseball's first organ and the first Ladies Day promotion, has maintained its basic personality since that renovation and many of those nuances still exist as visible reminders of years gone by.

Reminders such as the flags, banks of which fly atop the scoreboard, representing every National League team in order of that day's standings. Centering those banners is an American flag that is replaced after each game by either a

white flag with a blue "W" signaling victory, or a blue flag with a white "L" signaling defeat. Two Hall of Fame numbers fly atop the foul-pole flags—Banks' 14 in left, Williams' 26 in right, and team flags circle the inner rim of the park.

Wrigley also has been known for two things you didn't see.

For many years, the Cubs refused to add lights, giving the ballpark distinction as the champion of daytime baseball—a Wrigley trademark embraced by fans and baseball locals. Baseball in the sunshine, the way "it was meant to be played," endured until 1988, when Cubs officials finally gave in, installed light standards and played the first night baseball on Chicago's North Side.

The team always has refused to plaster advertisements all over the park, helping Wrigley maintain a clean, natural look that few other parks can claim. To this day, Wrigley remains relatively advertisement free, except for a Budweiser sign across the foot of the scoreboard and a "Torco" sign that hangs from a rooftop beyond the right field wall.

But all of that Wrigley ambience would be cosmetic without the laid-back, fun-loving atmosphere created by some of the most social fans in baseball. Unlike the blue-collar South Siders who go to a White Sox game to watch them win, Cubs fans are interested in having a good time. They heckle opposing players, shower affection on their favorite Cubs and throw back any home run not hit by a hometowner—like a fish that's too small.

Such affection is not reserved just for Cubs in uniform. For years, fans reveled in the distinctive "Hey, heys" of broadcaster Jack Brickhouse and the 1980s sight of retired—and shirtless—Bill Veeck in the outfield bleachers. But nobody captured Wrigley's flavor more than the colorful, beer-drinking Caray, who would lean out of his broadcast-booth perch behind home plate, wave to the adoring masses below and exhort them to join in one of the most popular seventh-inning stretch traditions in baseball history.

"C'mon everybody! Let me hear you now! A one, and a two, and a Take me out to the Ballgame ..."

A panoramic view of packed Wrigley Field with Harry Caray at the microphone (below)—it doesn't get any better for Chicago North Siders.

Yankee Stadium

Where Dodger Sandy Amoros raced into corner to rob Yogi Berra and save Game 7 of 1955 World Series

MONUMENT PARK
Miller Huggins, Ruth, Lou Gehrig, DiMaggio and Mickey Mantle

Grover Alexander comes out of bullpen to face Tony Lazzeri in '26 Series

Where Dodger Al Gionfriddo made spectacular catch of DiMaggio's long drive in Game 6 of '47 World Series

Where Johnny Lindell's slide into Whitey Kurowski was turning point of '43 Series

She stands as a cathedral, a monument to glories past—made over, spruced up and overhauled beyond the recognition of many old-timers who worshiped there. Yankee Stadium might not be the grand old lady she used to be, but her eloquence stretches well beyond the borders of baseball time. Her patrons have witnessed more drama, her heroes have inspired more prose and her championship banners have produced more emotion than any athletic arena in the world.

To walk through her gates is a religious experience. An aura of greatness, an unexplainable mys-

BABE RUTH, the Sultan of Swat. 714 lifetime home runs, .690 career slugging average, 60 home runs in '27, 177 runs scored in '21

Yankees post A.L.-record 114 wins and overall 125-50 mark en route to record 24th World Series crown and second in three years, 1998

THE PERFECT PLACE
Don Larsen shocked the baseball world with his perfect game in 1956 World Series. David Wells also was perfect on May 17, 1998, and David Cone on July 18, 1999

38

Remodeled Yankee Stadium opened April 15, 1976

1999 Yankees close out century with another World Series win—team's 25th in 77 years

Where Roger Maris hit homer No. 61, Oct. 1, 1961

Mickey Mantle hits shot off facade, May 22, 1963

Mickey Mantle hits 500th career homer, May 14, 1967

K.C.'s George Brett hits third-deck homer that cooks Yankees' Goose in Game 3 of the 1980 ALCS

CASEY STENGEL managed 10 pennant winners: '49, '50, '51, '52, '53, '55, '56, '57, '58, '60

Where Chris Chambliss hit ALCS-winning home run in 1976

Where 12-year-old Jeffrey Maier made the catch of his life on Derek Jeter's home run bid in Game 1 of 1996 ALCS

Site of K.C. third baseman George Brett's Pine Tar tirade, July 24, 1983

Chicago's Tom Seaver wins 300th game, Aug. 4, 1985

JOLTIN' JOE DIMAGGIO, center fielder for 9 World Series champions. He started 56-game hitting streak here, May 15, 1941

Lou Gehrig Day, July 4, 1939
A farewell to the Iron Horse, "the luckiest man on the face of the Earth"

Grand, pennant-filled Yankee Stadium provided the perfect backdrop for Babe Ruth's farewell to New York fans in 1948.

tique hangs over the great edifice like a thick fog. This is the Temple of Sport, where the New York gods created a masterpiece and dressed it in pinstripes.

This is where Babe Ruth hit 60 home runs while leading the charge for the most feared team in baseball history. This is the former home of Murderer's Row, the Iron Horse, the Yankee Clipper and the Old Professor. This is where Don Larsen pitched his perfect World Series game, Lou Gehrig delivered the Gettysburg Address of baseball, Mickey Mantle launched a stadium-threatening rocket and Roger Maris set off a record-shattering bomb.

"Where have you gone Joe DiMaggio?" wasn't merely a line from a song here—it was a lament that drifted through the Bronx for years after his 1951 retirement. "Mr. October" wasn't just a nickname here, it was Reggie Jackson's ticket into New York's elite postseason society.

"Elite" is an adjective that fits Yankee Stadium, the home of 25 championship teams and 98 World Series games in the 20th century. Well over a quarter of the 95 World Series played have been won by the Yankees, which explains the dignified, almost-arrogant aura that grips every visitor who walks through the turnstile.

The tradition has been a constant, from that April 18, 1923, day when "The House That Ruth Built" opened its gates for the first time. But this is actually a tale of two stadiums, one reflective of the quiet elegance inspired by Jacob Ruppert, Tillinghast Huston, Ed Barrow, Miller Huggins, Joe McCarthy and all the workmanlike Yankees championship teams through the 1973 season, and another featuring the Bronx Zoo atmosphere

A 1950s bullpen view shows the park's imposing grand stand and trademark facade. Fans (below) were warned about the team's strict rules of conduct.

of a refurbished Yankee Stadium, inspired by George Steinbrenner.

The Good Old Days

Early Yankee Stadium commanded a reverence that differentiated it from other arenas of its generation. Whereas Ebbets Field, located across the East River in Brooklyn, was known for its rollicking fun and zany characters, visitors to Yankee Stadium behaved with a more reserved dignity, a "we're better than you" arrogance supported by the quiet, businesslike manner in which their team went about winning pennants and championships. Ebbets was a cozy, home-style ballpark; Yankee Stadium was a massive, corporate-minded stadium.

It was expansive beyond the imagination of anybody setting foot through its gates for the first time. It rose up around you like a baseball canyon, its farthest third-deck seat about three or four echoes distant. It was big, like the city that surrounded it and the egos of the baseball teams that competed there.

Quirks and personality were exhibited in many forms. The roof that jutted over the upper stands was rimmed by a pale green facade that gave the park a distinctive, almost regal look. A scoreboard rose from ground level above the open right-center field wall, where passengers on the elevated train could get quick glimpses of action and freeloaders on rooftops and a train station platform could watch an entire game. Green wooden seats seemed to blend into a lush grass carpet that was maintained with obsessive diligence.

The Yankees added a huge helping of character in 1932 when a monument to former manager Huggins was erected in dead center field, in fair ground under the flagpole, about 10 feet in front of the wall. Ruth and Gehrig monuments joined Huggins in 1941, with plaques of former owner Ruppert and others adding to the mystique. The Yankees further charmed their fans by allowing them to exit every game through the center field gate, after pausing and paying homage to their departed heroes.

Over the years, the team's proud tradition became more and more a part of the Yankee Stadium experience through championship photos that greeted visitors outside the gates and expansive action photos of individuals that grabbed their attention once inside.

But nowhere were the Yankee Stadium quirks more pronounced than on a playing field tailored to the power stroke of Ruth. True to form, the Bambino dedicated the giant structure in 1923 with a three-run homer into a short right field porch that measured only 296 feet down the line.

"The biggest crowd in baseball history rose to its feet and let loose the biggest shout in baseball history," reported the New York Times, accepting an official record fan count of 74,200 that officials later admitted was padded.

While lefthanders were taking shots at the short right field porch, right-handers were losing would-be home runs in the vast left-center field pasture known as "Death Valley." The left field line was only 301 feet, but the fence arced deeply toward a distant center field wall that measured 461. That's where the monuments were positioned, forming a frustrating obstacle for center fielders who allowed balls to get over their heads.

That didn't happen often to the Yankees, who spoiled fans for more than three decades with the superior center field play of DiMaggio and Mantle.

The overview (above) shows old Yankee Stadium with the Polo Grounds in the background, just across the Harlem River. Improved transportation helped make Yankee Stadium a New York showplace by 1925 (right).

Something New

You stand at the main entrance of refurbished Yankee Stadium, in the

Monuments of Huggins, Gehrig and Ruth once stood in fair territory at Yankee Stadium. Now they're part of a Monument Park display beyond the left-center field fence.

shadow of a giant bat that stands majestically on one end, and you're filled with the same sense of awe that greeted fans of yesteryear. It still rises above you in all of its expansive glory, it still reeks of success and heroic deeds and it still smells and feels like the Yankee Stadium of Ruth and Gehrig and Gomez must have felt decades ago.

But make no mistake, this is not the Yankee Stadium of Ruth and Gehrig. It's a younger, slimmer, sleeker, prettier and more modern Yankee Stadium, the championship playground of Jackson, Munson, Guidry, Nettles and Randolph.

There are reminders. Nostalgic team and individual photographs still overpower you when you step through the turnstiles, the expanse and atmosphere still trigger emotions and the calming, perfect-diction words of public address announcer Bob Sheppard still provide elegant respites. They're illusions that mask

Ticket booths were plentiful and grandstand prices were right outside old Yankee Stadium.

what really is a facsimile of the old Stadium.

Patrons no longer are subjected to coronary-inducing climbs to the upper deck, thanks to a series of escalators and elevators. Gone are the sight-impeding pillars that supported the two upper tiers, giving every seat in the house a near-perfect sight line. Gone, too, is the roof and the facade that once gave the facility its regal air.

It's hard to keep your eyes off a massive 560-foot-long scoreboard that covers a wall blocking view of the once-prominent elevated trains and neighboring rooftops. The new wall is topped by a concrete facsimile that reminds fans of the old facade. Also missing are the center field monuments, which now reside in a special "Monument Park" located behind the left-center field fence.

While the general shape of the field has been retained over the years, the fence distances have become much less imposing for righthanded hitters and the coloring of the stadium has changed from green to bright blue with a stately white trim. Even the feel of the games is different.

With the makeover has come a different breed of team and a new, less-patient generation of fan. Gone is the dignified approach of those amazingly consistent championship teams featuring Ruth, Gehrig, Lefty Gomez, Waite Hoyt, Bill Dickey, Yogi Berra, Whitey Ford and Mantle. The Steinbrenner Yankees have featured more volatile personalities like Billy Martin, Thurman Munson, Ron Guidry, Jackson, Sparky Lyle, Graig Nettles, Willie Randolph and Don Mattingly. The Bronx Bombers have given way to the Bronx Zoo and fans, suffering through the first serious pennant drought in the Stadium's 50-year history, have become impatient, loud and occasionally rowdy.

The defining moment of 1976, new Yankee Stadium's first season, came in

Yankee Stadium's scoreboard operator in 1948 viewed games through small slots, hidden from general view inside the giant right-center field structure.

Game 5 of the American League Championship Series against Kansas City, when Chris Chambliss secured the first Yankee pennant in 12 years with a home run, then feared for his life as he attempted to circle the bases while being mobbed by crazed fans.

The end result is a different kind of Yankee Stadium—still the House of Champions, but now catering to a rowdier, younger crowd that is tougher for opposing players and those Yankees not performing up to expectations. Through the transformation, the winning mystique continues. World Series championships in 1996, '98 and '99, with players like Derek Jeter, Bernie Williams, Paul O'Neill, David Cone and Mariano Rivera operating with the businesslike efficiency of old, brings the curtain down on an incredible century of baseball excellence.

And the proudest, grandest stadium the sports world has ever produced.

YANKEE STADIUM (1923-)

Facing eviction from their Polo Grounds home, a home they shared with the rival Giants, owners of the Polo Grounds, the Yankees purchased the lot of land on which Yankee Stadium stands in 1921. In a mere two years, Yankee Stadium was designed and constructed, and play began there in 1923.

Original plans called for a three-deck grandstand to encircle the stadium, however those plans were scaled back and the original grandstand didn't reach the foul poles. In 1928, the grandstand in left field was extended to its current point, and in 1937, the right field grandstand was expanded around the foul pole.

In 1946, lights came. In 1967, the green grandstand seats were painted blue. And in 1976, after two seasons in Shea Stadium to allow for major renovations, a new Yankee Stadium, one without supportive steel pillars that obstructed the view of the fans, opened.

The greatest legacy of Yankee Stadium is its 25 World Series championships, the last three under manager Joe Torre (right).

Through it all, the one element that has remained constant is the stadium's most-recognized feature, the facade. While it once adorned the rim of the grandstand, today it spans the top of the scoreboard from the left field grandstand to the right field grandstand.

Even with all of that history oozing at you from every corner of the ballpark, there's nothing like Monument Park, a memorial that today resides behind the wall in left-center field and honors Yankees greats. And you can't get much greater than Ruth, Gehrig, Mantle, DiMaggio. ...

First game: April 18, 1923. Babe Ruth christened the new stadium with a home run in the Yankees' 4-1 victory over the Boston Red Sox.

■ Site of 34 World Series (1923, '26, '27, '28, '32, '36, '37, '38, '39, '41, '42, '43, '47, '49, '50, '51, '52, '53, '55, '56, '57, '58, '60, '61, '62, '63, '64, '76, '77, '78, '81, '96, '98, '99)

■ Site of three All-Star Games (1939, '60, '77)

The Middle Ages

They were products of baseball's Middle Ages, that period from 1953 through 1969 when the game relocated and expanded to parts unknown.

Milwaukee's County Stadium, Los Angeles' Dodger Stadium and the Oakland Coliseum were either built or renovated for teams shifting operations from other cities; Anaheim Stadium, New York's Shea Stadium and San Diego's Jack Murphy Stadium were built for expansion teams.

They have undergone cosmetic changes, even major surgery, to help them make the transition to a new millennium. Some have even changed their personality, from baseball-only to multi-purpose.

But their time is fleeting, some with more immediacy than others, as plans are being drawn and votes are being cast. They're starting to hear the whispers, sometimes shouts, of inadequacy, that it's time to rebuild for a new generation of fan.

Anaheim
Stadium

Also known as Edison International
Field of Anaheim (1997-)

Destination of Dave
Henderson homer off
Donnie Moore in Game 5
of 1986 ALCS—a stunning
blow that denied Angels
first pennant

Where Rod
Carew (left)
drove a pitch
from Minnesota
lefty Frank Viola
for 3,000th
career hit,
Aug. 4, 1985

T he Big A, banished to a corner of the Anaheim Stadium parking lot, still towers majestically over the mortality below. Long removed from its perch beyond the left field fence, it now flashes its giant halo at passing motorists, spreading the good news of Angels' victories. At first glance, the 230-foot, A-framed former scoreboard seems over-qualified for such work. But in this world of retro-fitted, fan-friendly, throwback ballparks, it provides a powerful and necessary reminder of humble beginnings.

Anaheim Stadium is perfect testimony to the adage, "What goes

NOLAN RYAN
struck fear
into opposing
hitters with
his powerful
right arm, 1972-79

Alex Johnson becomes
Angels' only batting
champion . . .
.329 in 1970

Lefthanded complement:
Frank Tanana, Chuck
Finley, Mark Langston,
Clyde Wright, Jim Abbott
find success in Anaheim

Don Baylor and Fred Lynn power
Angels in Games 1 and 2 of 1982
ALCS, but Brewers rally for three
straight wins at Milwaukee

A.L. West champs 1979, '82, '86 —
always an ALCS bridesmaid

The "Big A" undergoes facelift, changes from open to enclosed stadium, 1981

Bobby Grich's 11th-inning single completes big comeback in Game 4 of 1986 ALCS and gives Angels three-games-to-one edge over Red Sox

Reggie Jackson hits 500th career homer on Sept. 17, 1984—same date and place where he hit first major league homer 17 years earlier for A's

Don Baylor (36 homers, 139 RBIs) 1979 A.L. MVP

Ryan blows away 383rd batter in Sept. 27, 1973 game vs. Twins, sets major league single-season strikeout record

Bo Jackson, Wade Boggs hit back-to-back homers leading off game, trigger 5-3 A.L. All-Star win, July 11, 1989

Tony Perez's 15th-inning homer off Catfish Hunter ends longest game in All-Star history, July 11, 1967

Yankees reliever Ron Davis strikes out eight straight Angels, May 4, 1981

George Brett collects fourth hit of game, 3,000th of career, off Tim Fortugno, Sept. 30, 1992

Where Ryan posted two of his four Angels' no-hitters, beating Twins 4-0 in 1974 and Orioles 1-0 in 1975

Don Sutton (left) pitches Angels to 5-1 win over Rangers, notches 300th career victory, June 18, 1986

BRIAN DOWNING: Angels' career leader in runs, hits, home runs, total bases, RBIs and extra-base hits

Three Angels top 100 RBIs in 1995— Jim Edmonds (107), Tim Salmon (105), J.T. Snow (102)

around, comes around." It opened in 1966 as a baseball-only facility, was enclosed in a 1979-80 cookie-cutter renovation that added 20,000 seats for football's Los Angeles Rams and was given a 1996-97 Disney makeover that knocked out 20,000 seats, reopened the outfield and transformed the stadium back into a ballpark—with splashy Camden Yards and Coors Field-type retro trimmings.

You don't get the glitzy, Hollywood feel of Los Angeles neighbor Dodger Stadium, but you quickly get the idea that Anaheim Stadium is a production—choreographed and directed like the visitor-friendly Disneyland, which is located only two miles away in suburban Anaheim. You are greeted at the gate by two giant caps and the main-entrance awning is supported by huge baseball bats. The exterior has been modernized, garden-like greenery and palm trees circle the facility and everything is immaculately clean, from the outdoor plazas to the well-lit concourses and precisely-placed concession stands.

And, of course, you are served by the most courteous attendants and ushers in baseball. "Convenience, Comfort and Courtesy" has always been the Anaheim Stadium motto and that hasn't changed. But the Disney Angels also are obsessed with the park's visual impact—much of which has been borrowed from other facilities.

Intimacy is the goal and Anaheim Stadium was originally designed with that in mind. Limited foul territory puts seats close to the field and a well-designed three-tiered grandstand stretches from foul pole to foul pole, with the highest seats seemingly close to the action. On a clear day, the newly-opened outfield provides a wonderful view of the San Gabriel Mountains and The Pond, the arena where Disney's Mighty Ducks play hockey, can be spotted over the left-center field fence.

This park can make out-of-towners feel at home. A Coors Field-like retro scoreboard looms over outfield bleachers in right-center, complete with video board, JumboTron display and other state-of-the-art goodies. A Jacobs Field-like out-of-town scoreboard is built into the right-center field fence, Camden-like terraced bullpens are visible in left and a rock pile in left-center is a clever disguise for a Kauffman Stadium-like water display. Behind-the-plate dugout suites offer a field-level view, similar to Dodger Stadium.

Two Anaheim Stadium quirks have remained constant through all of its makeovers—a 4.75-foot high home run fence in both corners, where the ends of the grandstand jut into play, and the laid-back, late-arriving Southern California fans who often seem more interested in the social experience and less passionate about winning and losing than fans in other ballparks.

The distances down both lines are 330 feet, but that's where the symmetry ends. Both short fences, which sometimes force outfielders to wrestle eager fans for potential home run balls, roll out quickly to deep power alleys that turn Anaheim into a pitcher's park. The power alley in right-center is 370 feet, 26 shorter than its counterpart in left center. The 408-foot center field crest fronts an 18-foot fence and a dark

When Anaheim Stadium opened in 1966, the halo-topped Big A was a hulking presence over the left field fence (below, right), a combination scoreboard and landmark. During a later renovation, the Big A, no longer a scoreboard, was relegated to its current location in the stadium's parking lot (right inset).

hitter's backdrop. A small bleacher section in left and extended bleachers in right offer prime views of the action.

Anaheim Stadium has come a long way since its 1966 debut—when the Los Angeles Angels, then under the fatherly direction of "Singing Cowboy" Gene Autry, relocated there and changed their name to California Angels. The grandstand layout and beautiful grass carpet were much the same then and the outfield was open, without the retro frills of today. Light standards and the Big A, which served as the park's original scoreboard, were the only obstructions for balls launched toward the nether reaches of Anaheim.

"The first chill I ever received in this game came when I walked into the Polo Grounds for the first time. I received another when I walked into this park," said then-Angels manager Bill Rigney after getting his first look at what soon would become known as "the Big A."

This was the Anaheim Stadium of Jim Fregosi, Alex Johnson, Bobby Knoop, Frank Tanana, Clyde Wright and a young, flame-throwing Nolan Ryan. The later, 65,000-seat enclosed version belonged to the Rod Carew, Don Baylor, Fred Lynn, Brian Downing, Bobby Grich, Wally Joyner, Doug DeCinces, Bobby Witt and Mark Langston teams that won three division titles and even came within one pitch of securing the Angels' first

ANAHEIM STADIUM (1966-)

Renamed Edison International Field
of Anaheim (1997-)

Upon the awarding of an expansion franchise, the Angels — Los Angeles Angels until 1965 — knew one of their first orders of business was finding a place of their own.

So while they played in temporary quarters — L.A.'s Wrigley Field in 1961, and as tenants, unhappy tenants, of the Dodgers in Dodger Stadium from 1962-1965 — they searched out a place to build their own stadium.

Farmland in Anaheim, with easy access to major highways, was selected as the site, in part because of population studies that showed that it would be the center of a growing metropolitan area. Another candidate, Long Beach, was eliminated in part because the team objected to the city's wish that the team's name be changed to Long Beach Angels. The team insisted that Los Angeles or California was to be the team's name, which became ironic when the team changed its name to Anaheim Angels after the 1996 season.

First game: April 19, 1966. Chicago White Sox pitcher Tommy John, who would play for the Angels 16 years later, is the winning pitcher in a 3-1 Chicago victory.

■ Site of no World Series
■ Site of two All-Star Games (1967 and 1989)

Two giant caps and a baseball bat-supported awning greet visitors at the main entrance (above) of the renamed Edison Field. A rock pile water display (right) dresses up the scenery over the left-center field fence.

World Series appearance—a hope that was denied by Boston center fielder Dave Henderson's 1986 ALCS home run, one of the most shocking blows in baseball history.

It was the kind of drama that appeals to today's impact-minded Disney Angels, but not before editing that would allow the local heroes to prevail. And Anaheim Stadium to play host to its first World Series championship in a happy ending.

Dodger Stadium

Ironman Mike Marshall (a record 106 games) becomes first reliever to win Cy Young, 1974

Jack Clark's ninth-inning, three-run homer off Tom Niedenfuer shocks Dodgers in Game 6 of 1985 NLCS

In short there's simply not a more congenial spot, for happily ever-aftering than here in Ca-me-lot.

King Arthur would have approved of Dodger Stadium. He would have liked the laid-back atmosphere of the place and the way color literally explodes before your eyes. And the trees and the flowers and its near perfect harmony with nature. And, of course, the weather—it couldn't rain until after sundown in Camelot; in Chavez Ravine, it seldom rains at all.

But unlike Camelot, Dodger

Back-to-back seventh-inning homers by Pedro Guerrero, Steve Yeager give Jerry Reuss 2-1 win over Yankees in Game 5 of 1981 World Series

Where Cubs' Rick Monday snatched American flag away from protestors who were trying to burn it, April 25, 1976

Walter Alston won his 2,000th game as manager, July 17, 1976

SANDY KOUFAX: Dominated N.L. hitters here from 1961-66 with five straight ERA titles, four strikeout titles, one MVP and three Cy Youngs

1965 switch-hitting infield: We Parker 1B, Jim Lefebvre 2B, Mau Wills SS, Jim Gilliam 3B

Where Orel Hershiser compiled many of his record 59 consecutive scoreless innings in 1988

Giants score four runs in ninth, defeat Dodgers 6-4 in third game of playoff to determine N.L. pennant, Oct. 3, 1962

Orioles reliever Moe Drabowsky strikes out 11 Dodgers in Game 1 of '66 World Series

Rookie Fernando Valenzuela becomes baseball sensation en route to 1981 Cy Young

Cardinal Fernando Tatis goes where no player has gone before—two grand slams in one inning, April 23, 1999

World Series champs in 1963, '65, '81, '88 World Series losers in 1966, '74, '77, '78

Where gimpy Kirk Gibson hit dramatic two-out, two-run, ninth-inning homer off Dennis Eckersley to beat A's in Game 1 of 1988 World Series

Four balls have been hit out of Dodger Stadium: Willie Stargell 1969, 1973; Mike Piazza 1997; Mark McGwire 1999

Where Willie Davis made three errors in fifth inning of World Series Game 2 vs. Orioles, Oct. 6, 1966

Where Phillies' Garry Maddox dropped Dusty Baker's line drive, setting up winning run in 1978 NLCS

Maury Wills finishes record-breaking 1962 season with steals 103 and 104 in finale of pennant playoff series vs. Giants

Site of Koufax's perfect game vs. Cubs, Sept. 9, 1965 . . . Where he set N.L. single-season strikeout record with 382 in 1965

1974 MVP STEVE GARVEY: Top gun of long-running infield that included Ron Cey, Bill Russell and Davey Lopes

Don Drysdale shuts out Yankees on three hits, posts club's first World Series win at Dodger Stadium, Oct. 5, 1963

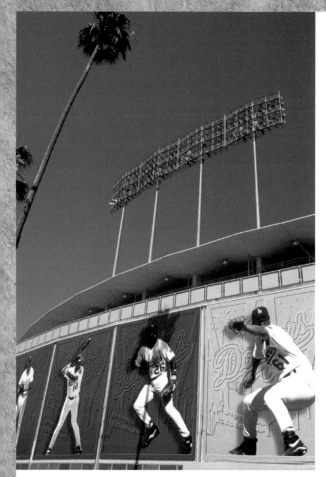

Huge photographic 'banners' of current Dodgers decorate the outside facade at Dodger Stadium, providing an inspirational beginning to a fan's baseball experience.

Stadium is no mythical wonderland. Its one brief shining moment has been sustained for almost four decades in one of the most pristine baseball settings imaginable. Nestled in the tree-lined Elysian hills, with the purple San Gabriel Mountains standing guard to the north and a breathtaking view of downtown Los Angeles available to the south, it looks like an Arthurian castle, perched on a pedestal for approaching visitors to look up to and admire.

The approach, from the network of expressways that feed into 21 terraced lots, is a memorable part of the Dodger Stadium experience. It glitters high above you in the bright sunlight; it offers a beautiful light show at night. Your eyes become locked on the structure, oblivious to the magnificent landscaping—more than 3,400 trees, grassy landings, colorful flowers—that surrounds you as you ride the escalator up, up, up.

The Dodgers take great pride in the look—and the almost obsessive cleanliness—of their summer playground. The concourses of Yankee Stadium and Fenway Park are old, dingy reminders of baseball past. The corridors of Dodger Stadium are colorful, freshly-painted hallways, with floors so clean you could eat off them.

It almost becomes too much—that antiseptic sense of perfection. But then you step into the field area and back to reality—baseball reality, complete with sparkling green grass, rich brown dirt and all the sights and sounds you might expect from a ballpark visit.

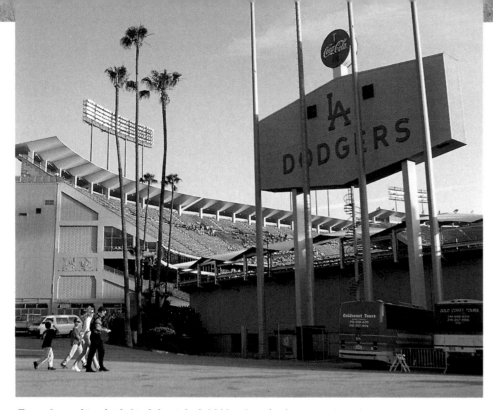

From the parking lot behind the right field bleachers (top), approaching fans can get a close look at palm trees and the wavy pavilion roof that is distinctive to Dodger Stadium. This panoramic view (right) shows colorful Dodger Stadium looking out on the tree-lined Elysian hills beyond the outfield fences.

Dodger Stadium struggles with the intimacy issue, but it's a huge, five-tiered, aging arena that still manages to retain most of the classic ballpark feel. An upper tier wraps from just beyond first base to just beyond third. The other four levels stretch from foul line to foul line, cut off from single-level fair-territory bleachers by bullpens shaded by palm trees. Distinctive wavy-topped roofs hang over the back few rows of the outfield bleachers, a challenging target for gargantuan home runs in what has always been a pitcher's park.

For anybody who has watched a Dodgers game on television, the sight of radar gun-toting Mike Brito is locked in memory. Brito is always standing behind home plate, clocking pitches, in the dugout-level boxes that wrap behind home plate, giving fans a field-level view of the game. Fans in the outfield areas are kept abreast of game progress by field-level auxiliary scoreboards on the sides of both dugouts.

This has been the basic look of Dodger Stadium since 1962, the year it opened as "the Taj Mahal of baseball"—a symmetrical 330 feet down both lines,

DODGER STADIUM (1962-)

Dug out of a hilly section of earth known as Chavez Ravine two miles from the center of the city of Los Angeles, Dodger Stadium was hailed as baseball's Taj Mahal when it opened for business in 1962.

When the Dodgers moved west in 1958, they played four seasons in the Los Angeles Memorial Coliseum, in less-than-ideal baseball configurations. The left field line was just 251 feet away, and even with a 40-foot-high screen it was an inviting home run target.

Four seasons there was a small price to pay for their eventual permanent home — Dodger Stadium. To this day, it's considered one of baseball's best settings, with nearly ideal weather conditions (15 rainouts in its history) and its sweeping picturesque view.

So when you visit L.A., endure the traffic, wallow in the historical tributes to Dodgers greats on the outfield fence, tune in to Vin Scully on the radio and bask in the setting.

First game: April 10, 1962. The Reds defeated the Dodgers, 6-3.

■ Site of eight World Series (1963, '65, '66, '74, '77, '78, '81 and '88)
■ Site of one All-Star Game (1980)

Dodger Stadium, with its explosion of color and lights, is a glittering wonderland that lures you into its baseball clutches.

the open feel of the outfield, expansive foul territory, especially the area between the dugouts and the infield foul lines, state-of-the-art score and video boards in left- and right-center and 3-foot right and left field fences that connect the foul lines to the bullpens, making shots into the corners a test of restraint for souvenir-hungry fans.

"This edifice is one of the important steps in a new era of the game," raved baseball commissioner Ford Frick after his first look at the facility in 1962. "I expected it would be great. But my wildest imagination did not foresee anything this remarkable."

Attention to detail and Dodgers class have kept it among the best parks in the game. Little things matter here, from the bright, perfectly-pressed uniforms of ushers to comfortable plastic seats and the precise efficiency of the grounds crew between innings. The powerful voice of former public address announcer John Ramsey, Vin Scully at the mike, Dodger Dogs and the trick-shot peanut-delivery artistry of vendor Roger Owens add to the color. But fans are the dimension that sets Dodger Stadium apart from contemporary parks.

They arrive late and leave early, partly because of the horrid Los Angeles traffic and partly because this is the California way. The entire Dodger Stadium experience is very Los Angeles, a stereotypical laid-back, fun and trendy thing to do, complete with stars, starlets and other pretty faces. There's a definite Hollywood feel. Forget the baseball, what better place to watch the sunset on a clear summer night?

But that's not to say fans don't support their Dodgers—and that they aren't rewarded for doing so. This was baseball's first 3-million attendance ballpark, and it's usually full. The Dodgers have rewarded them with eight National League pennants, four World Series winners, eight N.L. West Division crowns and a Who's Who player roster that includes such names as Koufax, Snider, Drysdale, Wills, Sutton, Garvey, Cey, Guerrero, Gibson, Hershiser and Piazza.

Say what you want, but it's hard to ignore the diversity of a ballpark that speaks to you from as many levels as Dodger Stadium. It's beautiful, it's painfully clean, it exudes an old-style charisma, it mimics the personality of its fans and it reeks of success. A real Dodger-blue Camelot in the City of Angels.

County Stadium

Two-time homer champ Gorman Thomas (right) patroled center field for Brewers from 1973-83 . . . second baseman Jim Gantner anchored infield from 1976-92

Stan Musial homers in 12th inning to win 1955 All-Star Game

Brewers have unprecedented distinction of competing here as member of both A.L. and N.L.

Giants' slugger Willie Mays ties record with four homers vs. Braves, April 30, 1961

Cleveland rookie John Farrell stops Paul Molitor's hitting streak at 39 games, Aug. 26, 1987

Where Phillies beat Braves to end modern-record losing streak of 23 games, Aug. 20, 1961

Lefty WARREN SPAHN: 1957 Braves Cy Young winner recorded nine 20-win seasons and won 300th game here, Aug. 11, 1961

Rollie Fingers (right), Brewers' 1981 MVP and Cy Young winner; Pete Vuckovich, '82 Cy Young

Baseball, Milwaukee-style, begins in the parking lot, where lazy summer nights and afternoons have all the feel of aromatic, nobody's-a-stranger family reunions. It happens like clockwork before every game. Baseball's most accomplished tailgaters arrive early, set up their grills and tap kegs, quickly transforming a gray, working-class area into a friendly, vibrant playground.

It's all about fun, a social obsession Milwaukee fans can't seem to resist. The smell of their bratwurst and burgers embrace you, the sounds of their laughter and happy voices give you a sense of what to expect the rest of the night, win or lose. The casual visitor can be overwhelmed by the

Pirates' Harvey Haddix pitches 12 perfect innings, only to lose 1-0 in 13th, May 26, 1959

Where Hank Aaron started his career, 1954-65 with Braves . . . and ended his career, 1975-76 with Brewers

St. Louis' Mark McGwire hits homers 64 and 65, Sept. 18, 20, 1998 . . . No. 66 is disallowed by umpire's controversial ruling

Cardinals rookie center fielder Willie McGee kills Brewers in Game 3 of 1982 World Series with two homers, four RBIs and two sensational catches

Hank Aaron hits final home run of career, No. 755, July 20, 1976

Hank Aaron's 11th-inning homer wins pennant for Braves, Sept. 23, 1957

Where Eddie Mathews hit his 10th-inning homer to beat Yankees in Game 4 of 1957 World Series

Chicago's Sammy Sosa hits homers 64 and 65 . . . Cubs left fielder Brant Brown drops bases-loaded fly ball in ninth, giving Brewers three runs and 8-7 win, Sept. 23, 1998

Robin Yount singles for career hit No. 3,000, Sept. 9, 1992

Where Chicago White Sox played 20 "home games" in 1968, '69

Two-time MVP and leader of Harvey's Wallbangers, the 1982 A.L. pennant-winning team

Where Nolan Ryan beat Brewers for milestone 300th win, July 31, 1990

Cecil Cooper (left) and Don Money (right) hit grand slams in same inning, April 12, 1980

COUNTY STADIUM (1953-)

Milwaukee Braves	Milwaukee Brewers
(1953-1965)	(1970-Present)

Built as a facility for the Brewers, the Braves' top farm team, County Stadium was completed in March of 1953. Three days after having been opened to the public, the Braves announced the team would relocate from Boston to Milwaukee. Just a month later the stadium would host its first major league game. It was hailed as the first major league ballpark built with lights included and built entirely through public funds.

It has seen National League baseball — the Braves through '65, and the Brewers when they moved to the NL in 1998 — as well as American League baseball — the Brewers from '70 to '97 and the Chicago White Sox played a total of 20 home games there in 1968 and '69.

Baseball in Milwaukee, baseball at County Stadium, is about having fun. There's no place else where you can tailgate on beer and brat outside the park, get Bob Uecker on the call and watch Bernie Brewer slide into his mug of beer.

First game: April 14, 1953. Billy Bruton hit a 10th-inning home run to give the Braves a 3-2 victory over the Cardinals.

■ Site of three World Series (1957, '58 and '82)
■ Site of two All-Star Games (1955 and 1975)

contagious enthusiasm and a party atmosphere usually associated only with football.

Big, gray and commanding, County Stadium serves as a backdrop for these pregame festivities. You know this will be a special experience the moment you drive into the parking lot and hear an attendant say, "Welcome to County Stadium"—a greeting he really seems to mean. You quickly get caught up in the tailgating, which has become so ingrained in the ballpark experience that the Brewers installed restroom facilities outside the gates.

Soon everything reverses. The enthusiasm, like the mouth-watering smell of ballpark delicacies on the grill, wafts into the park and becomes the backdrop for baseball, which has been played in much this context since 1953—when the Braves moved to Milwaukee from Boston. The city's love affair with major league baseball still exists almost a half century later, although the Braves have been replaced by the Brewers, winning baseball has been replaced by mediocrity and a grand old stadium is ready to be replaced by the modern, high-tech facility being built a line drive away in the same parking lot.

There has never been anything high-tech about County Stadium, and that's one of its endearing qualities. Baseball here is much like the people it entertains—down to earth, no-frills and friendly with an upper-Midwest toughness. This is bleacher

County Stadium was host to the 1957 and '58 World Series, prompting long lines at ticket booths (right) and a fan-friendly atmosphere (above). Eddie Mathews (41, below) and Hank Aaron walk the long tunnel to the Braves' clubhouse.

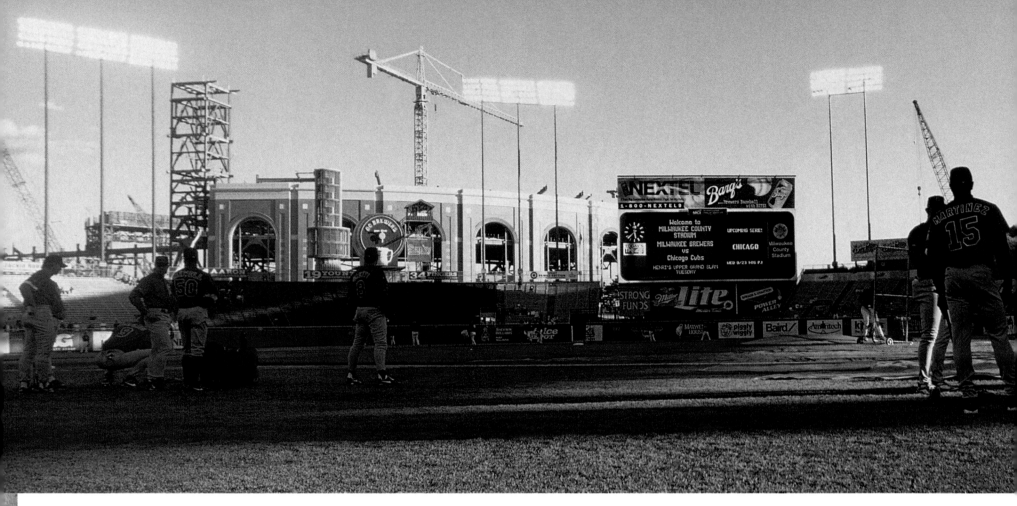

baseball, reflecting a quintessential blue-collar town filled with factories, breweries and a yearning to have fun.

It's no coincidence that many of the closest seats are in the outfield bleacher sections—one that stretches from straightaway left field to the center field backdrop; another between the backdrop and the massive right-center field scoreboard; and another from the scoreboard to straightaway right field. The bleacher seats are benches without backs, the concourses are dingy and cramped and the scoreboard has a video screen that shows replays in black and white—no complaints.

The single-deck bleachers give the outfield an open, airy, baseball-only feel,

belying County Stadium's four decades as host for two or three Green Bay Packers games per year. Double-decked, roofed grandstands wrap from foul pole to foul pole, with lower-deck field boxes sitting right on top of a beautiful, symmetrical grass field and higher-seat sightlines obstructed by support pillars.

County Stadium has undergone several expansions over the years, raising its original capacity of 36,011 to its current 53,192, and the relationship between players and fans has changed. But otherwise, it's basically the same functional park the Braves called home in 1953. Players for the Braves, who stayed there 13 mostly wonderful years, can remember fans who turned out in record numbers, gave them

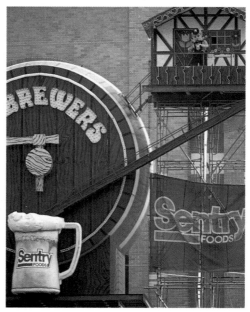

With new Miller Park looming over the right-center field fence, batting practice before 1999 games at County Stadium had a nostalgic feel (left). Bernie Brewer's chalet and beer mug (above) were stadium fixtures for many years.

success. Fans worshiped Warren Spahn and Hank Aaron, who began and ended his pursuit of Babe Ruth here, and they identified with Johnny Logan and Eddie Mathews, tough-edged players in the Milwaukee mold. Beer-drinking Gorman Thomas was vintage Milwaukee, as was disheveled 1982 Cy Young winner Pete Vuckovich. Robin Yount and Paul Molitor were models of the Midwest work ethic.

Most fans, however, will tell you it's the little things that make the difference at County Stadium. And the Brewers lean hard on their relationship with the community.

Like when Bernie Brewer, positioned over the center field backdrop, slides from his chalet into a giant mug of beer every time a Brewers player hits a home run. Or when County Stadium turns into a hypnotic, hand-clapping frenzy during "The Beer Barrel Polka," which is played at the seventh-inning stretch. Nothing brings down the house faster than a good Brat Race, a daily sprint around the warning track by four daring souls dressed like a Polish sausage, Italian sausage, bratwurst and hot dog. And where else in the major leagues is a relief pitcher delivered to the mound in the side car of a locally-produced Harley Davidson?

Only in Milwaukee, where everybody knows how to have fun—and the Brewers seem to care that they do. The Brewers spoke to their fans for 23 seasons through the gentle voice of public address announcer Bob Betts, whose nightly reminder, "Please drive home safely," will live long beyond the concrete walls of County Stadium.

gifts, brought food and birthday cakes to them at the park and showered them with an affection unlike anything found in most other major league communities.

The Braves rewarded them with two National League pennants, a 1957 World Series championship—and their defection to the greener pastures of Atlanta after the 1965 season. The relationship with the American League Brewers, who relocated to Milwaukee from Seattle in 1970 and from the A.L. to the N.L. in 1998, has not been quite so personal, although the Harvey's Wallbangers team of 1982 brought pennant fever to Milwaukee with a close-but-no-cigar World Series run.

But Milwaukee has always been more about players and having a good time than

Shea Stadium

Aging Willie Mays celebrates New York return debut with game-winning homer vs. Giants, his former team, May 14, 1972

Tug McGraw's "You Gotta Believe" motto rallies Mets to '73 pennant

Dodgers' Kirk Gibson settles Game 4 of 1988 NLCS in 12th inning wi solo home run

Phillies' Johnny Callison ends 1964 All-Star Game with dramatic three-run, ninth-inning homer

Phillies' Jim Bunning pitches perfect game on Father's Day, June 21, 1964

Where Cincinnati's Pete Rose was pelted with garbage after his Game 3 fight with shortstop Bud Harrelson in 1973 NLCS

Where Yankees played their home games in '74 and '75

Ninth-inning rally beats Marlins, ends Anthony Young's record 27-game losing streak, July 28, 1993

1999 infield as good as gold: John Olerud (1B), Edgardo Alfonzo (2B), Rey Ordonez (SS), Robin Ventura (3B)

DWIGHT GOODEN: Doc, 20, became youngest pitcher to win Cy Young and youngest 20-game winner in century, 1985

Lenny Dykstra's two-run, ninth-inning homer beats Astros 6-5 in Game 3 of 1986 NLCS

I t was a child of the '60s, home of the Amazin' Mets, "New Breed" fans and the craziest kind of baseball ever conceived. Shea Stadium is all grown up now, more mature and sophisticated, but age cannot wipe away the memories. This was the house of Casey Stengel and no-holds-barred fun, where ineptitude didn't matter, wins and losses were meaningless and there was always reason to smile.

That early innocence is long gone now, the smiles have become jaded and, like it or not, winning does matter. But today's Shea Stadium delivers a more enduring kind of charm. Many New Yorkers

Mets lose to Giants in 23-inning marathon—the second game of doubleheader—that lasts 7 hours, 23 minutes, May 31, 1964

Mets lose to Cardinals in 25th inning when wild pickoff throw to first allows Bake McBride to scurry around bases, Sept. 11, 1974

Casey Stengel called shots for Amazin' Mets. il Hodges guided Miracle Mets. Davey Johnson choreographed 1986 championship.

Where Robin Ventura hit game-winning, bases-loaded "single" in 15th inning, ending 1999 NLCS Game 5

Where Seaver struck out 10 straight Padres and 19 total, April 22, 1970 . . . where he topped 200 strikeouts for nine straight seasons

The Big Apple celebrates Mets home runs

Where Ron Swoboda made his diving catch in Game 4 of '69 Series

Where Tommie Agee robbed Orioles Elrod Hendricks, Paul Blair with game-saving catches in Game 3 of '69 World Series

Where Boston's Bill Buckner missed Mookie Wilson's (right) grounder, allowing Ray Knight to score winning run in World Series-saving Game 6 miracle

Where six-time Mets Gold Glover Keith Hernandez (below) dazzled fans . . . Home of power men Gary Carter, Howard Johnson

TOM SEAVER:
Three-time Cy Young winner provided anchor for '69 World Series champs, '73 pennant-winners

Mets

still view it as a big, blue, concrete bowl in the heart of Queens—a distant challenger to the incredible New York ballpark legacies of Ebbets Field, Yankee Stadium and the Polo Grounds—but what Shea lacks in history and charisma, it more than makes up for with personality.

To fully appreciate Shea Stadium, you need to understand the context of its first six seasons—a rollicking stretch of fun and unadulterated joy. When Shea made its major league debut in April 1964 as a spectacular showcase stadium in Flushing Park, it was located only a long fly ball or two from the World's Fair, which would draw millions of tourists through 1965. And it offered a different kind of baseball, the bumbling, sometimes-bizarre kind played by the expansion Mets, who had lost 231 games in two seasons under Stengel. Shea was fun and trendy, a place, unlike Yankee Stadium, where younger fans could cut loose.

It was a comedy act that played to rave reviews through 1968, thanks also

Shea glowed (above) in 1964 when it opened amid the hoopla surrounding the nearby World's Fair, the grounds of which can be seen in the upper left and center of the photograph. Shea is much more than a big, blue, concrete bowl, although that wasn't obvious from this 1999 parking lot view (right).

to the shifting of allegiance by jilted Dodgers and Giants fans. There was something going on here and, unlike anywhere else, losing was acceptable. The Mets drew 1.7 million fans in their first Shea season, 400,000 more than the pennant-winning Yankees. And so the fun continued.

But then, just as the comedy was wearing thin, the Amazin' Mets transformed into the Miracle Mets and Shea Stadium played host to its first World Series. Ironically, the 1969 Mets, managed by former Dodgers hero Gil Hodges and led by Cy Young winner Tom Seaver, posted the team's first winning record, won the first of the franchise's two championships—and changed the way Mets fans would view their teams forever.

Shea was a grand showcase when it opened, a high-tech curiosity and the trigger for the so-called cookie-cutter ballpark explosion of the late 1960s and '70s. Pirates manager Danny Murtaugh, who watched his team beat the Mets in the Shea inaugural, called it "a showplace. This will become one of the must visiting places for all tourists to New York, like the Empire State Building, Radio City or the Statue of Liberty," Murtaugh raved.

But later reviews were not so kind. Shea was fingered as a leader in the age of round, symmetrical, turf-covered, multi-purpose facilities that briefly changed the face of baseball. But it dodged much of the criticism that relentlessly dogged later stadiums in Cincinnati, Pittsburgh and Philadelphia. Shea was never enclosed by grandstands, which camouflages its circular shape; its open outfield gives it a baseball-only feel; and real grass and several distinguishing features make it easy to forgive its symmetrical lack of imagination.

The first thing you notice is the openness, a baseball characteristic the National Football League's Jets had to live with for 20 seasons. But your eyes drift quickly to the giant scoreboard that commands much of the right-center field view. The scoreboard, one of baseball's biggest in 1964, now is balanced by a Diamond Vision video display in left-center, a backdrop for the park's few bleacher seats. Next to the scoreboard in center field is the "Big Apple", which celebrates Mets home runs.

More than 90 percent of Shea's blue and red seats are located in foul territory, which adds to the open feeling. But that is offset by the five-tiered grandstands that climb precipitously high above the field. A curious architectural quirk can be found down both lines, where the grandstands edge inside the 338-foot foul poles, providing small fair-territory targets for home runs.

A visit to Shea is not complete without the roar of passing planes into and

The Mets' 1969 title triggered a wild celebration that resulted in serious damage to Shea Stadium (above).

out of nearby La Guardia Airport—a noise so deafening that players often step out of the batter's box until the roar subsides. Over the years, other recognizable sounds have been provided by organist Jane Jarvis and the rhythmic chant of "Let's Go Mets, Let's Go Mets."

Signs have always been an important part of the Shea landscape, encouraged by the Mets in deference to Yankee Stadium's no-banner rule. Big white-letter slogans adorned the stadium's exterior in the early years—"Watch the Stars Come Out", "Catch the Rising Stars", "Ya Gotta Believe"—and fans have always been willing to contribute their own expressive work. Who can forget Shea regular Sign Man, wearing his distinctive pie-hat, or Doc Gooden's "K"

SHEA STADIUM (1964-)

Left without a National League team since the Dodgers and Giants departed in 1957, New York, primarily because of the efforts of a young attorney named William Shea, was awarded an expansion franchise in 1960. The Mets would open play in 1962 and play two seasons in the Polo Grounds while their new stadium, named Shea Stadium to honor William Shea, could be built in the borough of Queens.

Opened in 1964, it has withstood the test of time. It was built with natural grass and an open center field, and has remained that way, unlike other parks that have switched to artificial turf and been enclosed.

Shea is an oasis in a desert of New York City concrete. Visitors who fly into nearby LaGuardia Airport often get a beautiful aerial view of Shea, the red and blue seats and the rich green grass.

First game: April 17, 1964. Pittsburgh slugger Willie Stargell broke the stadium in with the first hit, a home run in the second inning, to lead the Pirates to a 4-3 victory.

■ Site of three World Series (1969, '73 and '86)
■ Site of one All-Star Game (1964)

count? Shea's annual Banner Day promotions have ranked among the most popular in baseball.

At night, the exterior of Shea is like a wonderful Christmas light show for travelers on the network of expressways that connect Queens with the distant skyline of Manhattan and surrounding areas. Part of that show is provided by a series of lights that form the outline of bigger-than-life players in various poses (batting, pitching, catching, etc.) on the stadium facade. Part also comes from the distinctive lighting system that rims the inside of the grandstands and the two towers beyond left- and right-center fields.

Shea will not be named on many most-beautiful-stadium lists, but it's a good place to watch baseball and it has always been fun. From the craziness of Stengel and the Mets' improbable 1986 World Series comeback victory to the idiosyncrasies of coach Joe Pignatano's bullpen tomatoes and broadcaster Lindsey Nelson's wild and crazy sports jackets, fans have always gotten their money's worth.

And that, the Mets will assure you, is what baseball's all about.

The Big Apple (above) celebrates Mets home runs. More than three decades after Shea Stadium's opening, its outfield remains open (left) and its right-center field scoreboard (right) still dominates the view of fans.

Oakland Coliseum

Also known as Oakland Alameda County Coliseum; Network Associates Coliseum (1999-)

I t's a tough, imposing baseball factory, placed strategically in the hard, rigid, industrial community it serves. The Oakland Coliseum tries hard not to be flashy, hip or beautiful—and succeeds on all counts. Comfort and convenience are overrated accessories; charisma and charm are frivolous values. This is working-class baseball, the kind you have to labor, sweat and fuss over to appreciate.

You sense the need for such pain well before you even see the Coliseum complex. A gray, drab, rundown industrial neighborhood surrounds it, a sprawling parking lot and train tracks add to its isolation. At first

Milwaukee's Hank Aaron hits 750th career home run, June 18, 1976

1973 A.L. MVP Reggie Jackson hit 269 home runs in Athletics uniform

1972-73-74 world champions— The Mustache Gang

Where Henderson slid safely into record books with 939th career steal, passing Lou Brock, May 1, 1991

Finley tries to "fire" Mike Andrews after second baseman makes two errors in Game 2 of '73 World Series

CHARLES O. FINLEY: A's colorful and controversial owner, 1960-80

Tim Raines' 13th-inning triple snaps scoreless deadlock and gives N.L. 2-0 All-Star Game win, July 14, 1987

Right fielder Jose Canseco becomes baseball's first 40-40 man, 1988

Joe Rudi's seventh-inning, Game 5 homer off Dodgers ironman Mike Marshall decides 1974 World Series

1988-89-90 pennant winners—The Bash Brothers

Where Reds completed shocking World Series sweep of A's in 1990

Where Catfish Hunter pitched perfect game vs. Twins, May 8, 1968

Where Mark McGwire launched his amazing career with rookie-record 49 homers in 1987

Four A's combine for no-hitter vs. Angels, Sept. 28, 1975 (Vida Blue, Glenn Abbott, Paul Lindblad, Rollie Fingers)

Big pitch: Dave Stewart records four straight 20-win seasons, 1987-90; Bob Welch claims Cy Young with 27-6 record, 1990; Dennis Eckersley wins MVP and Cy Young, 1992

Sprinter Herb Washington serves as Finley's "designated runner" in 1974-75

Darold Knowles pitches in all seven games of 1973 World Series

Where Bert Campaneris hurled his bat at Detroit pitcher Lerrin LaGrow in Game 2 of 1972 ALCS

RICKEY HENDERSON: Baseball's all-time and single-season (130 in '82) basestealing king

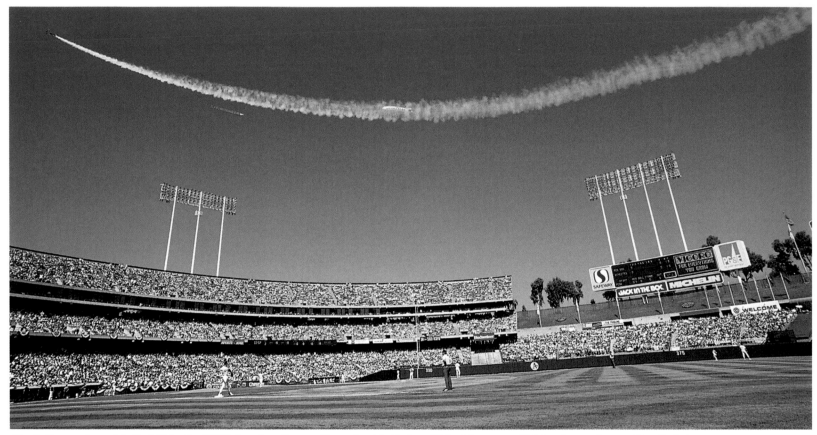

The Coliseum, dressed to the hilt for the 1990 American League Championship Series, still had its open outfield and a much more friendly feel.

glance, the huge, bowl-shaped Coliseum seems to rise up out of the pavement, overpowering its surroundings and the smaller, sleeker Oakland Arena, home of the NBA's Golden State Warriors.

It's no illusion. The floor of the Coliseum is dropped 21 feet below sea level, making its gray, nondescript facade less imposing than it could have been. But not even a tree-lined pathway around the structure can disguise what it really is—a monument to exposed concrete. It still is huge, it still rises up, up and away and it still overwhelms a first-time visitor, not unlike a first viewing of Yankee Stadium or the Los Angeles Coliseum.

Your first real sense of baseball is a powerful one—a symmetrical, lush, green, grass carpet that spreads out below and sweeps you away. You enter the stadium at mid-level, between the first and second decks, to a panoramic view that suggests important things happened here. There is little physical evidence and the A's do little to promote their championship aura, but you are bombarded by subliminal reminders that great teams—rough-edged, hard-working, raw-power teams with Oakland-style personalities—competed here.

You can almost see the faces of Reggie, Rudi, Campy, Sal, Catfish, Vida and Rollie as they feuded with owner Charlie Finley, fought among themselves and battled their way to five consecutive division titles and three straight World Series championships in the early 1970s. You can feel the arm-throbbing pain delivered by the Bash Brother teams of Jose Canseco, Mark McGwire and Rickey Henderson as they powered their way to three straight division titles and another Series win in 1989. This wasn't corporate America bottom-lining another championship; this was baseball with an old-fashioned mentality.

As hard as the Coliseum tries to maintain its edge, there's an ample supply of subtle charms and idiosyncracies to win over the toughest fan. Baseball has always been a pleasant experience here, especially before a 1995-96 football renovation enclosed the center field area and blocked a scenic view of a grassy knoll and the distant East Bay Hills.

It doesn't take long for your eyes to connect with the park's signature features. Expansive foul territory down both lines turns normally harmless out-of-play popups into easy outs. The backstop, which has been shortened from 90 feet to 60 behind the plate, appears to be notched into the box seats with side runways that provide a working area for photographers and feed directly into the dugouts and player clubhouses. Mirrored areas of sectioned steps over the left and right field fences—apparently going nowhere—send well-targeted home runs pinballing wildly in unpredictable directions.

The triple-decked grandstand wraps from foul pole to foul pole, curving away from the lines to create the large foul territory. For years, the Coliseum boasted one of the most raucous bleachers in baseball—two sections of single-decked seats, separated in center by an open runway, that connected the left and right field grandstands. The retainer wall above the bleachers was decorated by a line of pennant and team flags and three separate scoreboard units—including one of the first and best Diamond Vision boards in baseball—were perched atop the outer wall.

The entire center field structure changed with the 1995 renovation to accommodate the prodigal Raiders, who were making a triumphant return from Los Angeles. Now a massive wall of seats and skyboxes rise above the stadium rim, creating an edifice known among baseball fans as "Mount Davis," a sarcastic reference to Raiders owner Al Davis. The bleachers are gone, as are the flags and a concourse that allowed fans to pass above the bleacher sections. New video boards are perched on the stadium rim down the left and right field lines.

Mount Davis, the massive wall of seats and skyboxes that rise above the stadium rim in center field (bottom left), is equipped with retractable seats that can extend forward for football (center left). Like all modern stadiums, the Coliseum has its share of luxury boxes (above left) filled with amenities.

The stadium now has a football feel and small crowds get lost in its cavernous sprawl. When the house is full, fan enthusiasm makes the place jump. When it's not, baseball can be a lonely experience.

These are fans who know how to have fun and celebrate. They cut their major league teeth on the always-controversial Finley and his creative promotions when the team relocated there in 1968, and they survived the late-1970s, when Finley's tight-fisted management helped turn the stadium into the "Oakland Mausoleum." This is the reputed birthplace of video dot racing and the current or former home of drum-beating Crazy George, Charley O. the Mule, deep-voiced public address announcer Roy Steele and the wave. Bay Area bragging rights are locked safely away in a Coliseum vault, thanks to the A's 1989 World Series victory over the Giants.

What Oakland doesn't have—thankfully, A's fans will tell you—is San Francisco flavor or Candlestick Park weather. Coliseum patrons can put up with chilly night games and occasional wind-blown pop flies—as long as baseball is played there with old-fashioned values like hustle and hard work.

OAKLAND-ALAMEDA COUNTY COLISEUM (1968-)

Also known as Oakland Alameda County Coliseum;
renamed Network Associates Coliseum (1999-)

After years of threats and attempts to move from Kansas City, Charlie Finley finally succeeded in the fall of 1967. Though Oakland had been one of his intended targets for years, Finley had been studying two markets for potential relocation: Oakland and Seattle. Oakland was selected, in part, because it had a stadium already built.

In addition to being the home of the A's, the Coliseum also has been the home of the NFL's Raiders, from 1966 through 1981 and again since 1995. The stadium underwent a transformation in 1995 for the Raiders' return, with the addition of center field stands and skyboxes. With that addition, the wind patterns in the ballpark changed, and made it a park where fly balls carry better.

First game: April 17, 1968. With Governor Ronald Reagan on hand to throw out the first pitch, the A's lost their Oakland debut, 4-1, to the Orioles.

■ Site of six World Series (1972, '73, '74, '88, '89, '90)
■ Site of one All-Star Game (1987)

The circular Coliseum provided a spectacular panorama from center field (right) in 1991, before Mount Davis took away its tree-lined view (below).

Jack Murphy
Stadium

Also known as San Diego Stadium
(1969-1980); renamed
Qualcomm Stadium (1997-)

I t's situated in the lush, rolling
Mission Valley countryside, a
few miles from where Father
Junipero Serra established the
first California mission more than two
centuries ago. Beautiful downtown
San Diego lies about six miles to the
southwest, the Pacific Ocean eight
miles to the east and the San Diego
River four or five long fly balls to the
south, diverted from its natural banks.
If there's such a thing as sunshine
heaven, it's in the right field
bleachers, where you can get a tan
while offering strategy and advice to
Padres first citizen Tony Gwynn.

What's not to like about Jack
Murphy Stadium?

The Dodgers and
Orel Hershiser stop
catcher Benito
Santiago, who had
hit in rookie-record
34 straight games,
Oct. 3, 1987

Where new owner
Ray Kroc blasted his
players in 1974
home opener. He
yelled over public
address system:
"This is the most
stupid ballplaying
I've ever seen."

Giants pinch hitter Will
Mays hits career homer N
600 off rookie Mike
Corkins, Sept. 22, 1969

Montreal's Pedro Martinez,
perfect through nine innings,
allows 10th-inning double to
Bip Roberts in eventual 1-0
victory, June 3, 1995

TREVOR HOFFMAN

Birthplace of the
San Diego Chicken

78

Cardinals' Lou Brock sets modern major league record with 893rd stolen base, Aug. 29, 1977

Padres beat Braves 4-1, take shocking 3-0 lead in NLCS en route to second N.L. pennant, Oct. 10, 1998

Three Cy Youngs: Randy Jones (left) 1976, Gaylord Perry (right) 1978, Mark Davis 1989

Dodgers' ace Orel Hershiser works 10 scoreless innings vs. Padres, stretching record streak to 59, Sept. 28, 1988

Clay Kirby, who trails 1-0 after pitching eight hitless innings vs. Mets, is lifted for pinch hitter in controversial conclusion to eventual 3-0 loss, July 21, 1970

Where Steve Garvey hit ninth-inning, Game 4-winning home run vs. Cubs in must-win 1984 NLCS battle

Tigers storm past Padres in five-game 1984 World Series; Yankees sweep Padres in 1998 classic

Where Hoffman converted 53-of-54 save opportunities for a single-season record .981 percentage in 1998

Where Steve Garvey's ironman streak ended at 1,207 games when he dislocated thumb while sliding vs. Atlanta, July 29, 1983

TONY GWYNN: Mr. Padre is a member of baseball's 3,000-hit club and owner of eight N.L. batting titles

There are a few things—a 1997 renovation that enclosed a once-open right field; its multi-purpose feel—but it's hard to escape San Diego without a good baseball experience. It's all about atmosphere and casual fun here, the national pastime with a soft edge. On a perfect, sunshiny spring or summer afternoon, it's like a day at the beach—without the water.

The first thing you notice about Jack Murphy is the pastoral surroundings, once pristine but now more commercial with intruding hotels, restaurants and gas stations. It's a river area, always green and favorable to wildlife if you really take time to look. The 122-acre parking lot is an attraction in and of itself, an expansive area used for events like drag racing and skateboarding and a tailgating paradise for baseball and football fans who have been known to import sand, set up volleyball courts and even flavor their atmosphere with potted palm trees. Trolleys roll in and out of the lot, dropping off passengers from downtown San Diego or nearby Old Town—the historic mission district.

Entrance to the open-air concourses also is an experience. You can take the conventional escalator route to your desired level or you can be more adventurous and walk one of the distinctive concrete swirls that sit outside the main structure—ramps that look like giant springs ready to uncoil skyward. No matter where you're located at Jack Murphy, you can always feel the gentle breezes off the Pacific—the park's natural air-conditioner.

For many years, the field was shaped like a horseshoe, with five-level grandstands wrapping behind home plate from the right field foul pole all the way through left field to center. The open right field, which once offered a nice view of the rolling hillsides, now is closed—with grandstands butting up to a giant, high-tech scoreboard in right-center field. This obviously is a football stadium, but it somehow retains a reasonable baseball feel.

You have to be careful not to overdose on Jack Murphy's colors, a virtual rainbow of blues, reds, oranges and greens that surround you the moment you step into the field area. The green looks like an Augusta putting surface, spread out below on one of the best-kept natural carpets in the game. The coup de grace is provided by miniature palm trees that occupy the dead area between the outfield fences and bleacher retaining walls, inviting targets for home runs.

If you can get past the sense of enclosure and the park's near symmetry (327-405-330), you'll pick up on subtle quirks that make Jack Murphy distinctive. Such as a left field foul pole that stands 2 feet behind the outfield fence, 1 foot in from of the retaining wall—

The sparkling green grass and high-rising grandstands provide the backdrop for San Diego-style baseball.

Horseshoe-shaped Jack Murphy Stadium, renamed Qualcomm Stadium in 1997, is a monument to concrete, complete with giant swirling ramps (above, below) that take visitors to desired seating levels. The outside experience is active and quaint, enhanced by colorful trolleys (right) that deliver and carry away baseball-loving fans.

making it possible for a line drive to cross the fence in fair territory and hook in front of the pole into foul. And the lights that ring the rim of the stadium, making the typical hulking standards unnecessary.

Perhaps of more consequence are field boxes that arc from the dugouts toward the deep outfield foul lines, coming to a point before covering the bullpen mounds. The protruding stands obstruct umpires' sightlines for balls hit into foul territory in the corners and the bullpen pitcher's mounds touch the foul lines, making life hazardous for relievers with their back to the action.

The color and sunshine provide perfect backdrops for a Southern California experience—energetic fans who seem ready, willing and able to bring good cheer to the ballpark. The Padres, who cater to disparate age groups, always have been mindful that promotions, special events (the Beach Boys and other concerts) and giveaways are necessary to compete with the entertainment options of a tropical paradise. This was, after all, the birthplace of the San Diego Chicken, a mascot creation of Ted Giannoulas, who took his hilarious act on to national fame.

"Baseball under the sun" became a Padres theme years ago and Thursday afternoon games are now a popular tradition. It's not uncommon during well-attended afternoon contests to see fans dressed casually, some in bathing suits, working on their tans, batting beach balls up and down and doing the wave. Night games usually are more family-friendly and fans who get there early to watch batting practice often are treated to major league sunsets.

Fun is the name of the game at Jack Murphy Stadium and you get that sense from your first bite into a delicious fish taco to your first sighting of a tinsel star dangling from the end of a fishing pole out of Jerry Coleman's broadcast booth—his "You could hang a star on that one!" tribute to a spectacular play.

Baseball has been a laid-back experience at Jack Murphy for more than three decades. Built in 1967 as a lure for major league baseball, San Diego Stadium (its name until 1980) became the immediate home of the NFL's Chargers and a 1968 home for the Pacific Coast League's Padres. The expansion big-league Padres began play in 1969 and suffered through serious growing pains until 1984, when they won their first division title and National League pennant. Stadium expansions eventually lifted The Murph's baseball seating capacity to 66,307 and the 1998 pennant-winning Padres attracted six postseason crowds in excess of 62,000.

That might have been a coming-of-age for Padres fans, who have been entertained by such players as Gwynn, Fred McGriff, Joe Carter, Dave Winfield, Ozzie Smith, Gary Sheffield, Randy Jones, Rollie Fingers, Trevor Hoffman and Tony Fernandez, but still are looking for that final piece to a championship puzzle.

Jack Murphy, an explosion of color, has gradually transformed from a facility with an open right field to an enclosed, multi-purpose stadium.

JACK MURPHY STADIUM (1969-)

Also known as San Diego Stadium (1969-1980);
renamed Qualcomm Stadium (1997-)

Professional baseball arrived in San Diego in 1936. In that year, a Pacific Coast League team owned by Bill Lane, named Padres because of its proximity to a nearby mission, began play in Lane Field. The ballpark saw its share of future stars, including Ted Williams and Luke Easter. Lane Field, constructed in a federal employment program during the Great Depression, finally gave way in 1958 to Westgate Park.

In the mid-1960s, San Diego Union sports editor Jack Murphy began a crusade to build a new stadium, one that would attract a baseball expansion team and provide a home for the NFL's Chargers. In 1965, the San Diego city council approved plans for a new stadium. Two years later, after acquiring the land, diverting the flow of the San Diego River and finally construction, San Diego Stadium opened on August 19, 1967, with a football game between the Chargers and Detroit Lions.

In 1980, the stadium was officially renamed Jack Murphy Stadium, often shortened to simply The Murph, in recognition of Jack Murphy's efforts.

In 1998, the stadium earned the distinction of being the first to host a World Series and Super Bowl in the same calendar year.

Whether called San Diego Stadium, Jack Murphy Stadium or Qualcomm Stadium, the park is a wonderfully typical California experience — beautiful, cool and clear weather, palm trees swaying in the breezes and lush green as far as you can see.

First game: April 8, 1969. Behind a complete game and 12 strikeouts by Dick Selma, San Diego downed Houston, 2-1. One year prior, on April 5, 1968, the first exhibition game was played in the stadium, between the Indians and Giants.

■ Site of two World Series (1984 and 1998)
■ Site of two All-Star Games (1978 and 1992)

The Turf Era

They have survived scorn and ridicule for three decades while filling a basic need for fiscal responsibility. The Turf Era parks have always gotten a bad rap because of the round, cookie-cutter mentality, look-alike symmetry and artificial surfaces that were a shocking departure, technologically and aesthetically, from their quaint and curious predecessors.

But St. Louis' Busch Stadium, Philadelphia's Veterans Stadium, Pittsburgh's Three Rivers Stadium and Cincinnati's Riverfront Stadium are multi-functional arenas that have served their communities well by increasing revenue streams. Their larger dimensions and speed-enhancing turf fields also have affected the way the game is played.

Purists have welcomed the turf-to-grass switch at Busch and Kansas City's Kauffman Stadium and they look forward to the prospects of new retro parks in Pittsburgh and Cincinnati. But it seems inevitable—and in a strange way even sad—that this chapter of ballpark history is rapidly approaching its conclusion.

Riverfront
Stadium

Renamed Cinergy Field (1996-)

Bench hits final career homer (No. 389) on "Johnny Bench Night" vs. Houston, Sept. 17, 1983

Hank Aaron hits record-tying 714th home run off Jack Billingham, April 4, 1974

Reds score 14 runs on 16 hits in first inning of 18-2 win over Astros, Aug. 3, 1989

Where A's catcher Gene Tenace hit balls in first two at-bats in 1972 World Series

Shortstops Dave Concepcion and Barry Larkin (left) have anchored Reds' infield for three decades

Inside, it's a mirror image of its cookie-cutter brethren in Philadelphia and Pittsburgh. Outside, it's one of the most endearing venues in the major leagues, protected on one side by the mighty Ohio River and caressed on the other by Cincinnati's inviting downtown skyline. Riverfront Stadium is exactly what its name implies. And its legacy will always be closely tied to a Big Red Machine that methodically perpetrated baseball mayhem there.

Riverfront is not given to exaggeration or window dressing. What you see is what you get, a

Catcher JOHNNY BENCH: N.L. MVP in '70 and '72, was anchor for Cincinnati's Big Red Machine

Reds lefty Tom Browning joins the "perfect club" when he retires all 27 Dodgers in 1-0 win, Sept. 16, 1988

Where Boston catcher Carlton Fisk collided with Ed Armbrister, helping Reds claim controversial victory in Game 3 of 1975 World Series

Sparky Anderson's Big Red Machine produced pennants in '70, '72, '75 and '76

Bench's dramatic ninth-inning homer vs. Pirates ties Game 5 of 1972 NLCS . . . Reds secure pennant later in inning when George Foster scores on wild pitch by Bob Moose

Mets' Al Leiter stops Reds on two hits in one-game playoff to decide wild-card playoff berth, Oct. 4, 1999

St. Louis' Mark Whiten ties two long-standing records with four homers, 12 RBIs in second game of doubleheader vs. Reds, Sept. 7, 1993

Rose's 3,000th career hit (May 5, 1978) is merely an appetizer for the big one—record-breaker 4,192 off San Diego's Eric Show on Sept. 11, 1985

Second baseman Joe Morgan wins consecutive MVP awards in '75, '76

1990 World Series champs—unlikely hero Billy Hatcher gets seven straight hits in Games 1 and 2

PETE ROSE: Charlie Hustle was baseball's all-time hits king

Where Tom Seaver pitched only no-hitter of his career, vs. St. Louis, June 16, 1978

Where Rose bowled over Ray Fosse, giving N.L. a 12-inning win in 1970 All-Star Game

Ron Robinson, one out away from perfect game, surrenders single, homer before Reds finally beat Expos 3-2, May 2, 1988

Phillies pitcher Rick Wise makes history when he fires no-hitter and hits two home runs, June 23, 1971

Cincinnati fact of life since its June 1970 grand opening. The multi-purpose stadium was a state-of-the-art wonder then, the first to feature an all-artificial turf field with mound and base cutouts, and the only thing to change has been public perception—yesterday's marvelous and high-tech is today's sterile and antiseptic.

That's certainly not the case outside, where the circular, concrete structure sits like a flying saucer ready to take off at the first sign of trouble. Riverfront's unimaginative architecture is well camouflaged by serene, almost-quaint surroundings that lull you into a sense of how baseball is experienced in a picturesque Midwest community.

You can approach the stadium from downtown Cincinnati, over a skywalk that traverses a major expressway. A little shopping or dinner before baseball? The stadium's outside ramps offer a perfect excuse for

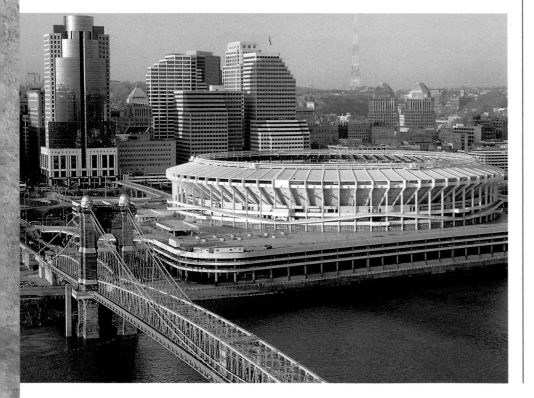

Riverfront Stadium sits in the shadow of the Cincinnati skyline (left, right), connected to Kentucky by an old suspension bridge and the mighty Ohio River. Fans were in a lingering mood in 1990 (above) as they waited for the gates to open for a World Series game against the Oakland A's.

lingering with your thoughts—a serenade of horns from old-fashioned riverboats paddling up and down the Ohio, a mesmerizing stream of cars crossing an ancient suspension bridge that connects Kentucky and Ohio. The Cincinnati skyline, brightly lighted at night, cradles Riverfront like a spoiled child.

You can feel the electricity of baseball on the streets when the Reds are playing well. When they're not, the fans still bask in the aura of Sparky Anderson-style baseball, which literally drips off the rafter-like overhang that circles the rim of the stadium. A quarter century later, the Big Red Machine is still running roughshod through everybody's mind.

The park is a model of symmetrical (330 down both lines) precision. But who needs quirks, crannies or architectural personality when you've got Johnny Bench, Joe Morgan, Pete Rose, Tony Perez, Dave Concepcion, George Foster, Eric Davis, Barry Larkin and five National League pennants? Before Riverfront was even a year old, it had played host to an All-Star

Cardinals slugger Mark McGwire, the newly crowned 1998 home run king, stands in the shadows, ready to take his best batting-practice shots at Riverfront's distant seats.

Game, an NLCS game and two World Series contests. Before it was 7, the Big Red Machine had hammered its way to four pennants and back-to-back championships.

You enter Riverfront on the plaza level—a stadium without bowels—and immediately are greeted by the green, artificial field. Plastic chairs rise around you steeply in color-coordinated schemes and your gaze quickly settles on the expansive fourth-level upper-deck red seats, where only a few sluggers have ventured with their mightiest home run swings. High, on the stadium rim over center field, is a long, skinny, horizontal scoreboard that stretches into left- and right-center field with myriad forms of information and advertising.

There is nothing really wrong with Riverfront—it's a typical baseball/ football facility that's simply devoid of the quirky physical characteristics baseball fans now demand from their ballparks. This is a stadium that expects you to focus squarely on the game without the frills and distractions of younger major league parks. It's comfortable, modern, attractive and obsessively clean. It's baseball without a ballpark atmosphere, strange bounces or unusual ground rules.

But that's not to say Riverfront is without distinctions. After the 1966 All-Star Game at St. Louis, Casey Stengel commented that Busch Stadium sure holds its heat well. So does Riverfront. Be prepared on a hot August afternoon because the humidity descends over the field, forced to hang like a blanket over turf that can only reflect, not absorb, its heat.

For a decade and a half, the Riverfront atmosphere included colorful owner Marge Schott, her dog Schottzie on a leash, parading around the field, chatting with players and surveying her kingdom. Schott, a sixth-generation Cincinnatian, also was visible during games in her "Blue 108" seat—an owner having fun with the fans instead of tucked away in a stuffy corporate box.

In what other city can you park below the stadium? Riverfront is one of few parks with a rimmed lighting system rather than towering standards. Replicas of the team's five retired uniforms hang from the facade above the left field fence, distances are painted metrically on the outfield walls and bullpens still are located in foul territory down both lines.

Baseball at Riverfront, which offers some of the lowest ticket prices in baseball, is only occasionally an ear-shattering experience. These are high-standard fans who can't resist the temptation to create a good wave, but otherwise reserve their emotion for just the proper moment. There have been a few.

This is, after all, where Hank Aaron tied baseball's all-time home run record in 1974 and hometown hero Rose broke the game's all-time hits record 11 years later. Where Cardinals outfielder Mark Whiten rocked the Reds with an incredible four-homer, 12-RBI explosion and the 1990 Reds rocked baseball by pulling off one of the most shocking World Series upsets in history.

Where a well-oiled Big Red Machine once pounded its way to the pinnacle of baseball and, in the process, lifted a city and its cookie-cutter stadium to glory beyond anybody's wildest dreams.

RIVERFRONT STADIUM (1970-)

Renamed Cinergy Field (1996-)

For most of the '60s, it was the subject of dreams and discussions, delays and debates. When Riverfront finally opened, its greatest strength was its size. Opened in time for the rise of the Big Red Machine, a whole lot more fans — Riverfront has 50,000-plus seats — could see the dynasty in action.

Built on the edge of the Ohio River, the name Riverfront made obvious sense, and the unnamed project took on that name unofficially. There were other suggestions for the stadium's name — Queen City Stadium, Red/Bengal Stadium, as well as the thought of recognizing prominent figures such as President Eisenhower, Powel Crosley and Neil Armstrong — but eventually the unofficial name became official.

Until 1996. On September 9, 1996, naming rights for the stadium were sold and the official name was changed to Cinergy Field.

First game: June 30, 1970. The Braves' Hank Aaron, who would tie Babe Ruth's all-time home run record of 714 in Riverfront in 1974, homered in the stadium's first game, an 8-2 Braves victory.

■ Site of five World Series (1970, '72, '75, '76 and '90)
■ Site of two All-Star Games (1970 and 1988)

Kauffman Stadium

Also known as Royals Stadium (1973-1993)

Carlos Beltran becomes first rookie since 1975 to drive in and score 100 runs, 1999

Where Cookie Rojas and Fred Patek celebrated Royals' clinching of '76 division championship by jumping into water fountain

Minnesota's Paul Molitor gets 3,000 career hit, a triple, on Sept. 16, 199

Brett goes 4-for-4, hits two homers in clutch ALCS Game 3 win over Blue Jays, Oct. 11, 1985

Misplayed fly ball gives Brett inside-the-park homer and allows him to edge teammate Hal McRae for controversial batting crown, Oct. 3, 1976

21-year-old Bret Saberhagen wins first of two Cy Youngs, 1985

GEORGE BRETT: Three-time batting champ wrote his own Royals record book en route to Hall of Fame

How do you spell relief? Dan Quisenberry (1979-88), Jeff Montgomery (1988-99)

I t is an I-70 jewel, a must-look landmark for anybody driving to or from downtown Kansas City. The seats of Kauffman Stadium seem to bristle in the daylight, a reflection of all the lustrous baseball moments they have witnessed since 1973. Hundreds of thousands of drivers zip past the stadium on a daily basis, momentarily distracted by the sudden dash of color and the back of a giant, crown-shaped object that stands guard over the facility.

That's the 12-story-high scoreboard, a replica of the Kansas City Royals' logo and one of the two

Where Mark Quinn belted record-tying two homers in his first big-league game, Sept. 14, 1999

Bret Saberhagen shuts out Cardinals as Royals win all-Missouri Series and claim first championship, Oct. 27, 1985

Hal McRae collects 54 doubles in 1977, a major league DH-record 133 RBIs in 1982

Brett's .390 average, MVP exploits help Royals capture first A.L. pennant, 1980

Where Amos Otis (left) and Willie Wilson patroled for more than two decades

Royals defeat A's, Sept. 15, 1977, for 16th straight win, the longest major league winning streak in 24 years

Where Angels' Nolan Ryan fired first career ɔ-hitter, first at Royals Stadium, May 15, 1973

Where umpire Don Denkinger made his infamous call on Jorge Orta's ground ball in Game 6 of '85 World Series

FRANK WHITE: Winner of eight Gold Gloves as one of premier second basemen in baseball history

illie Wilson ties switch-hitting ecords with 230 ts and 100 hits om each side of plate, 1980

Brett kisses home plate, to delight of fans attending his final Kauffman Stadium performance, Sept. 29, 1993

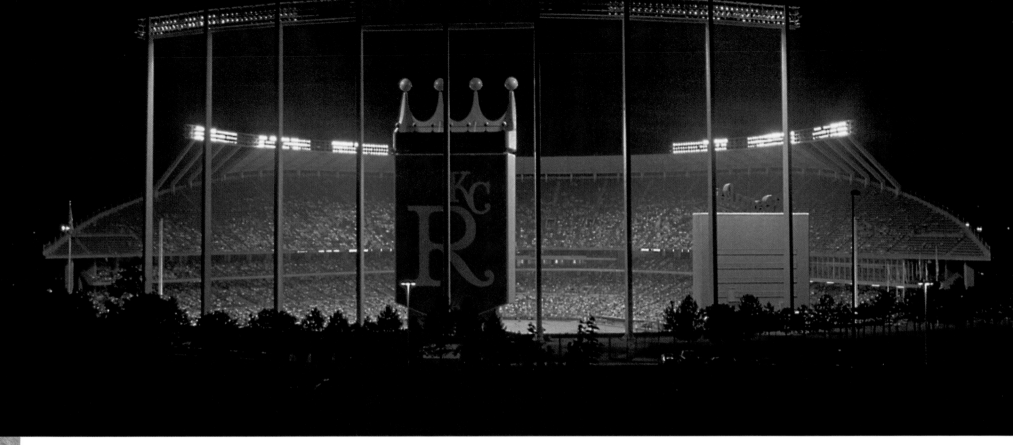

signature features of a ballpark that somehow escaped the depressing cookie-cutter stigma of the 1970s. You see the scoreboard coming, you see it going—and it commands your attention for significant spans during every game.

Kauffman Stadium has always been a structure of vision, and that becomes apparent the moment you enter a massive parking lot that serves two masters. Kauffman, a k a Royals Stadium, was built as a base-ball-only ballpark in the era of sterile, nondescript, multi-purpose facilities that sprung up in St. Louis, Philadelphia, Cincinnati and Pittsburgh. Next door, a couple of football fields away, stands Arrowhead Stadium,

The trademark crown-shaped scoreboard (above) dominates the view of Kauffman Stadium, home of the Royals, from Interstate 70. The stadium (right) has always been known for its beauty, both during its turf and grass eras.

the equally impressive home of Kansas City's Chiefs.

On Sunday mornings during the fall, this parking lot would be filled with the aroma of the best barbecue any taste bud could hope to savor and the sights and sounds of fans who have turned tailgating into an artform. But baseball appetites are less demanding and the real experience begins with your first gaze on a travelogue-like playing area.

You can't avoid the giant JumboTron video board stationed on the left field hillside or the vertical scoreboard, which rises up, up, up on the stadium's outer wall in dead center field, framed by towering light standards and flanked on both sides by a 322-foot-long waterfall that covers most of the area beyond the fences in both left and right. The water is mesmerizing, whether shooting skyward, cascading or merely reflecting a variation of colored lights.

It's hard to sit anywhere in the ballpark, gaze upon the open outfield expanse and not appreciate what a distinctive backdrop the fountain provides. You might understand the charm of Ebbets Field or Fenway Park, the charisma of Yankee Stadium or Wrigley, but it's still hard to imagine baseball in a brighter, cleaner or more beautiful setting. The park's pastoral effect was punctuated before the 1995 season, when the Royals finally replaced their artificial surface with grass.

The geometrically-perfect and symmetrical Kauffman (330 feet down both lines, 400 to center) looks and feels almost like a painting, unlike the quirky and colorful atmospheres of many old-time ballparks. It lacks the colorful frenzy of some parks, the boisterous cheers and jeers of others. Kauffman has the feel of a small community relationship with a serenity that can almost lull you to sleep. But the Royals teams of the late 1970s and early '80s inspired as much fervor and baseball passion as you'll find anywhere in the country.

These were the Royals of George Brett, Hal McRae, Amos Otis, Frank White, Willie Wilson and Paul Splittorff—the six-time West Division champions who provided a blueprint for expansion success. This was a team filled with warriors who stood toe-to-toe and traded punches with the powerful Yankees in four memorable American League Championship Series.

Colorful, high-rising fountains form a spectacular backdrop for hitters and a scenic view for Kauffman visitors.

KAUFFMAN STADIUM (1973-)

Also known as Royals Stadium (1973-1993)

An expansion franchise that began play in 1969, the Royals played for four seasons at Municipal Stadium, which had also been the home of the Kansas City Athletics.

Since its opening in 1973, the former Royals Stadium has undergone remarkably few major changes. In 1993, the stadium was renamed Kauffman Stadium, a tribute to former owner Ewing M. Kauffman, and the artificial surface was replaced by natural grass before the 1995 season.

Kauffman Stadium is a warm, summer evening, the outfield opening to invite those driving by on I-70 to take a peek inside and the water fountains dancing beyond the outfield walls.

First game: April 10, 1973. The Royals beat the Rangers, 12-1, behind Paul Splittorff.

■ Site of two World Series (1980 and 1985)
■ Site of one All-Star Game (1973)

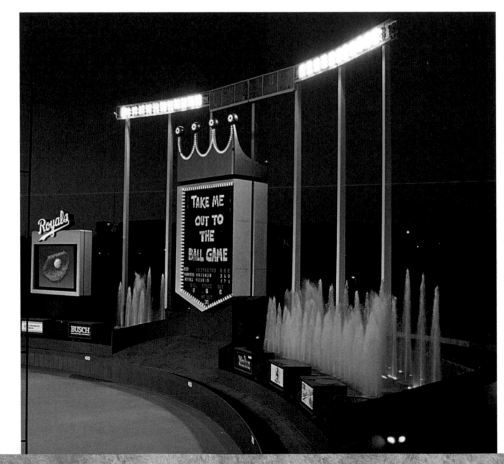

It's hard to visit Kauffman without getting a special sense of Brett, the multi-talented third baseman who helped make the small-market Royals a nationally respected championship contender. You can still see him, standing on second base, tipping his cap to a delighted crowd as the scoreboard flashes ".401" in the background. He's at the plate, crouched, weight back, ready to uncoil into another pitch. He's making that "in your face" home run trot in the first inning of Game 5 of the 1980 World Series.

But other images are just as prominent. Who can forget Cookie Rojas and Freddie Patek jumping into the fountains to celebrate a division title? Or Bo Jackson's titanic home run over the center field fence? Or a Patek-to-White-to-Mayberry double play, a Bret Saberhagen no-hitter, a U.L. Washington toothpick, an Otis running catch?

The pain still burns deep from that 1977 ALCS loss to the hated Yankees, but the joy still bubbles

Kauffman Stadium (above right) and Arrowhead Stadium, home of the NFL's Chiefs, sit side-by-side—an innovative stadium double that has served Kansas City's professional sports needs since 1973. A sunset over Kauffman (below) is as good as it gets in baseball.

over from that incredible Game 6 comeback win over Whitey Herzog and the cross-state Cardinals in the 1985 World Series. Fans will never forget Dick Howser, hugging his players after the Game 7 championship-sealing victory, a smiling, waving Ewing Kauffman or the sight of reliever Dan Quisenberry, hose in hand, showing compassion for sweltering fans hanging over the side wall of the right field bullpen.

Kauffman Stadium is a place of community, a reflection of the Midwest values that often are scorned by the more hard-core fans of other regions.

But that laid-back approach also is a big part of the flavor that makes it so special. Through the Royals' 1976-85 run, the facility stood as a Camelot among ballparks, that near-perfect blend of success, beauty and personality.

Maybe the most appropriate tribute to Kauffman Stadium was made, fittingly, by Brett in his final career home game in 1993 when he sent the crowd into a frenzy by getting down on his knees to deliver a goodbye kiss to home plate—the final stop on his path to the Hall of Fame.

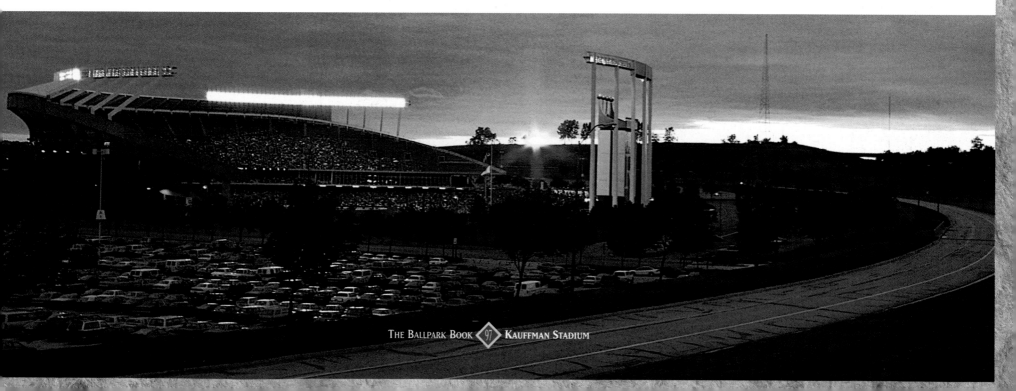

Veterans Stadium

It opened in 1971 to rave reviews, a baseball showcase mirroring state-of-the-art facilities already in use at St. Louis, Cincinnati and Pittsburgh. Almost three decades later, Veterans Stadium stands as a monument to nondescript, one of the ultimate cookie-cutter stadiums that have drawn the everlasting scorn of ballpark purists. Somewhere between those extremes is the real Vet, the home of three National League pennant winners, the franchise's only World Series champion and the most emotional, vocal fans in baseball.

The only real problem with Veterans Stadium is perception—it was built for comfort and multi-purpose durability, not as a charming reflection of a city or team's personality.

The "Bull Ring", where Greg Luzinski bought tickets for various youth organizations

Where smooth-fieldi shortstop Larr Bowa patrole for 11 seasons

Carlton wins 15th straight game, Aug. 17, 1972

Blue Jays score six runs in eighth inning and claim wild 15-14 win in Game 4 of 1993 World Series

STEVE CARLTON won Cy Youngs in '72, '77, '80 and '82

Carlton finishes 1977 season with 17-3 record at Veterans Stadium

Gary Matthews' three homers, eight RBIs help Phillies to a four-game NLCS win over Dodgers and fourth pennant, 1983

Dave Johnson hit two pinch-hit grand slams in 1978

Curt Schilling shuts out Blue Jays, gives Phillies temporary life after five games of 1993 Series

Where Greg Luzinski drove a 500-foot homer off old Liberty Bell, May 16, 1972

Greg Luzinski's homer wins Game 1 of 1980 Championship Series

Eddie Murray crashes two Game 5 homers as Orioles dash Phillies' hopes for 1983 World Series championship

Home-field advantage? N.L. pitchers hold A.L. batters to a single run in 7-1 (1976) and 6-0 (1996) All-Star Game wins

Tug McGraw holds off Royals in sixth 1980 World Series game, giving Phillies first championship

Bake McBride's three-run homer helps Phillies beat Royals in Game 1 of '80 World Series

me of 1983 and 1987 y Young winners— John Denny, Steve Bedrosian

Schmidt ties N.L. record with 11th home run in April of 1976

Three-time MVP third baseman MIKE SCHMIDT owns numerous team offensive records and 10 Gold Gloves

Pete Rose singles for N.L.-record hit No. 3,631, Aug. 10, 1981

It lacks the quirks and nuances of the baseball-only parks of yesteryear, it doesn't have a lot of distinctive features and it's not Camden Yards, the blueprint for today's retro parks. What it does have is simplicity— Veterans Stadium is a comfortable place to watch baseball for demanding patrons who would gladly substitute success for beauty.

To appreciate the Vet, you first have to put it in perspective. The stadiums of the 1970s were built in the shadow of Houston's Astrodome, the biggest, baddest, most wondrous superstructure ever erected—the sports arena that lifted the concept of multi-purpose practicality to a new level. This was not the age of ballparks—it was the era of high-tech, durable, no-nonsense facilities that could serve two masters, baseball and football, while attracting non-sports events ranging from revivals and concerts to rodeos and tractor pulls.

For many years, the Big Three venues in Philadelphia sports were (right to left) Veterans Stadium, the Spectrum and John F. Kennedy Stadium.

When Veterans Stadium opened its doors, it was hailed as a masterpiece, a circular, enclosed, concrete-based sports nirvana located within a few dribbles of two other South Philadelphia sports arenas—the Spectrum and John F. Kennedy Stadium, now the site of First Union Center. Not only was the Vet splendid and hip, its baseball field was a symmetrical work of art (330 feet down both lines, 371 to the power alleys, 408 to center), covered with a durable, low-maintenance AstroTurf carpet that had dirt cutouts around home plate, the bases and the pitcher's mound.

"It's got to be the best new park in baseball," raved then-Montreal manager Gene Mauch. "It looks like they've taken the good things from all the other new parks, added some things of their own, and whipped them into a pretty good place."

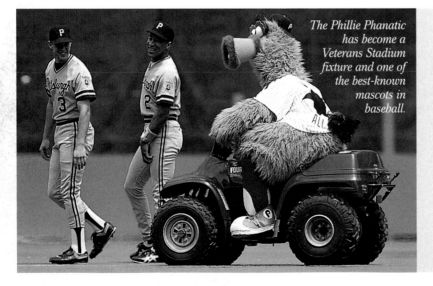

The Phillie Phanatic has become a Veterans Stadium fixture and one of the best-known mascots in baseball.

VETERANS STADIUM (1971-)

Opened for play in 1971, the Vet was a product of talk of a new stadium that began in 1953. Numerous disagreements delayed ground-breaking until 1967 and further delays pushed the unveiling until '71.

Public opinion polls conducted in newspapers showed a preference for names such as the Philadium and Philadelphia Stadium, but legislation was passed in the Philadelphia city council to name the stadium Philadelphia Veterans Stadium in honor of the city's war veterans.

It's difficult to savor the experience of the Vet, a relatively non-descript park. But you know you've visited the Vet when you see the Phillie Phanatic. Borne out of a team marketing meeting, the Phanatic made its debut in 1978 and is, behind the San Diego Chicken, the most well-known mascot in American sports.

First game: April 10, 1971, a 4-1 Phillies victory over the Expos and a win for Hall of Famer Jim Bunning.

■ Site of three World Series (1980, '83 and '93)

■ Site of two All-Star Games (1976 and 1996)

THE GREAT WALLENDA

The brilliance of that 1970s Vet is contrasted by today's perception of a big, sterile sports amphitheater. It's simply a matter of bad timing. As the 1970s notions of hip and trendy died away, words like "atmosphere," "charm" and "character" began creeping back into the ballparks vocabulary. Your first sense when gazing over the still geometrically-perfect, personality-challenged Vet is that this could be the model stadium if a mathematician became baseball commissioner and decided to standardize all playing fields.

Veterans Stadium, while comfortable, has no skyline and few other distinguishing characteristics. A statue of Connie Mack, the venerable ruler of Philadelphia baseball for a half century, stands guard on the corner of Broad Street and Pattison Avenue and an unidentified player remains locked in midslide, elevated on the outside of the stadium near the Phillies offices. But few of the original inside landmarks remain.

Opening day, Veterans Stadium-style, has featured everything from misguided parachutists to tight rope-walking Karl Wallenda (above). Phil and Phyllis (left) were early mascots, modeled after mechanical dolls that were part of a Liberty Bell display in center field. A Connie Mack statue (right) is still a fixture outside the Vet.

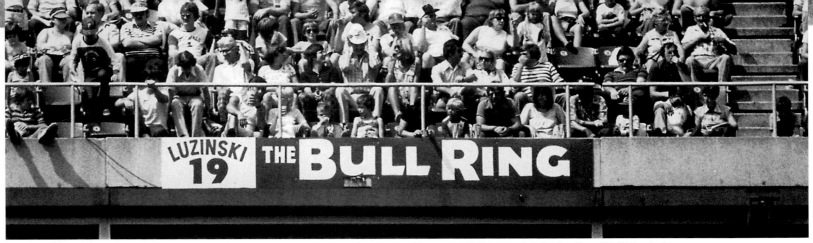

The "Bull Ring" was a former special section of the left field stands named in honor of longtime Phillies star left fielder Greg "Bull" Luzinski.

The Liberty Bell, once part of the Phil and Phyllis display that celebrated home runs at the base of the upper deck in dead center field, now rests on the stadium roof in center, a moonshot away from the plate. Phil and Phyllis, a pair of huge, computer-controlled dolls dressed in colonial garb, are gone, as are the massive twin scoreboards in left and right-center fields and the team logos that formerly decorated the black backdrops just above the outfield fences. Two state-of-the-art video boards entertain fans from high in the blue-seated center field bleachers and two recently installed scoreboards catch your attention from behind the open, glass-fronted, ground-level bullpens in left and right field. The "worst turf in baseball" is faded and the outline of the football field never completely disappears.

What the Vet lacks in personality it tries to make up for with promotional gimmicks. The Phillie Phanatic has become one of the best-known mascots in baseball and the team is constantly entertaining fans with promotions ranging from its one-year American Phanstand to its long-standing tradition of delivering first balls on opening day in creative ways—by air, horseback, cannon and even by Karl Wallenda, who crossed boldly above Veterans Stadium on a high wire.

One of the enduring images of the Vet came from Game 6 of the 1980 World Series, as the Phillies were on the verge of wrapping up the first championship in the franchise's long history. Surrounding the field from corner to corner, positioned on the foul-territory warning track, were helmeted police on horseback, nightsticks at the ready and snarling attack dogs ready to pounce. Phillies fans, already regarded as the

most antagonistic in baseball, never lived it down.

But Phillies fans also are among the most enthusiastic and loyal, when the players give them a reason to care. And the lack of Veterans Stadium atmosphere, a major contrast to Camden Yards less than two hours away, is never a problem when the baseball is right.

It simply doesn't get any better than Mike Schmidt facing Tom Seaver, no matter where the game is played. And how can you improve on Steve Carlton vs. Dave Parker or Curt Schilling staring down Barry Bonds? A Greg Luzinski home run would be impressive in any ballpark, as would a Larry Bowa diving stop or a Lenny Dykstra running catch.

There's no doubt Veterans Stadium has lost its cutting-edge appeal—it exists as a relic from better times. But memories are in the eyes of the beholder and Phillies fans have plenty to choose from. Love it or hate it, there's no place like home—even if it is Veterans Stadium.

Phillies fans can be antagonistic, but they also are among the most enthusiastic and loyal in baseball. That enthusiasm was on full display during 1996 All-Star Game festivities.

Three Rivers Stadium

Three Rivers
Stadium

Seven-time NLCS losers, including 1990, '91 and '92. Braves' John Smoltz shut out Pirates 4-0 in Game 7 of 1991 series here

Braves owner Te[...] Turner plays "Manager for a Da[...] May 11, 1977

Temporary home of Barry Bonds, MVP in '90, '92

Honus Wagner stands proudly on his Gate C pedestal, watching as another line drive sails toward the distant Pittsburgh skyline. Gate A is manned by Roberto Clemente, off and running after his vicious shot over the mighty Ohio River. Outside Gate D, quietly pondering the view of his beloved city, sits Art Rooney, the venerable founder and former owner of the NFL Steelers.

The sea of concrete that surrounds Three Rivers Stadium is nothing if not sentimental. It's also set dramatically into one of the most beautiful baseball backdrops ever conceived. Stationed strategically at the point where the Allegheny River joins the Monongahela River to form the Ohio, Three Rivers is only a fly ball or two

Bill Madlock won N.L. batting titles here in '81, '83

Clemente's 3,000th career hit, a double, is also his last, Sept. 30, 1972

Mr. Pirate ROBERTO CLEMENTE batted .414 with 12 hits in 1971 World Series victory

Baseball's first World Serie[...] night game: Reliever Bruc[...] Kison keys Pirates' 4-3 win o[...] Orioles in Game 4, Oct. 13, 1[...]

Stargell becomes first big-leaguer to hit 11 home
runs in April, April 27, 1971

Phil Garner hits grand slams in
consecutive games, Sept. 14 and 15, 1978

Extra, Extra—a no-hitter. Francisco Cordova (9)
and Ricardo Rincon (1) stop Astros in first
combined extra-inning no-hitter in baseball
history, July 12, 1997

Phillies star Mike Schmidt makes 500th career
homer a dramatic one—a three-run, ninth-inning
shot that beats Pirates, April 18, 1987

Pirates lose third and final game of
'75 Championship Series, despite
John Candelaria's 14 strikeouts

"Pops" Stargell, head of Pittsburgh's 1979 "Family",
led the Bucs to World Series win over Baltimore

After allowing leadoff
single vs. Braves, Jim
Bibby retires next 27
batters, May 19, 1981

Where Phillies second baseman Mickey
Morandini turned the first unassisted triple
play by N.L. player since 1927, Sept. 20, 1992

Bob Walk fires Game 5
three-hitter vs. Braves and
keeps Pirates' flickering
hopes alive in 1992 NLCS

WILLIE STARGELL belted four upper-deck
home runs, all of which are marked by
stars on the seats where they hit

The Clemente statue (right), scenic views from the Ohio River side of Pittsburgh's Golden Triangle (opposite page) and fan participation (left) are part of the Three Rivers experience.

away from picture-postcard ecstasy.

You'll never get that sense from close-up photographs that reveal a round, gray, concrete mass, similar to the cookie-cutter multi-purpose facilities in Philadelphia and Cincinnati. Aside from the statues, there is little in sight to suggest character or charm. But when you put Three Rivers in the context of its surroundings, you see an almost stately structure that tries hard to fit in with an aggressive downtown skyline.

Three Rivers at night can be spectacular. Lights from downtown buildings reflect off the Allegheny, providing a laser-like escort for tugs and other boats chugging along the water. The outlines of bridges add color, as do the lights from houses atop the hills on the distant Ohio bank. Activity on the Duquesne Incline, with a tram delivering patrons to a nightlife strip on the top of Mount Washington, provides an alternative sidelight on the opposite banks of the three-river confluence, slightly upriver from Pittsburgh's Golden Triangle.

If nothing else, the scenery puts you in a receptive mood. That's good because what you get inside is a symmetrical expanse of artificial turf with base and home plate cutouts and a bowl-like feeling of enclosure. Like Riverfront Stadium (Cinergy Field) in Cincinnati and Veterans Stadium in Philadelphia, this is a facility designed for football with little to offer by way of distinctive features.

One thing it does have is color—a kaleidoscope of reds, yellows, blues and greens that explode from each of the five seating levels and the playing surface. A tarp covered with decorative championship logos covers most of the outfield upper deck, relieving the feeling of emptiness that comes with consistently sparse crowds. Just below the tarp, still visible, are painted numbers on four upper-deck seats—landing spots for prodigious Willie Stargell home runs.

For predominantly blue-collar Pittsburgh fans, Three Rivers Stadium, devoid of the frills and trappings that fans in other cities have come to expect, is a satisfactory 47,972-seat ballpark. This is the Steel City, home of the rugged Steelers and one of the most successful baseball franchises in history. Names like Clemente, Stargell, Dave Parker, Bill Madlock, Al Oliver, John Candelaria, Kent Tekulve, Barry Bonds and Doug Drabek have passed through, leaving a three-decade legacy of nine East Division titles, two pennants and two World Series victories. Combined with the Steelers' stunning Super Bowl success in the 1970s, Three Rivers has been a well-honored championship venue.

In July 1970, it was simply a glittering, state-of-the-art baseball wannabe, a major departure from the old-style Forbes Field

THREE RIVERS STADIUM (1970-)

It sits on the same site as Exposition Park, where baseball was played as far back as the 1880s, but Three Rivers is a far cry from Exposition and its immediate predecessor, Forbes Field.

After the NFL's Steelers vacated Forbes for Pitt Stadium, and with the University of Pittsburgh, which had purchased Forbes Field, in need of expansion, Forbes' days were numbered.

Ground was broken for Three Rivers in April of 1968, and the intention was to open the stadium for the 1969 season. Delays pushed the debut to the middle of the '70 season.

The 2000 baseball season is scheduled to be the last at Three Rivers. The Pirates open 2001 in a new facility, PNC Park (naming rights were sold to PNC Bank Corp.), plans for which were announced in 1998. PNC Park, with a 21-foot wall to honor the number of Pirates great Roberto Clemente, will be located on the Allegheny River, within striking distance of a 450-foot home run. It will be adjacent to Federal Street, a site just east of the Three Rivers Stadium site.

First game: July 16, 1970. In a stellar pitching matchup of the Reds' Gary Nolan and the Pirates' Dock Ellis, Cincinnati beat Pittsburgh, 3-2. Coincidentally, it was the same score as Forbes Field's debut game in 1909, a 3-2 Chicago victory.

■ Site of two World Series (1971 and 1979)
■ Site of two All-Star Games (1974 and 1994)

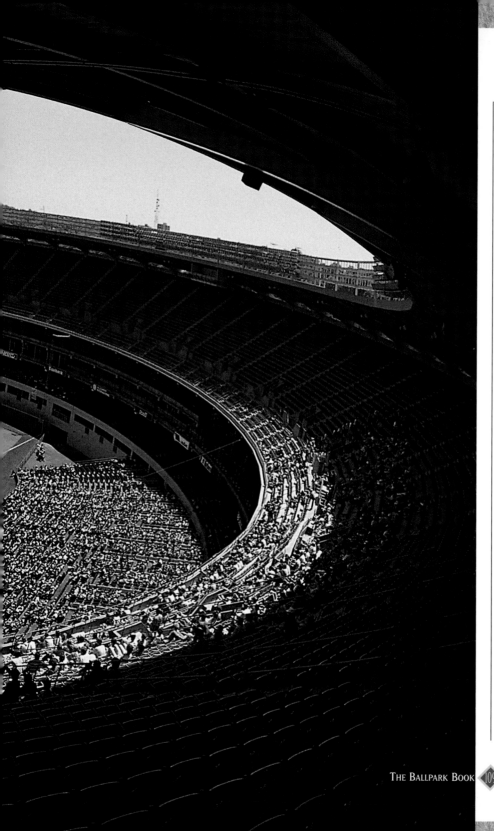

atmosphere that Pirates fans had absorbed since 1909. Three Rivers' only connection with the past was its location (the former site of Exposition Park, the team's home before Forbes Field), the Wagner statue that had stood behind Forbes' left field wall and artifacts from Forbes that were placed in the Allegheny Club—an 8-by-12-foot section of the brick outfield wall, 12 Romanesque window frames and a Babe Ruth plaque marking his 714th home run.

In 1971, the Pirates' first full season at Three Rivers, Clemente led them to the franchise's fourth Series championship. Before the '70s were complete, the

The Wagner statue (left) stands guard at Three Rivers (far left), much as it did for years at Forbes Field.

Pirates had secured four more division titles and another championship—the 1979 "We Are Family" charge sparked by Pops Stargell. Three Rivers, only 10 years old, already had witnessed more postseason excitement than many stadiums do in a lifetime.

Not much has changed cosmetically over the years. The original scoreboard, a narrow horizontal strip that stretched from left-center field to right-center, not far above the 10-foot inner fence, was removed and a new board was installed just below the stadium's upper rim in straightaway center—a binoculars view for fans behind home plate. Two hard-to-ignore giant billboards now sit on top of the rim—between light standards and above the scoreboard.

Three Rivers is short on quirks, but it does have fenced-off bullpens down the lines and dugout-view seats behind the plate. It also has a few amenities that might interest even the most baseball-intense fans. The Bullpen Cafe allows diners to watch game action from just over the left field fence, the Allegheny Club offers a nice blend of refreshment and nostalgia from its third- and fourth-level perch in foul territory down the first base line and a Three Rivers Stadium Hall of Fame keeps patrons aware of Pittsburgh's rich sports heritage.

But the stadium's greatest asset is the beautiful, progressive city it has served with quiet competence from its riverside perch along Roberto Clemente Memorial Park—the ground upon which George Washington-led troops once fought for Fort Duquesne in the French and Indian War. Three Rivers Stadium is a modern-day battleground—with a view.

BUSCH Stadium

The Gateway Arch towers in the skyline above Busch Memorial Stadium, an ever-vigilant sentry guarding its St. Louis treasures. Jewels, past and present, like Bob Gibson, Lou Brock, Joe Torre, Ted Simmons, Bob Forsch, Ozzie Smith, Willie McGee and Mark McGwire. Diamond memories of Cardinals, Clydesdales, baseball magic and World Series moments, all colored in a sea of red.

Rumor has it the Arch sways happily to every beat of the Budweiser theme song, which has filled the downtown St. Louis air around 250 Stadium Plaza for more than three decades. So do the bronze statues of Stan "The Man" Musial, Gibson, Brock, Enos Slaughter, Red Schoendienst and Jack Buck,

Big Mac Land

Landing pads for Mark McGwire homers Nos. 62 and 70 during historic 1998 season

Mark McGwire hits career homer No. 500 (Aug. 5, 1999), follows up record-breaking 1998 season with 65

Tom Lawless' second career homer, a three-run shot, helps Cardinals beat Twins, Frank Viola in Game 4 of 1987 World Series

OZZIE SMITH: The Wizard of Oz performed magic on left side of Cardinals' infield from 1982-96

Steve Carlton strikes out 19 Mets but loses game 4-3, Sept. 15, 1969

N.L. prevails 2-1 on 105-degree afternoon in hotly-contested All-Star Game, July 12, 1966

Lou Brock sets single-season record with 104th and 105th steals en route to 118, Sept. 10, 1974 . . . slashes 3,000th career hit off hand of Cubs pitcher Dennis Lamp, Aug. 13, 1979

Keith Hernandez: 1979 co-MVP and big gun in 1982 World Series championship

Where Mark McGwire's 545-foot blast off Marlins' Livan Hernandez dented sign, May 16, 1998

Site of Gibson's overpowering 17-strikeout performance in Game 1 of 1968 World Series vs. Tigers

Ozzie Smith's first career lefthanded homer shocks Dodgers in Game 5 of 1985 NLCS

BOB GIBSON: Five-time 20-game winner, two Cy Youngs, 1.12 ERA in 1968

Where Curt Flood misjudged Jim Northrup's fly ball, opening gates to seventh-game Tigers win in 1968 World Series

Roosting place of "Cha Cha" Cepeda, MVP cheerleader for 1967 El Birdos

Where Larry Jaster shut out Dodgers for fifth straight time in remarkable 1966 performance, Sept. 28

Where "Mad Hungarian" Al Habosky meditated before striking out another batter

Where Vince Coleman, the Cardinals' 110-steal rookie, was gobbled up by automatic tarp before Game 4 of NLCS, Oct. 13, 1985

Line drive by Pirates slugger Roberto Clemente breaks Gibson's leg, July 15, 1967

Mark McGwire has added a missing ingredient to the Busch Stadium mix, defying its long-standing image as a cookie-cutter ballpark.

strategically placed outside the stadium to greet visitors and provide inspiration—to properly prepare them even before they walk through a gate.

Inspiration is everything for St. Louis fans, who have always blanched at the nonstop verbal shots Busch Stadium has endured from ballpark purists. From its 1966 opening through its impressive 1990s facelift, Busch has carried the tag of "cookie-cutter" original—the first of the sterile, plastic, boringly symmetrical, Astro-Turf, multi-purpose facilities that sprang up in the late 1960s and '70s. "I stand at the pitcher's mound in Philadelphia and I don't know if I'm in Pittsburgh, Cincinnati, St. Louis or Philly," former major leaguer Richie Hebner once complained. "They all look alike."

Critics took one look at the nearly-round, cavernous, bowl-like Busch in 1966 and labeled it an "airport"—with seats, a scoreboard and little by way of personality. They were appalled when it became the assembly-line blueprint for a wave of unimaginative stadiums affected by the desire for big seating capacities and the need to convert back and forth between baseball and football.

But fans who have worshiped there, who have experienced five World Series and countless memorable moments there, remember early Busch for a subtle beauty that emanated from its proud Cardinals tradition and a personality supplied by special players and successful teams.

BUSCH MEMORIAL STADIUM (1966-)

Named for August A. Busch Jr., then the chairman of Anheuser-Busch, Inc., which owned the Cardinals from 1953-1995. Alternately known as Busch Stadium, this is actually the second Busch Stadium. Sportsman's Park, home of the Cardinals from 1920-1966, was renamed Busch Stadium in 1953.

Known as a turf stadium, Busch Stadium's first surface actually was natural grass. It was a grass field from 1966 through the '69 season, replaced with artificial turf for the 1970 season and returned to natural grass for the '96 season.

Perhaps its most endearing feature, however, is outside the stadium. Outside the northeast section stands a 15-foot bronze statue of Cardinals great Stan Musial. Over the years, Stan has been the meeting place for fans attending the game, and in recent years has been joined by statues honoring other Cardinals greats in the Plaza of Champions.

First game: May 12, 1966, a 4-3 Cardinals victory over Phil Niekro and the Atlanta Braves in 12 innings. The first home run hit in the ballpark was by the Braves' Felipe Alou, who hit two that day.

■ Site of five World Series (1967, '68, '82, '85 and '87)
■ Site of one All-Star Game (1966)

The early Busch Stadium experience was Gibson and McCarver, Maxvill and Javier, Torre and Cepeda, Brock and Coleman, Smith and Herr, Clark and Hernandez, Pendleton and Simmons, Hendrick and McGee, Tudor and Andujar. It was waves of red, the color of choice for the self-professed "best baseball fans in America," line drives into the gap, a man-eating automatic tarp, the Wizard of Oz, Whitey Ball, Harry Caray, Buck and Mike Shannon in the broadcast booth and the Budweiser song, which never failed to whip Cardinals supporters into frenetic fits.

It was a massive two-sectioned scoreboard, one side occupied by a Anheuser-Busch eagle that flapped its magnificent wings in approval, the other by an electronic Redbird that flew back and forth during a seventh-inning stretch or in recognition of a Cardinals home run. It was team owner August A. Busch triumphantly circling the stadium in a beer wagon pulled by a team of Clydesdales, an Ozzie Smith body flip or a seat in the left field bleachers, as close as a young fan could get to childhood hero Brock.

The Cardinals know how to celebrate their heroes. The 15-foot Stan Musial statue (left), a Stadium landmark since its dedication (above) in 1968, has been joined in recent years by statues (below) of Bob Gibson, Lou Brock, Enos Slaughter, Red Schoendienst and Jack Buck on the Plaza of Champions.

Busch Stadium was proactive, which allowed fans to ignore unfavorable comparisons to ballpark favorites Wrigley Field, Fenway Park and the Polo Grounds. There were no unusual angles, dimensions or nuances to spice up play—little personality beyond that supplied by the people who played and cheered there. Dimensions were a standard 330 feet down both lines and 386 to the power alleys. Center field was 414 (later 404) and the AstroTurf, installed in 1970, was hard and fast, features that fit the profile for a team dependent on speed and defense.

Supporting the Cardinals meant appreciating aggressive, fundamental play—and, of course, the stolen base, which Brock and Vince Coleman turned into lethal offensive weapons. The home run, which would become such an important factor in the 1990s, was a 1970s and '80s afterthought. Whitey Herzog's 1982 world champions hit 67 homers, three fewer than McGwire hit in his record-setting 1998 season, while recording 200 steals.

But Big Mac wasn't the only thing new about the 1990s Cardinals. New ownership, no longer content to let one of baseball's premier franchises play in a no-frills setting, retro-fitted Busch Stadium into one of the fan-friendliest playgrounds in the game. For St. Louis baseball fans, the Cardinals' house became a home.

The turf, at long last, was removed and replaced by grass. The outer walls in left- and right-center field were spruced up, one area, decorated by flags, celebrating all the retired numbers in Cardinals history. The bullpens were moved from the first and third base foul lines to areas behind the left and right field fences. And a more modern scoreboard in left-center was mirrored by a replay/highlights screen in right-center.

New interactive attractions, picnic areas, extended bleachers and an upper-deck seating area named Big Mac Land became hot locations, primarily because of McGwire's headline-generating home run prowess.

A fan who had not been to a game since the 1970s might not have recognized the new Busch. Sleek, modern and attractive to the first-time visitor, the stadium became an attraction on its own merit—an eye-pleasing structure and a fitting depository for the moonshot blasts launched by McGwire into the outer limits.

The house that a beer baron had built in 1966 was officially transformed into a warm, inviting corporate showcase for one of the greatest baseball shows on earth.

The Dome Era

They were heralded as technological wonders and later regarded as offensive to our baseball senses. What the dome really gave us was relief from game-inhibiting elements and a sense of what baseball luxury could become.

They came to us with good intentions—baseball Utopia, where it was never too hot or too cold, too wet or too dry, too rainy, too snowy or too breezy to play. Whether permanent or retractable, the roof meant the show would always go on in Houston's Astrodome, Seattle's Kingdome, Minnesota's Metrodome, Toronto's SkyDome or Montreal's Olympic Stadium, which finally was crowned after more than a decade of political hassling.

The Astrodome and Kingdome are gone now, and their legacies, ironically, are less about what was above than what was below. The most significant measure of dome ball has been the artificial surface it introduced to the sport.

Baseball has never been the same since.

The Metrodome

Indoor baseball, complete w
fiberglass roof, lighting and
acoustical problems, artifici
turf and a "Hefty Bag" linin
that serves as right field wa

Consecutive at-bat popups by Detro
Rob Deer ricochet off ceiling to
shortstop Greg Gagne, May 30, 199

Dan Gladden's grand slam sparks 10-1 win over Cardinals in first indoor World Series game, Oct. 17, 1987

Unimpressed writers have nicknamed it the Hump, Humpty-Dump, Homerdome, Thunderdome, Sweat Box, Sweatrodome and Metrodish. More generous visitors observe diplomatically that it looks like a big, rectangular-shaped mushroom— without the stem. By any name or description, the Hubert H. Humphrey Metrodome is a baseball anomaly, an indoor ballpark that still stirs passion in much of the outdoor-loving community it has served for almost two decades.

Twins players and hard-core fans have another nickname for the white-topped structure that sits defiantly on the east edge of downtown Minneapolis, guarded by one of the

KIRBY PUCKETT: Popular Kirby was .318 career hitter and six-time Gold Glove center fielder

Atlanta's Lonnie Smith commits Game 7 baserunning gaffe that helps Twins win worst-to-first World Series . . . Gene Larkin gives Jack Morris 1-0 Series-clinching win with 10th-inning single, Oct. 27, 1991 ite of 1985 All-Star Game—a 6-1 N.L. victory

Roof suffers slight tear due to high winds, causing
nine-minute delay in game vs. Angels, April 26, 1986

Gary Gaetti homers
twice vs. Tigers in
ALCS opener and
Twins win first
postseason game since
1965, Oct. 7, 1987

Milwaukee's Ben Oglivie hits
longest homer in Metrodome
history—a 481-foot rocket
into second deck, July 27, 1983

Puckett goes 3-for-4, makes sensational leaping
catch and hits 11th-inning homer to beat Braves
in Game 6 of World Series, Oct. 26, 1991

Where Hrbek hit his Game 6 grand slam in 1987
World Series vs. Cardinals

Frank Viola (right) goes 24-7,
wins 1988 Cy Young . . .
Scott Erickson wins 20 in
1991, Brad Radke 20 in 1997

Where Hrbek gave
Atlanta baserunner Ron
Gant a lift and tagged
him out in Game 2 of
1991 World Series

Chili Davis hits towering fly ball that bounces
off speaker and caroms to Orioles second
baseman Mark McLemore, transforming sure
homer into pop out, July 5, 1992

Oakland's Dave Kingman hits ball
into one of roof's drainage holes
and it never comes down,
resulting in ground-rule double,
May 4, 1984

First baseman KENT HRBEK: 293
homers, 1,086 RBIs from 1981-94

Home Sweet Home for Twins, who win
all eight World Series games played
there in 1987, 1991

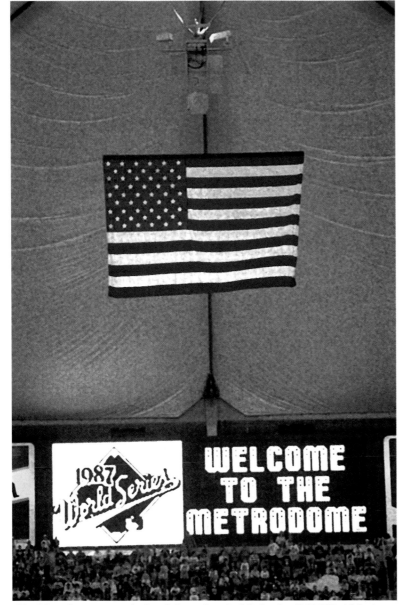

The Metrodome was packed and dressed to the hilt for the 1987 World Series, one of the two fall classics that would be decided there over the most prosperous five-year period in Twins history.

friendlier skylines in big-city America. They call it "home" and, putting aside the frustrations you must endure as a player there, you will not find a greater field advantage for any team in professional sports.

"The Twins have a very good ballclub—in their park," manager Whitey Herzog grumbled after watching his Cardinals lose four times at the Metrodome in a seven-game 1987 World Series. "But their guys didn't look all that good down in our park, did they?" The Twins, 85-77 during the 1987 regular season, won all six of the postseason games they played at the Metrodome and five of six they played there en route to the 1991 Series championship. No question, the world's largest air-supported dome does have its advantages.

The exterior roof is coated with Teflon, giving the outer building a white glow. But the inner lining, made of fiberglass, is a dirty white color that combines with the lighting system to swallow balls hit into the air. The Twins play there regularly and have learned how to deal with the problem of disappearing fly balls, but it's more of a problem for visiting teams. "This ballpark is a joke," Yankees manager Billy Martin said in a 1985 moment of anger. "It should be banned from baseball. Why don't they spend a hundred grand to paint the ceiling blue and this stuff won't happen?"

Teams, especially when the Metrodome is filled, become overwhelmed by the noise, which reverberates around the dome and almost makes the building rock.

HUBERT H. HUMPHREY METRODOME (1982-)

Faced with a decaying facility in Metropolitan Stadium, the city unveiled its plan to provide a new home for the Twins and NFL Vikings. That plan, for a new indoor stadium, was approved in 1979 with financing to be provided by the state of Minnesota. Ground-breaking followed in December of that year.

Named in honor of Hubert H. Humphrey, a former mayor of Minneapolis, U.S. Senator and U.S. Vice President, the facility opened in 1982 as baseball's third dome (behind Houston's Astrodome and Seattle's Kingdome) and the largest air-supported dome in the world.

The oft-criticized Metrodome, where outfielders have trouble picking up fly balls against the dirty-white ceiling, was the first facility to host a World Series, All-Star Game, Super Bowl and NCAA basketball championship game in its history.

First game: April 6, 1982. Foreshadowing the offense-favoring nature of the dome, Seattle beat the Twins, 11-7, in the stadium's debut game.

■ Site of two World Series (1987 and 1991)
■ Site of one All-Star Game (1985)

Twins fans waved their Homer Hankies in 1987 and created such a din that noise experts measured Game 2 at an average of 98.5 decibels and equated it to three straight hours without earplugs in a printing plant or standing behind a running Lawnboy. The Cardinals in '87 and the Braves in '91 were clearly affected by the numbing Thunderdome atmosphere.

The Metrodome, while artificial and sterile when compared to many outdoor ballparks, is filled with quirky nuances you normally don't find in domed stadiums or the multi-purpose facilities. You can't come into Minneapolis once or twice a year and expect to play baseball with any degree of efficiency.

Variations of the outfield fences (an irregular 343-408-327) are both fascinating and frustrating. The park's signature feature is a 7-foot padded right field wall topped by a 16-foot piece of stretched canvas that has been dubbed the "Hefty Bag." Balls hitting the hard padding shoot back toward the infield but balls hitting the Bag drop straight to the ground.

For years, the 7-foot padded left field wall was topped by a 6-foot section of plexiglass, providing an outfield view much like you find at a hockey game. The recently removed glass, erected to cut back on ground-rule doubles off the hard turf, made for fast and difficult bounces as well as impaired viewing. The 7-foot center field fence, immortalized by the home run-stealing catches of Kirby Puckett, is made from a thin sheet of canvas that gives on impact, allowing center fielders to snag balls actually hit 2 or 3 feet beyond the barrier.

Another oddity is an irregular curvature behind the plate that creates a right field lean and forces passed balls to bounce off the backstop toward first base. A secondary result is that fielders have more foul-territory room on the right side than the left and fans in the third base boxes are closer to the action than those on the first base side.

Nothing about the Metrodome is conventional, from the way the roof is supported to the shape of the field, a result of the building's rectangular form. It is

Umpires still feel the heat under the air-conditioned dome (left) and a plexiglass barrier (below) once gave left field fans a hockey-like feel. Homer Hanky-waving fans (below left) made the dome rock during the 1987 World Series.

covered by more than 10 acres of Teflon-coated fiberglass and the dome requires 250,000 cubic feet of air pressure per minute to remain inflated. You enter through revolving doors, getting a quick rush of air that makes you feel like you're walking against the wind. That department-store feel is reversed when you exit, the air rush practically vaulting you through the doors and onto the stadium plaza.

The inside experience feels cozier, less imposing, than what you found at Houston's Astrodome or Seattle's Kingdome. The ceiling has a puffy, quilted look and looms overhead with speakers dangling precariously in a high-wire act. From those speakers come all the sounds of a high-tech ballpark and the perpetually angry-sounding voice of public address announcer Bob Casey, a local celebrity dating back to the Twins' Metropolitan Stadium days.

The three-level stands circle the field, awash in a dark blue coloring matched by the outfield walls and the Bag, which covers some of the 7,600 retractable seats that are unfolded for football. The long, paneled scoreboard and videoboard dominate most of the left field view atop the upper grandstand and a 200-foot-long curtain stretches from deep left-center to the right field corner, covering seldom-used upper-deck seats and giving the dome less of an empty feel. The curtain, 51 feet high, is decorated with massive portraits of former stars and banners that highlight the Twins' postseason accomplishments.

There have been many such highlights since 1982, when the Metrodome opened without air-conditioning (the Sweat Box, Sweatrodome) and quickly gained renown as one of the friendliest home run parks in the game (Homerdome). Many focus on Puckett, one of the most popular players in Twins history, and stars like Kent Hrbek, Frank Viola, Greg Gagne, Gary Gaetti, Jack Morris, Chuck Knoblauch and Brad Radke. Others revolve around the Metrodome and the numerous special effects—like them or not—it has brought to the game.

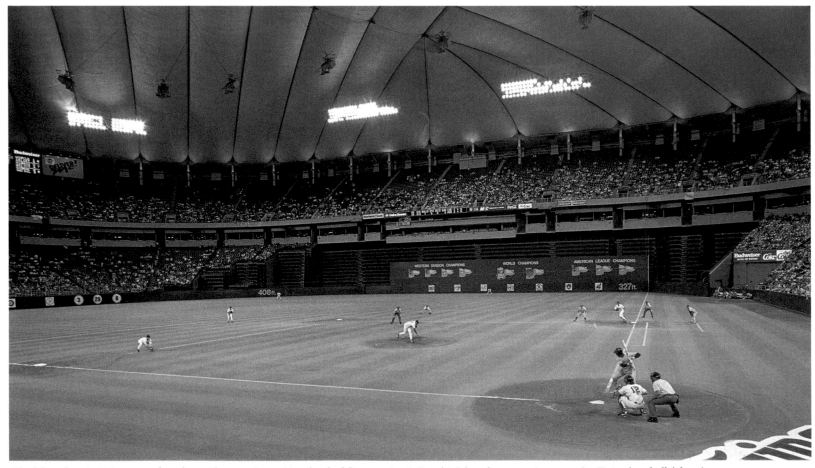

The Metrodome's Teflon-coated roof provides a quilty cushion for the Minneapolis skyline (right) and a protective cover for Twins baseball (above).

Olympic Stadium

Steve Carlton and Phillies ruin Montreal's Olympi[c] Stadium debut and disappoint 57,592 fans with a 7-[?] victory, April 15, 1977

Big crowd watches Expos shell Red Sox and former hero Pedro Martinez in 13-1 victory, June 9, 1999

Tim Raines (right) sets modern rookie stolen base record with 71 in 1981

Padres star Tony Gwynn joins baseba[ll] exclusive 3,000-hit club, Aug. 6, 199[?]

The Reds end Vladimir Guerrero's team-record 31-game hitting streak, Aug. 27, 1999

It has been criticized, scorned, ridiculed, mocked, despised and laughed at—in two different languages. Some locals call it a white elephant; others think it looks like a white spaceship, ready to transport an alien sport back into the galaxy from which it came. It's a good thing Olympic Stadium has a thick, concrete skin because no venue in sports history has endured more controversy and received less affection.

Strip away all the political posturing, miscalculations, unforeseen costs, bad decisions and untimely mishaps and what you have left is a friendly ballpark. Look past all the contempt and you see a facility with

ANDRE DAWSON (225 homers) was Expos' offensive anchor from 1976-86

N.L. wins 4-1, records 11th straight All-Star Game victory, July 13, 1982

Ron LeFlore (below) leads N.L. with 97 stolen bases in 1980

Where Pirates' slugger Willie Stargell hit 535-foot shot on May 20, 1978—the longest homer in Olympic Stadium history

Pete Rose accentuates his short Montreal career with hit No. 4,000, April 13, 1984

The stadium was built for 1976 Summer Olympic Games before being converted to baseball

Steve Rogers (1973-85) holds franchise records in most pitching categories

Rookie Bill Gullickson strikes out 18 Cubs, Sept. 10, 1980

Where Rick Monday drove a two-out, ninth-inning pitch from Steve Rogers in Game 5 of 1981 NLCS, winning a pennant for Dodgers

Where Warren Cromartie's drive caromed off wall, hit Dodgers center fielder Rick Monday on head and bounced into stands for ground-rule double, May 10, 1977

Third baseman Tim Wallach: Career leader in mes, hits, at-bats, doubles, total bases and RBIs

No. 10 Rusty Staub: One of three Expos numbers to be retired.

Carter allowed only one passed ball in 152 games in 1978

GARY CARTER: Former catcher ranks near top of Expos career lists in many offensive categories.

Where San Francisco lefty Dave Dravecky collapsed in pain with broken arm after delivering pitch to Expos hitter Tim Raines, August 15, 1989 a proud sports heritage—site of the opening ceremonies and all track and field events at the 1976 Summer Olympic Games, home base for the Expos, one of the two major league baseball franchises that play their home games outside the continental United States.

This is a stadium that lives in two dimensions. In one you can't dispute the two-plus decades of well-publicized financial problems (it has cost more than $1 billion so far) and ill will the structure has generated among French Canadians in the province of Quebec—and its awkward physical appearance, which has shaped the perception of outsiders. In the other, you discover that baseball is not an unpleasant experience in this east Montreal stadium, which once entertained Queen Elizabeth while serving as the centerpiece for a world of athletes in the Olympic Village.

The former Olympic complex still serves as a nostalgic backdrop. Just northwest of the stadium is one of the world's largest botanical gardens, complete with the largest insectarium in North America. Directly north is attractive Park Maisonneuve, perfect for pregame picnics, and next door is a world-class biodome, on the site of the former Olympic cycling track. The area is attractive, clean and largely residential—10 minutes from downtown Montreal. The stadium's trademark feature, of course, is the tower—that 575-foot leaning monstrosity that has been at the center of every Olympic Stadium debate from day one.

The tower, almost 20 feet taller than the Washington Monument,

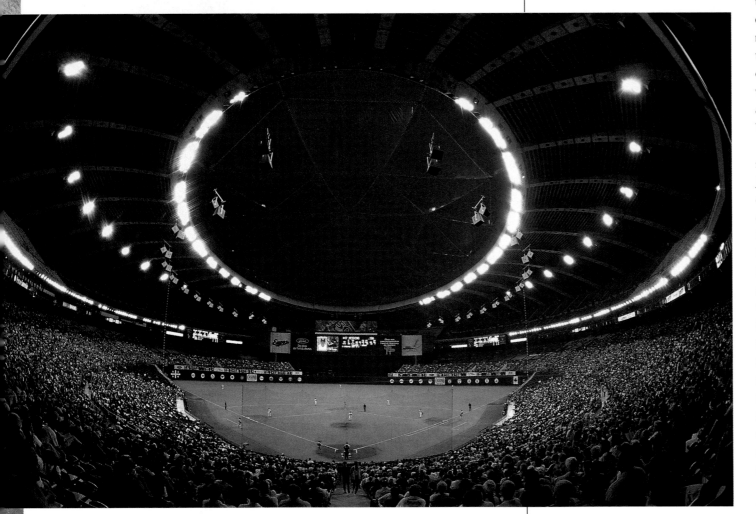

The orange roof at Olympic was replaced in 1998 with a roof which is beige on the outside but deep blue inside, giving the impression of a night game under the sky.

leans at a 45-degree angle—considerably more than the Tower of Pisa—and is the world's tallest inclined structure. It hulks over the stadium, huge cables dropping from its apex. Original plans called for the cables to hoist and drop an

Olympic Stadium, with its tower and flying saucer-like look, has become a fixture in east Montreal, on the former site of the 1976 Olympic Village.

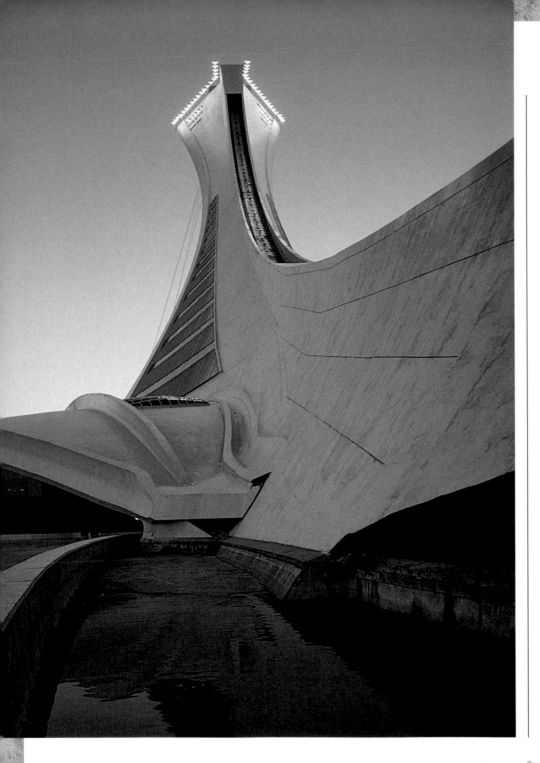

umbrella-like top over the structure—baseball's first retractable roof—as weather dictated. But it would take more than a decade of bickering and financial dickering before anything close to that plan could be implemented.

From 1977 through 1986, fans endured the unpredictable whims of spring and fall weather in Montreal—much as they had since 1969 when the expansion Expos, baseball's first non-U.S.-based team, began play at open Jarry Park. The three-tiered Olympic oval was completely enclosed with a steel-and-concrete rim that extended over the seats like a protective roof, leaving only an oval hole at the top. Through the hole, beyond center field, stood the half-finished tower in all its intimidating glory.

The roof, a high-tech synthetic cloth-like material called Kevlar, remained in storage for a dozen years before finally being installed in 1987. But generator problems kept the roof—a gaudy orange umbrella that looked like the meringue on top of a pie—in place for two years before it finally became retractable in 1989. It worked only briefly, because of tears, leaks and other persistent problems. The stadium was closed for 72 days in 1991 when a concrete beam the size of a locomotive fell off the exterior of the stadium onto a concrete walkway.

The orange roof finally was removed in 1998 and the Expos played a full season in open air while a permanent-top dome was being installed. Baseball, 1999-style, came with a plastic fiber cover coated in Teflon—beige to outside viewers on the top, blue (like the sky) to inside viewers from below. The new blue roof, which coordinates well with the blue and yellow seats and a navy blue tarp that covers much of the upper deck to relieve a sense of emptiness that comes with small crowds, can be inflated to keep water from building in heavy pockets on its top.

It is symmetrical baseball (325-404-325) with air-conditioning, 12-foot walls and artificial turf, but everything here has a fresh and curious feel. Where else can you find coatrooms, mixed-drink vendors and the dressiest crowd on the major league circuit? The theater-like lobby that houses ticket booths is distinctive, as is the Jackie Robinson (he played with the minor league Montreal Royals before the Dodgers) statue outside the main entrance. Two national anthems (the fans here really sing) are played, all announcements come in two languages

Since starting play at Olympic Stadium in 1977, the Expos have worked under the ominous shadow of the hulking tower (left), a leaning roof support that is almost 20 feet taller than the Washington Monument. The Olympic tower is the tallest inclined structure in the world.

and every Expos rally is saluted with chair-banging fervor. This is baseball with a French accent.

The Big O is really a reasonable place to watch a game. Among the best visual features are an attractive, horizontal scoreboard that dominates your view just above a dead area beyond the center field fence and retired-number logos that adorn the outfield walls. Among the

The bright yellow seats at Olympic are especially noticeable because of the traditionally sparse crowds.

best seats are the left and right field bleachers and the field-level Catcher's Club behind the plate.

Through all the mishaps and unfortunate publicity, Montreal fans have formed a nice relationship with baseball and their teams, most of which have fallen well short of championship-caliber, but have usually been entertaining. Only once have the Expos captured a division title (in the strike-shortened 1981 season) and

only three postseason games have been played on the Olympic Stadium turf.

But just mention names like Rusty Staub (Le Grande Orange), Gary Carter, Tim Wallach, Tim Raines, Andres Galarraga, Steve Rogers, Larry Parrish, Andre Dawson, Pedro Martinez and current favorite Vladimir Guerrero and watch some eyes light up. It's much more fun than discussing political maneuvering, cost overruns and best-laid plans gone awry.

OLYMPIC STADIUM (1977-)

For the first eight years of their existence, from 1969 through 1976, the Expos played at Jarry Park. Awarded an expansion team in the summer of 1968 on condition that a suitable field would be found for the '69 season, the team selected Jarry Park, a recreational facility that had but 3,000 seats.

Expanded to accommodate a major league team, the facility proved less than adequate from the outset.

After the 1976 Summer Olympics in Montreal, the facility was outfitted for baseball and became the Expos' home at the beginning of the 1977 season.

Plans are in the works for a new baseball facility in the city. There are hopes that Labatt Park, to be constructed in downtown Montreal at Peel, St. James, Notre-Dame and Mountain streets, will be ready for the 2002 season.

First game: April 15, 1977. The Phillies, behind Steve Carlton, beat the Expos, 7-2.

■ Site of no World Series

■ Site of one All-Star Game (1982)

During the 1998 season, while the roof was being repaired, fans got to watch Rondell White (above) and the Expos play baseball outdoors.

SkyDome

Where an Aug. 27, 1990 game vs. Brewers was delayed 35 minutes when bugs swarmed field

Where Carter blasted his World Series-ending home run off Philadelphia's Mitch Williams, Oct. 23, 1993

Oakland's Mark McGwire reaches fifth deck with 488-foot bomb on July 25, 19... . . . Carter follows two day later with 483-footer

ALCS losers in '89, '91 at SkyDome before two-year championship reign

Oakland's Jose Canseco launches 480-foot rocket into fifth deck of SkyDome in Game 4 of 1989 ALCS

Home runs by Carter, Candy Maldonado in Game 6 of ALCS gives Canada its first pennant and World Series team, Oct. 14, 1992

1996 Cy Young winner
PAT HENTGEN

Call it a Magic Kingdom of sports, a massive complex that houses a 348-room hotel, a Hard Rock Cafe, several restaurants, a 300-foot bar and enough other amenities to make your Toronto baseball experience, well ... comfortable. SkyDome is not a ballpark, it's an urban megastructure with a split personality, thanks to the inside-outside magic of a remarkable four-paneled retractable roof. This is baseball with frills, the glitzy, high-tech side of America's national pastime.

That glitz is a perfect fit for Toronto, a cosmopolitan, vibrant city that takes pride in its social and cultural diversity and reputation as an architectural pioneer. SkyDome is located in the heart of Canada's largest city, within easy walking distance of the entertainment district,

(Left to right) Carlos Delgado (44) and Shawn Green (42) combine for team-record 86 home runs in 1999

(Left to right) John Olerud (.363), Paul Molitor (.332) and Roberto Alomar (.326) finish 1-2-3 in 1993 A.L. batting race, a baseball first in century

Dave Stieb loses perfect game when Yankee Roberto Kelly doubles with two out in ninth—Stieb's third no-hit bid that falls one out short, Aug. 4, 1989

1991 Blue Jays become first team to top 4 million in attendance

Cal Ripken's three-run homer gives A.L. fourth straight All-Star Game win, 4-2, July 9, 1991

ndy Maldonado's bases-loaded single gives Blue Jays Game 3 victory over Braves in first World Series ntest played outside of United States, Oct. 20, 1992

Bernie Williams hits eighth-inning grand slam off Billy Koch to tie game and Paul O'Neill hits ninth-inning slam off Paul Spoljaric to give Yankees 10-6 win over Blue Jays, Sept. 14, 1999

JOE CARTER recorded six 100-RBI seasons for Blue Jays, led them to '92, '93 World Series titles

Where Roger Clemens won his fourth and fifth career Cy Youngs, 1997 and 1998

SkyDome provides an architectural balance for the CN Tower, which rises majestically above Toronto's elegant skyline.

masked by a business-office look and interesting distractions like the gigantic sculptures depicting cheering, booing, pointing and binocular-viewing fans on its north facade.

It's not until you step inside that you get a true sense of SkyDome, the last of baseball's multi-purpose stadiums to be built. Open or shut, the roof overwhelms you—a lurking, hovering protector of the green artificial turf expanse below. When open, it rises up over center field like a giant whale preparing to swallow its prey. When closed, you get a sense of what Jonah must have felt like after the meal. The open roof exposes 100 percent of the field and 91 percent of the seats and it's worth the price of admission just to watch the sliding, rolling, twisting panels work their way open or shut in a fascinating 20-minute sideshow.

If you're not careful, baseball and the Blue Jays can get lost in this remarkable entertainment maze. The symmetrical, turf-covered field (330-400-330) is cookie-cutter ordinary with uniform 10-foot fences surrounding the outfield. But foul territory behind the plate is major league minimum, five-level circular grandstands offer a variety of viewing options and the Jumbotron video board (33-by-110 feet) provides near-perfect reproduction from its high center field perch.

The board is framed by windows of the 70 SkyDome (renamed Renaissance) Hotel rooms that overlook the field—the same hotel Roberto Alomar once called home. Several times those windows have provided shocking outside-in views for Blue Jays fans who caught hotel patrons in amorous encounters. Hard Rock dancers have similar window perches over the right field wall and bar patrons can watch the game without leaving their seat at the center field club level.

SkyDome is not an intimate ballpark experience—on its best days, it's a stadium without bleachers. But, surprisingly, it does not have the sterile, amusement park feel you might expect. When the roof is open on a sunny afternoon or clear summer night, it becomes a pleasant place to watch a game. When the roof is closed because of rain or cold, you're thankful for the wonders of modern technology.

SkyDome becomes a pitcher's park when the roof is open, the stationary panel serving as a wind scoop that causes a home run-hindering downdraft. The ball carries better with a closed roof, a result of the building's climate-controlled predictability. Joe Carter's 1993 World Series-deciding drive into SkyDome's left field seats off Philadelphia's Mitch Williams—one of baseball's most memorable home runs—came with the roof shielding appreciative fans from the cold winds of October.

the appealing Harbourfront Centre and Lake Ontario. It opened in 1989 as a companion to the world's tallest self-supporting structure—the 1,821-foot CN Tower, which challenges the stratosphere from its sentry point beyond the right field corner.

The contrast between the huge, white-topped oval dome and the towering needle is striking—visual counterpoints that help define the largeness of both. SkyDome is big and tall enough to hold a 31-story building inside its dome, which measures 282 feet (87 feet higher than Minnesota's Metrodome) at its apex and weighs 11,000 tons. But its hulking size and drab, concrete grayness are well

The hotel facade is adorned by a gigantic sculpture depicting cheering, booing, pointing and binocular-viewing fans.

The Blue Jays like to brag about their 150-plus private skyboxes and that most of their 50,516 blue plastic seats are located in foul territory. But that results in a steep climb to distant upper decks for fans who are not the most vocal or enthusiastic baseball supporters to begin with. The crowd noise is minimal at a packed SkyDome game, an atmosphere that sometimes ranges between heavy breathing and excited applause. Some of the perceived lack of enthusiasm can be attributed to the park's status as one of baseball's biggest tourist attractions.

You can never really escape the sense that this is an incredible piece of architecture, an engineering breakthrough with a cleanness and luxury never before witnessed in a sports venue. Other amenities include a health club with squash courts, a glass-enclosed promenade that circles much of the stadium, providing wonderful views of the city, a home clubhouse with health spa, weight complex and recreation room and dugout monitors that allow coaches to check activity in the bullpens, which were out of sight behind the left and right field fences before windows were installed for the 1999 season.

You are constantly reminded of baseball's American ties (McDonald's was the supplier of SkyDome concessions for the park's first 10-plus seasons). But banners honoring former Toronto Argonauts (CFL) stars give the place a Canadian feel as well. SkyDome's official baseball stamp of approval was delivered in 1992 and '93 when the expansion Blue Jays (1977) rose up to avenge 1985, '89 and '91 ALCS losses and give Toronto consecutive World Series championships—the first ever for a Canadian-based team.

Cutting through the glitter of SkyDome has never been easy, but Toronto fans have been entertained by a succession of great players and pitchers—Alomar, Carter, John Olerud, Paul Molitor, Rickey Henderson, Devon White, Tony Fernandez, Fred McGriff, Dave Stewart, Dave Stieb, Pat Hentgen, Todd Stottlemyre, Juan Guzman, Roger Clemens—who have kept the wandering spotlight on the field rather than the many distractions that surround it. That hasn't always been easy.

Ballpark comfort is a lounge chair and drinks inside your luxurious room at the Renaissance Hotel, within full view from left-center field of all the action on the field.

SkyDome (1989-)

Almost 3 ½ years in the making, SkyDome (no "the" and capital D) rests on a site under which a main water tunnel traveled. During the excavation for the facility, a number of artifacts, primarily bottles, were uncovered.

The site selection itself was a subject of debate. Chief concerns were the aesthetics of the area and the prospective traffic difficulties. Ultimately, the government of then-premier William Davis selected the site.

The SkyDome name purportedly came from a contest in which 12,879 different names were suggested. A number of people suggested SkyDome; their entries were put in a drum and one name was selected — an Ontario resident named Kellie Watson — as the contest winner. Why SkyDome? "It was a dome where you could see the sky?" she told the Toronto Globe and Mail.

First game: June 5, 1989. The Brewers' Paul Molitor, whose career would eventually take him through Toronto, opened the park with a first-inning double and the Brewers beat Toronto, 5-3.

■ Site of two World Series (1992 and 1993)
■ Site of one All-Star Game (1991)

The New Wave

They are the New Wave ballparks, feel-good venues that borrow the textures, feelings and emotional characteristics of their early-century predecessors.

A seat in Comiskey Park gives you the feel and visual impact of Old Comiskey; Camden and Jacobs give you a sense of Fenway and Wrigley; Coors Field hits you over the head with its Ebbets Field-like facade; The Ballpark in Arlington offers visual tributes to Tiger and Yankee. Bank One is SkyDome with grass and Tropicana is, well, a dome, not unlike the one that covers the Metrodome.

Some refer to them as retro parks—modern facilities that try to combine all the modern conveniences and technologies with old-time charm and charisma.

Only time will tell if they can accomplish that goal.

The Ballpark
in Arlington

One was a North Texas dinosaur, tough, functional and lacking in the frills and grace of today's modern sports venues. The other is a baseball oasis, a sparkling, quirky and refreshing breeze in the scorching Texas heat. The Ballpark in Arlington stands only a quarter of a mile from the site of old Arlington Stadium, but it's a world or two away from Arlington's oppressively hot, friendly-but-unsophisticated, minor league-like atmosphere.

It's not that old Arlington was a bad place to watch baseball. But The Ballpark was beautiful, upscale, charismatic and filled with amenities long-suffering Rangers fans had never dreamed possible. This was a mansion replacing a one-bedroom apartment—

JUAN GONZALEZ:
Career leader in runs, hits, doubles, homers, total bases and RBIs

Perfecto: Kenny Rogers retires all 27 Angels he faces in 4-0 masterpiece, July 28, 1994

1996 West Division champions: 35 years of frustration ends as franchise takes first postseason plunge

Home of two-time MVP Gonzalez, a 40-homer, 100 RBI machine

Rodriguez, Gonzalez and Rafael Palmeiro (left) combine for 121 homers, 389 RBIs as offense enjoys prolific 1999 season

West Division titles in 1998 1999 are followed by Divisio Series sweeps by Yankees . . Texas scores one run in 199 Division Series

Palmeiro's inviting right field porch.

Gonzalez drives in six runs, Dean Palmer (left) and Kevin Elster five apiece as Rangers blow away Orioles 26-7, April 19, 1996

N.L. manages only three hits, but all are home runs in 3-2 victory in first All-Star Game at The Ballpark in Arlington, July 11, 1995

The Ballpark plays host to first interleague game in major league history: Giants 4, Rangers 3, June 12, 1997

Gonzalez ties postseason single-game record with fifth home run, but Rangers still fall to Yankees in fourth and final game of 1996 Division Series

Rangers, en route to third A.L. West title in four years, get three-run homer in ninth from Lee Stevens (right) and game-winning homer in 10th from Gonzalez in 4-3 win over Royals, May 31, 1999

Catcher IVAN "PUDGE" RODRIGUEZ, the Man with the Golden Glove

and a defining commitment for sports in the Dallas-Fort Worth metroplex. With the 1994 opening of the shiny new facility came Arlington's first All-Star Game (1995) and West Division championship (1996) and clear signals that baseball was here to stay, the team would henceforth be competitive and the franchise, after 22 seasons in Texas, finally would be accepted into the major league fraternity.

Arched windows and entryways play a big role in The Ballpark's design (above) and a closeup of the center field office building (right) reveals many architectural nuances as well as a display base for advertisers.

corners is a nice blend of red brick, red granite and cast-stone reliefs of a Lone Star and steer heads alternating between the tops of giant, arched windows. Murals depicting Texas historical scenes circle the park between the upper and lower arches and a brick Walk of Fame rings the perimeter, honoring every Rangers team.

Once inside, you can entertain yourself for hours before even

Appearance means a lot in today's sports world and The Ballpark can match any facility in the major leagues, quirk for quirk. Hitters can deposit fly balls into a friendly Tiger Stadium-like right field porch, take aim at the distant Yankee Stadium-like white facade or bounce a line drive off one of the yellow foul poles from old Arlington. Fans can check out the Camden Yards-like brick exterior or the out-of-town Fenway Park-like manual scoreboard on the left field wall.

The Ballpark gives new meaning to the term "retro park." But it's also filled with innovative features and a sense of purpose never experienced by the once-lowly Rangers. The Ballpark, thanks to such stars as Juan Gonzalez, Ivan Rodriguez, Rafael Palmeiro, Will Clark and Kenny Rogers, played host to three West Division titles and the first three postseason series in franchise history—over its first six years. If clothes can make the man, then appearance definitely can make the ballpark.

And this one is an eye-grabber—from the moment you reach Nolan Ryan Expressway in search of a parking space. The square complex with the beveled

sitting down to watch a game. The concourses are spacious with restaurants, gift shops, a pizza place, an art gallery, a monument to Ryan and a scenic picnic area. But the best attraction is a 17,000-square-foot Legends of the Game baseball museum that might be second only to the facility at Cooperstown. The museum contains a 7,000-square-foot children's learning center with interactive exhibits.

The field area, set 22 feet below street level to ease the problem with summer winds, is a frenetic visual wonderland. There's so much to see that visitors often miss the obvious. One thing you can't miss is a four-story office building that dominates the landscape from left-center to right-center, a facility that encloses the normally open center field in most baseball-only parks.

The building, complete with large picture windows and white wrought-iron decor, houses the Rangers' offices (fourth floor), retail shops and ticket offices (first floor) and rental offices (second and third floors). Sitting atop the building are advertising panels and a 42-by-430-foot windscreen. To its right field side is the three-floor museum.

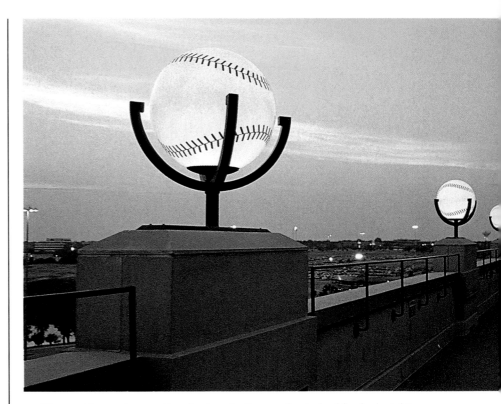

Cast-iron Lone Stars decorate all of the dark green plastic armchairs that make life comfortable for fans at The Ballpark in Arlington.

The park's most appealing feature is the 325-foot, double-deck right field porch that looks very much like the old stands at Tiger Stadium and provides an inviting home run target as well as a sense of intimacy. The state-of-the-art main scoreboard sits high atop the porch pavilion, a nice contrast for the manual board that's part of a 14-foot left field wall that measures 332 in the corner.

Home run hitters also can take aim at a grass incline in straightaway center that serves as the batter's eye, an area backed by the picnic park. It's fun to watch kids scurry onto the grass to chase home run balls, a practice not discouraged by the Rangers. On each side of the batter's eye are bleacher sections (bench-style seats from old Arlington Stadium) and the raised lower-deck seats in left field provide a special bleacher-like view.

One of The Ballpark's quirkiest features is a right-center field fence that angles awkwardly around an elevated Rangers bullpen, creating the possibility of unexpected bounces. The point where the bullpen fence

If attention to detail makes the ballpark, then Arlington can be proud of its baseball-shaped lamps (left) and the baseball-friendly atmosphere it provides for fans.

angles away from the right field wall is 381 feet; it jogs again at 377 feet and connects to the center field wall at the deepest point of the park—407 feet, 7 more than straightaway center.

The park's five levels rise up steeply around you, topped by a white hanging facade that circles the entire rim. The grass field seems to stand up well to the intense Texas heat and it blends well with the 49,166 seats—most of them dark green plastic armchairs adorned with cast-iron Lone Stars.

Everything about The Ballpark fits into one of two themes: baseball and Texas. From the parking lot, you can hear the sounds of the nearby Six Flags Over Texas amusement park and you are constantly confronted by detailed design elements that range from Lone Stars and steer heads to upper-concourse light fixtures shaped like baseballs.

The only detail that's missing is a championship—and that, at least, is a possibility now.

THE BALLPARK IN ARLINGTON (1994-)

From its first regular-season game on April 11, 1994, the Rangers' retro home, rising from a suburban landscape dotted with theme parks and restaurants, oozes Texas from its granite-and-brick and Lone Star-dotted facade.

With a quirky, asymmetrical playing field, home run porch in right field and architectural details that conjure up images of classic old stadiums, The Ballpark is the crowning achievement of the former ownership group led by then-managing partner George W. Bush.

If Arlington Stadium was an over-expanded minor league facility, then The Ballpark, located a quarter-mile southeast of its predecessor, is major league in every way, from the four-story office complex looming beyond the center field fence and an on-site baseball museum to the amphitheater and youth field that's a downsized replica of the stadium.

And clearly the Rangers have responded to their state-of-the-art surroundings. Try this on for size: Since moving into The Ballpark, they have won their division three times in six years and were in first place in 1994 when labor problems halted the season; in the 22 seasons up to that point, they had never won the A.L. West.

First game: April 11, 1994. Dave Nilsson's home run spoils the day as the Brewers' Jaime Navarro outduels Rangers starter Kenny Rogers, 4-3, before 46,056. Like their first season at Arlington Stadium, which was delayed by a players' strike, the Rangers' first season at The Ballpark was affected by labor problems. Although they were 10 games under .500 when the owners' lockout came in August, the Rangers were in first place in the A.L. West, a game ahead of the A's.

■ Site of no World Series
■ Site of one All-Star Game (1995)

Turner Field

Eight straight division titles, the last three at Turner Field: '91, '92, '93 in West; '95, '96, '97, '98, '99 in East

Javy Lopez (right) hits two-out, ninth-inning homer to tie Cubs 1-1. . . Chipper Jones singles home run in 10th, ending Game 2 of 1998 Division Series

Where Eddie Perez hit game-turning home runs vs. Mets in Games 1 and 2 of 1999 NLCS

Where Danny Bautista lost bases-loaded fly ball in lights during five-run NLCS Game 6 explosion that wrapped up 1998 pennant for Pad

Where Kevin Brown fought off flu and pitched Marlins to Game 6 win over Braves in 1997 NLCS, completing their Cinderella run to World Series

1999 MVP CHIPPER JONES

It's one of the classic misnomers in baseball history. Yes, Turner Field is a beautiful place to watch a game, a grass-covered jewel with all the sights, sounds, nuances and feels you associate with the ballparks of yesteryear. But a "field?" No way. This is a complex, a self-advertised "baseball theme park" with all the comforts of home—the kind Donald Trump or Bill Gates might choose to live in.

Turner Field is a gleaming example of baseball's new "it takes a village" philosophy. It's a fenced-off, self-contained suburban neighborhood in the downtown edge of one of the most

raves christen new Turner Field with come-
rom-behind 5-4 win over Cubs, April 4, 1997

Tom Glavine (left) goes 20-6 in 1998,
wins second Cy Young . . . Denny
Neagle joins 20-win ranks in 1997

Cal Ripken goes 6-for-6 with two homers and six
RBIs in Baltimore's 22-1 interleague win over
Braves, June 13, 1999

Where Sammy Sosa's 444-foot bomb
left the ballpark—longest homer at
Turner Field, May 22, 1998

Brewers' National League
debut is a losing one, 2-1 to
Braves in 1998 season opener

Chipper Jones single-handedly crushes Mets
with four homers in three-game sweep of
East Division contenders, Sept. 21-23, 1999

Michael Tucker ruins no-hit bid by Cardinals' Alan
Benes with two out in ninth . . . Braves win 1-0 in
11th on Andruw Jones' RBI single, May 16, 1997

Four-time
Cy Young winner
GREG MADDUX

Maddux . . . Tom Glavine . . .
John Smoltz (right) — 6
career Cy Youngs,
4 ERA titles for
pitching-rich Braves

The columns that help block off Turner Field's Monument Grove plaza once supported the temporary bleachers for Olympic Stadium at the 1996 Summer Games.

cosmopolitan cities in North America. You enter its gates to a montage of restaurants, shops, picnic areas, video arcades, day-care centers, museums, luxury suites and ATM machines—filled with enough money to ensure many hours of entertainment bliss. Baseball is the overriding theme, but it's not the only game in this town.

The Braves are quick to point out that the food, shops and sideshows scattered throughout the park are merely accessories for the National League's team of the decade, a group that won eight division titles, five pennants and one World Series in the 1990s. But they also know that when the glory days of Greg Maddux, Tom Glavine, John Smoltz, Chipper Jones and Andres Galarraga are over, Turner Field—the theme park—will be enough to keep the turnstiles moving.

So far, Turner has been on a massive ego trip. First it was a playground for world-class athletes competing in the 1996 Summer Olympic Games. Then it became a world-class retro-style ballpark for one of the best teams in the game. From Olympic Stadium to Turner Field, it has witnessed world-record-setting performances and baseball excellence that many facilities never achieve.

Turner Field was built with that double personality in mind. Olympic Stadium,

located in a former parking lot of Fulton County Stadium, was set up so it could be converted into a state-of-the-art baseball field. The columns that once supported Olympic Stadium's temporary bleachers now serve as posts for the fence that surrounds Turner's outer Monument Grove plaza. There you encounter statues of Hank Aaron, Phil Niekro and Ty Cobb, as well as various retired number statues that front a brick-and-limestone facade not too far removed from Camden Yards.

Adjacent to Monument Grove is a giant entry area that almost overwhelms the unprepared. A one-of-a-kind food court—Bison burgers or moon pies anyone?—works its way toward the Chop House restaurant and there's plenty for everybody, including an arcade area called Scout's Alley, photo kiosks, a retail store, a Hall of Fame and museum and a video wall with monitors broadcasting every in-progress major league game.

The emerald-green field, set 20 feet below street level, is contrasted by patriotic bursts of red, white and blue (the Braves' colors) everywhere you look. Even in the field area you can never really escape the distractions. One of the park's distinctive features is an advertisement—a 42-foot-tall, fireworks-spewing Coke

TURNER FIELD (1997-)

In order to host a world-class event like the Olympics, Atlanta required a new Centennial Olympic Stadium, built just a home run distance from Atlanta-Fulton County Stadium.

After the '96 Summer Olympic Games, eight months of retro-fitting converted the 1996 Olympic Stadium into Turner Field in time for the start of the 1997 season. While Atlanta-Fulton County Stadium still may have been adequate, the new facility was state-of-the-art.

Turner Field, named for Braves owner Ted Turner, may be too young to have a personality all its own, but it's worth the visit to wallow in the glory of great Braves of the past — Aaron, Mathews — and great Braves of today — Maddux, Glavine.

First game: April 14, 1997. With all of the individual pitching talent the Braves had in the '90s, the winner in the stadium's opener (5-4 over the Cubs) was Brad Clontz.

- Site of one World Series (1999)
- Site of no All-Star Games

bottle that commands your gaze from the grandstand roof down the third base line. That's where Coca-Cola's Skyfield area—a 22,000-square-foot grass-covered, attraction-filled pavilion—is located, 80 feet above the outfield.

A three-level grandstand backs the entire foul territory, extending a few feet inside both foul poles, and a video-enhanced scoreboard, topped by a scripted Braves logo over a tomahawk, rises to prominence above the hitter's backdrop in an otherwise open outfield. An out-of-town scoreboard—a relic from Fulton County Stadium—rests atop the Stadium Club in left, topped dramatically by Atlanta's towering skyline. Bleacher-like seats are popular in both left-center and right-center.

Turner's slightly assymetrical field (335-400-330) does not have the crazy angles that affect play in some of the newer parks, but the grass is meticulously maintained and the surface is one of the most beautiful in baseball. It's hard to find a bad view in the 50,062-seat facility, where first-row fans are 8 feet above the field and minimum foul territory keeps everybody close to the action.

Turner Field, nicknamed The Ted after Braves owner and namesake Ted Turner, also forces visitors to look back, particularly with its many tributes to all-time home run king Aaron. Every seat at Turner is decorated with Aaron's silhouette and his record-setting 715th home run ball can be seen in the Hall of Fame or in an enlarged photo at the main entrance. One of the streets bordering the park has been renamed Hank Aaron Drive and if you park across the street, where Fulton County Stadium once stood, you'll probably run across a memorial plaque marking the spot for homer 715.

It's that attention to detail that marks Turner Field as a new-wave ballpark that offers a glimpse of the past. Aaron, tomahawk chops and a Hall of Fame vs. arcades, interactive stations and ATMs—that's 21st century-style baseball.

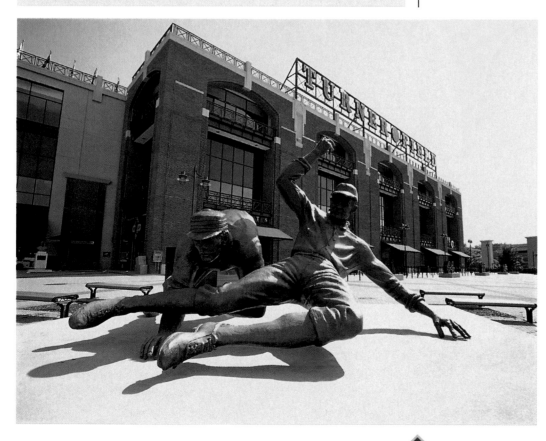

Georgia Peach Ty Cobb, in his familiar sliding pose, is one of the statues that greet visitors at the main entrance of Turner Field.

Camden Yards

Also known as Oriole Park at Camden Yards

Ripken takes a seat vs. Yankees, ending ironman streak at 2,632 games in final home game of season, Sept. 20, 1998

Eddie Murray, enjoying a one-season encore in Baltimore, hits career homer No. 500, Sept. 6, 1996

Ironman
CAL RIPKEN

Mussina allows one hit and strikes out 10 over eight innings in ALCS Game 6, but Indians win 1997 pennant when Tony Fernandez homers in 10th inning off Armando Benitez

Ripken plays in his record 2,131st consecutive game, passing Lou Gehrig and triggering one of most heart-warming celebrations in baseball history, Sept. 6, 1995

I t is nestled snugly within the contours of downtown Baltimore, a comfortable nook in the revitalization of a historic community. Old-timers who remember Camden Yards as a busy former railroad center now marvel at its bustling vitality as a trendy baseball complex. Camden Yards is a reminder of the past, a symbol of renewal and a vision of baseball future—all wrapped strategically in the intricate fabric of a vibrant, growing city.

Camden Yards is, first and foremost, a throwback—an appeal to the charm, charisma and intimacy fans remember from days when baseball

Where center fielder Brady Anderson hit 50 homers in 1996, leading Baltimore's charge to major league-record 257

Mussina, two outs away from a perfect game, surrenders a single to Indians catcher Sandy Alomar before completing his one-hitter, May 30, 1997

Boog's Bar-B-Q is a must-visit spot at Oriole Park

Ken Griffey Jr. went where no one else has gone in 1993, when he crushed a ball off B&O Warehouse during All-Star home run contest

L. 9, N.L. 3 in Camden's first All-Star Game in 1993

Rick Sutcliffe cut the ribbon for Camden Yards' grand opening with a five-hit, 2-0 shutout of the Indians, April 6, 1992

MIKE MUSSINA took center stage as Orioles' ace in 1992

This parking lot behind Camden Yards feeds into Eutaw Street, which becomes a 60-foot-wide promenade that separates the B&O Warehouse (left) from the ballpark. There are amenities for everyone on the promenade, including culinary delights from Boog's Bar-B-Q.

was an extension of community rather than an entertainment extravaganza. It is a marketing strategy, a deliberate attempt to return the game to its ballpark roots. When the park's designers mixed the enchanting nuances of Ebbets Field, Forbes Field, Shibe Park, Fenway Park, Crosley Field, Wrigley Field and the Polo Grounds, they produced a masterpiece of traditions, landmarks and memories that seem to mysteriously multiply with every pitch.

"The smell of Camden Yards is baseball," says admiring Seattle DH Edgar Martinez. And in the case of Camden, the aroma works its way from the outside in.

It starts with the arched brick facade that covers the outside of the stadium and blends subtly with the surrounding neighborhood, matching the field's most distinctive landmark—the all-brick B&O Warehouse that dominates the Eutaw Street skyline beyond the right field wall. You can't take your eyes off the warehouse, an imposing, 1,016-foot, eight-story structure that stretches almost a quarter of a mile and houses the Orioles' offices as well as a cafeteria, sports bar and gift shop.

The ballpark and warehouse are separated by a 60-foot-wide promenade, an extension of Eutaw Street where fans can arrive early to shop, view brass plates that mark landing spots for prodigious home runs, look at plaques honoring Ori-

oles Hall of Famers, take in the batting practice echoes that bounce off the warehouse wall and sample the tasty delight of Boog's Bar-B-Q and Bambino's Ribs.

Boog Powell never played here, but he's a Camden fixture and his barbecue sends tempting odors drifting through the ballpark during the game, luring helpless fans back to the busy concourse between innings. Many give in to its pull, but others are too captivated by what is happening on the emerald green grass field, carved into the ground 16 feet below street level.

It's an irregular-shaped field, framed by the warehouse in right, the downtown skyline in center and triple-decked left field stands that defy the open expanse of the rest of the outfield. A sun roof covers the upper deck, which wraps behind home plate from the right field corner to left field, and an ivy-covered outer wall provides a backdrop in center. An unusual two-tiered bullpen area offers a distinctive look in left-center.

Adding to the nostalgic mix is the knowledge that Babe Ruth, the same Bambino of New York Yankees fame, was born only two blocks from the site of the park, and that his father operated Ruth's Cafe, which was located in what is now center field at Camden Yards. The Babe might have felt right at home here, but

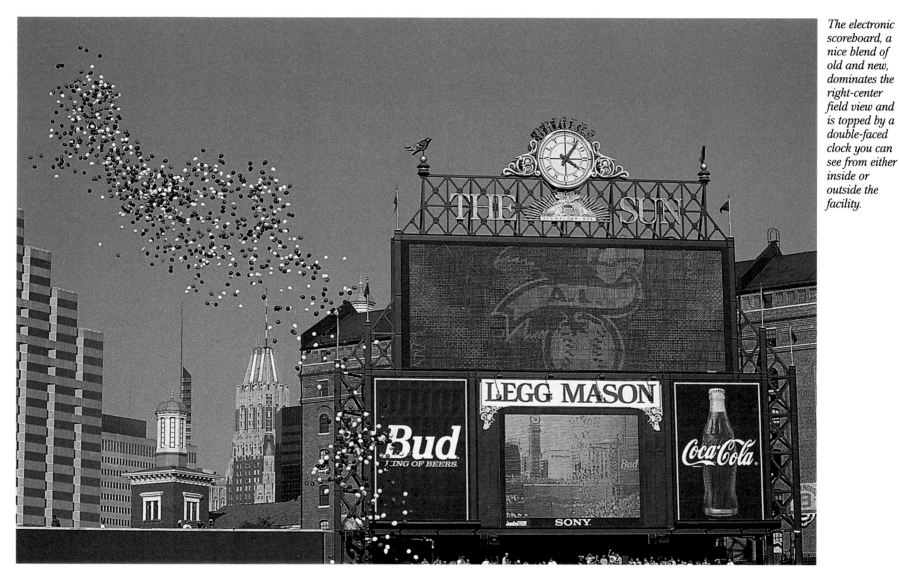

he would have been stunned by the accessories.

Such as the state-of-the-art electronic information boards on the scoreboard in right-center field, which are topped by a double-faced clock you can see from inside or outside the facility. Another electronic board, built into a 25-foot tall right field wall and topped by standing room area, simultaneously posts out-of-town scores.

There is no such thing as a bad seat at Camden, especially for those with tickets in the right-center field bleachers. This is a great place to watch a baseball game, even those that don't end with an Orioles' victory.

The still-youthful Camden Yards has become a symbol for the retro-ballpark mania that is sweeping through baseball, the inspiration for beautiful, old-style

The triple-decked left field stands form a visual barrier, but center field is open to the Baltimore skyline and the ever-present warehouse looms over the right field wall.

facilities that have sprung up in Cleveland, Seattle, Texas, Arizona and Denver with more on the way. All are spectacular, but so far none have been able to match the ambience and character of Oriole Park.

The only thing missing has been a World Series, but Camden Yards has not been lacking for baseball electricity. Ken Griffey Jr. supplied his share in 1993 when he became the first player to bounce a ball off the warehouse during the All-Star home run competition, Brady Anderson shocked everybody in 1996 when he hit 50 home runs and Mike Mussina helped power the Orioles into postseason play in 1996 and '97. But the national spotlight really focused on Camden Yards on a special September night in 1995.

What baseball fan can forget Cal Ripken, celebrating his new status as the greatest iron man in baseball history, circling the field at Camden Yards, glad-handing with elated fans and introducing millions of television viewers to the charms of a special ballpark. High above right field, hanging from the top of the warehouse, were the massive numbers 2,130, which changed to 2,131 before the eyes of a nation.

CAMDEN YARDS (1992-)

Also known as Oriole Park at Camden Yards

Its official name is Oriole Park at Camden Yards, but it's often shortened to Oriole Park and even more often to, simply, Camden Yards.

Camden Yards opened in 1992, a state-of-the-art replacement for venerable Memorial Stadium and quickly — and deservedly — gained the reputation as one of the best stadiums in baseball. Many have tried to imitate it — Jacobs Field, The Ballpark in Arlington, Coors Field among others — but none has duplicated the magic of Camden.

Part of the reason is its blend of past and present. It's hard to watch a game in Camden and not recall Babe Ruth, whose father's cafe was located roughly in Camden's center field, while at the same time watching Cal Ripken Jr. drive a double to the gap.

A perfect ballpark experience might begin with a shopping tour at Baltimore's popular Inner Harbor and a 12-minute walk to the Eutaw Street gate, which gains entrance to the warehouse concourse beyond center field. Or visit the Babe Ruth Museum, located just two blocks away and open before Orioles home games. Browsing not only is permitted at Camden Yards, it is encouraged. So are the sights and sounds of batting practice, as the baseball atmosphere literally floats you away.

First game: April 6, 1992. Behind Rick Sutcliffe, the Orioles beat Cleveland, 2-0.

■ Site of no World Series
■ Site of one All-Star Game (1993)

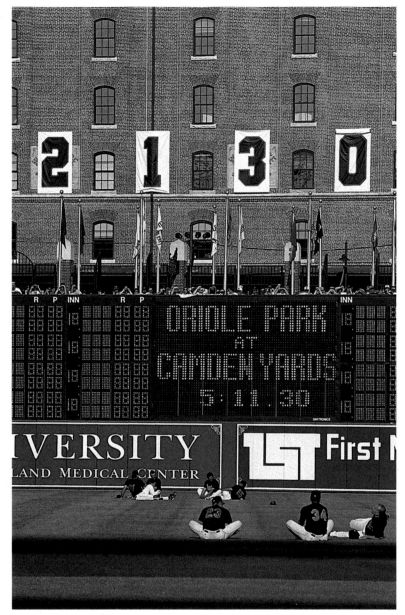

The 2130 sign on the warehouse facade paid tribute to Cal Ripken when he tied Lou Gehrig's all-time ironman streak in 1995.

Comiskey Park

Chris Singleton becomes fourth White Sox player to hit for cycle and first A.L. rookie since 1985, going 5-for-6 with four RBIs in 8-7, 10-inning loss to Royals, July 6, 1999

Where five-time Gold Glover Robin Ventura did great Brooks Robinson impression from 1990-98

OZZIE GUILLEN: Enthusiastic caretaker of shortstop position at both old Comiskey and new Comiskey

Bo Jackson hits three-run homer and White Sox clinch first A.L. West title in 10 years with 4-2 win over Mariners, Sept. 27, 1993

F or more than two years, they stood side by side, father and son, on the mean streets of Chicago's South Side. Comiskey Park, the venerable creation of Charles A. Comiskey in 1910; new Comiskey, the evolving protege and successor. This was an honorable passing of the torch, an old story with a new ending. For devoted White Sox fans, it also was an unusual opportunity to respect the past while catching a glimpse of the future.

The future in 1990 was a spiffy, gleaming, state-of-the-art facility

Thomas (.347) becomes first White Sox player to win A.L. batting title in 53 years and tops 100 RBIs for seventh straight season, 1997

Cubs post emotional 8-3 interleague win over White Sox in first regular-season meeting between teams that have competed for loyalty of Chicago fans since 1901, June 16, 1997

Albert Belle obliterates long-standing White Sox single-season records for home runs (49), total bases (399), extra-base hits (99), RBIs (152) and doubles (48), 1998

Jack McDowell: 1993 Cy Young winner

Tigers 16, White Sox 0 in a disappointing grand opening for new Comiskey, April 18, 1991

Where Dave Stewart shut down White Sox twice in ALCS as Blue Jays set stage for second straight World Series championship, 1993

Bo Jackson, becoming first major league player with artificial hip, homers with first swing of bat in home opener, April 9, 1993

FRANK THOMAS: Two-time MVP first baseman, '93 and '94

that would replace the decaying physical structure of old Comiskey, if not the spirit and character that had helped it become baseball's oldest ballpark treasure. New Comiskey was young and alive, dressy and hip. Such qualities as intimacy, charm and charisma would be judged over time.

"Beautiful," marveled Detroit manager Sparky Anderson after watching his Tigers win the new stadium's 1991 debut. "This place feels like a real ballpark. Looks like a real ballpark. ... This place is beautiful, but it's not gaudy. Everybody's going to want one of these now."

It seems ironic, almost a decade later, to hear it judged somewhat harshly — criticism based more on perception than fact. Hailed during its inaugural season as a masterpiece and the first baseball-only major league park to be built since Royals Stadium in 1973, it has become a victim of the very ballpark-building craze it triggered. The only real problem with new Comiskey is that it's not Camden Yards or Jacobs Field.

Eventually, that might not be so bad. As the retro parks continue to pop up around the country, each trying to out-quirk, out-charm and out-

COMISKEY PARK (1991-)

It triggered a ballpark-building craze, new stadiums with all of the modern conveniences that took visitors back in time for the baseball experience.

But Comiskey is more than just a ballpark that draws upon Chicago's baseball past. New Comiskey actually saved south side baseball for Chicago.

When it became evident that the days of old Comiskey were quickly passing by, the first intention was to move the White Sox out of their South Side roots to the Chicago suburbs. A second option was to move the team to St. Petersburg, Florida, where a stadium was already being built.

Addison, Illinois, voters rejected the notion to build a stadium in that suburb, and it took a last-minute save by the Illinois legislature to build a new stadium on the South Side site to keep the White Sox from fleeing south.

Comiskey often is criticized for what it isn't — it isn't Camden Yards or Jacobs Field — but it is a ballpark that gives you a sense of White Sox history beyond its years.

First game: April 18, 1991. The Tigers' Cecil Fielder broke it in with a home run as the Tigers ran away with a 16-0 win.

■ Site of no World Series
■ Site of no All-Star Games

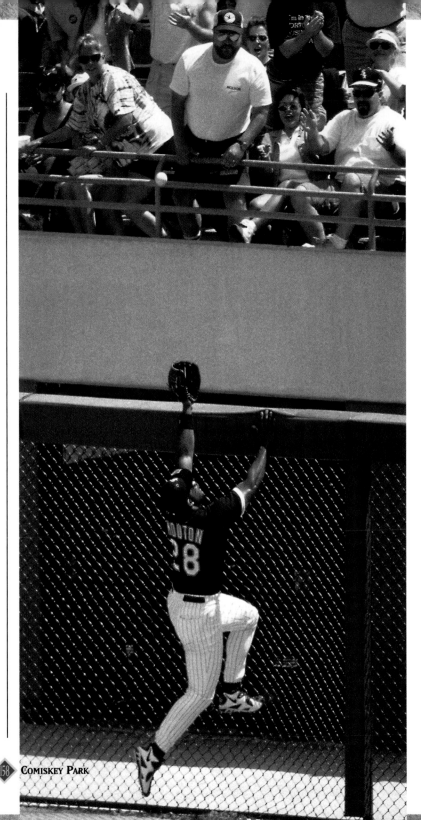

The fireworks-ready scoreboard dominates center field, and fans in the right field picnic area can watch action through a screened, field-level fence (right).

everything the other, new Comiskey stands as a traditional, symmetrical park with easy-viewing lines—and a few nice throwback touches mixed in. Comiskey does have a few negatives, but it's a down-to-earth, friendly place to take in a game.

To fully appreciate Comiskey, you have to understand that location and attitude are everything to hard-core White Sox fans, who have been attending games in the rough-edged area between West 35th Street and West 36th for nine decades. Baseball is serious business here, unlike the cuddly, warm-and-fuzzy Cubbies brand played on Chicago's North Side. You approach Comiskey with trepidation and are greeted by an imposing structure that seems much larger than the roofed, compact older version that once stood on the other side of 35th.

Inside, you discover why it looks so huge. The third-tier upper deck, which wraps behind the plate from foul pole to foul pole, sits well back from the field and covers only a small area of the lower grandstands, an architectural quirk that forces a steep rise to the stadium's rim. High upper deck is binocular territory and heavy breathing is encouraged there. Front-row upper-deck seats are located farther from home plate than those in the back row of the upper deck at old Comiskey.

Sections of the upper deck have been closed off when heavy winds come whipping off nearby Lake Michigan, creating potential safety problems. But the steep construction of the upper tier also is what makes the lower grandstand so appealing.

Because the upper deck sits so far back, the lower deck is open and exposed — a behind-the-plate bleacher seat. There are plenty of bleachers in the outfield as well, with four single-decked sections connecting the foul poles, divided in center field by a giant scoreboard and a dark hitter's backdrop. Some of the outfield openness is blocked, unfortunately, by two video boards and four equal-sized advertising billboards.

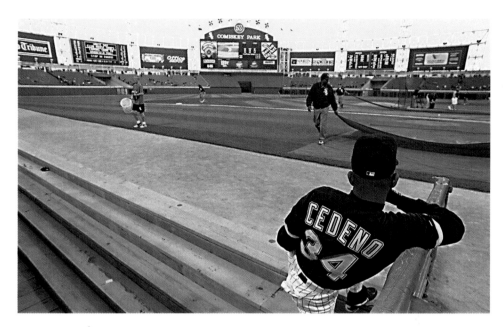

Players can enjoy a field-level view of new Comiskey from the bench or top step of the White Sox's third base dugout.

Comiskey has long been associated with its scoreboards and this one is easy to like. Explosive and eye-catching in the Bill Veeck tradition, the board is topped by the familiar pinwheels and responds to White Sox home runs with light-flashing, fireworks-shooting enthusiasm. It is framed on both sides by a white square-pieced, lattice-work design that also tops the outfield billboards and dresses up the light standards, adding a nice visual touch.

Comiskey's charms are demonstrated in other subtle ways. A mid-level concourse circles the stadium, allowing walkers to keep their eyes on the action from anywhere in the park. The visible concourse around the outfield has the look of a carnival midway, dotted with stands for cotton candy, hot dogs and other concessions. Right-center field picnickers can watch the action from field level through a screened fence below the bleachers, as can bar patrons in straightaway right. Aisles and concourses are wide; outdoor ramps protrude from the outer facade, guiding fans to their grandstand destinations.

Comiskey designers wisely avoided the temptation to create irregular dimensions, a tribute to the team's symmetrical tradition dating back to the early century, when most parks were nestled into the oddly-shaped contours of their surroundings. With dimensions of 347-400-347 and unpredictable winds that can send spring and autumn chills through the sturdiest of bodies, players have adapted to a roomy pitcher's park that defies the home run-happy game of the 1990s.

But nothing sets the tone for a great baseball experience better than the color shock you get the moment you step into the field area. Bright blue seats and fences frame a green grass playing surface that literally explodes before your eyes—a visual wonderland that makes it easy to understand why Ozzie Guillen was always smiling. Also prominent are the sounds of Nancy Faust on the organ, trains that chug and whistle behind the right field grandstands and the crack of the bat on a Frank Thomas, Carlton Fisk, Harold Baines, Robin Ventura or Ray Durham line drive.

The only thing missing from a potentially explosive atmosphere are the large, boisterous crowds of old and a team capable of taking the White Sox to their first World Series since 1959.

Jacobs Field

It's an architectural illusion, dropped like a jewel into the center of Cleveland's rehabilitated downtown skyline. Jacobs Field shines, sparkles and glimmers like a diamond, but it feels, smells and sounds like an old-fashioned ballpark. It's an irresistible blending of new and old, a spark that has rekindled a city's love affair with baseball.

The Jake's combination of beauty, character and flashy appeal is no accident. This park wasn't built—it was choreographed. While the exterior is designed to blend into

Where Mark McGwire's 485-foot bomb off Orel Hershiser hit left field scoreboard, April 30, 1997

Eddie Murray's 11th-inning single gives Indians 7-6 win over Braves in Game 3 of 1995 World Series—the team's first Series win since 1948

Manager Mike Hargrove: Five straight Central Division titles, tw pennants, 471 wir from 1995-99

CHARLES NAGY: Mr. Consistency won 15 or more games every season from 1995-99

Indians defeat Baltimore 3-2 and clinch A.L. Central — first title of any kind in 41 years, Sept. 8, 1995

Wayne Kirby's 11 inning single completes comeba gives Indians 4-3 v in Jacobs Field del April 4, 1994

Omar Vizquel fans on suicide squeeze attempt, Baltimore catcher Lenny Webster misses ball and Indians score winning run in Game 3 of 1997 ALCS

Sandy Alomar scores from second on daring baserunning gamble that helps Indians post 8-7 win over Orioles in Game 4 of 1997 ALCS

Cleveland celebrates as Sandy Alomar claims All-Star Game MVP honors with two-run, seventh-inning homer in 3-1 A.L. victory, July 8, 1997

Indians score 10 eighth-inning runs, hand Angels shocking 14-12 loss, Aug. 31, 1999

First-inning ejections of Mike Hargrove, starting pitcher Doc Gooden energize lethargic Indians, who rebound for 9-5 win over Red Sox in Game 2 of 1998 Division Series

Jim Thome homers twice, but Indians complete Division Series collapse vs. Red Sox with 12-8 loss, Oct. 11, 1999

Indians record first postseason win since 1948 when Tony Pena's 13th-inning homer ends Game 1 of Division Series vs. Boston, Oct. 3, 1995

Area patroled by Kenny Lofton, five-time A.L. stolen base champion

1999 Indians become seventh major league team to top 1,000 runs in season

Albert Belle's grand slam off Baltimore's Armando Benitez snaps 4-4 tie and helps Indians post 9-4 win in Game 3 of 1996 Division Series

Albert Belle hits franchise-record 50th home run vs. Kansas City, Sept. 30, 1995

MANNY RAMIREZ: Posted baseball's eighth-highest single-season RBI total with 165 in 1999

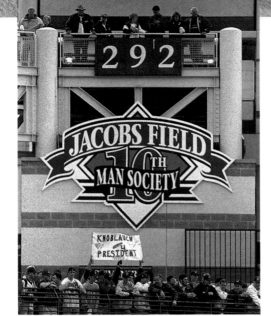

The Indians saluted enthusiastic fans in 1998 (right) with a '10th Man' sign in the left field standing area. The '292' was a running tally of consecutive sellouts.

the landscape of Cleveland's downtown renaissance, the interior works hard to combine hip and trendy with charming and old.

You sense that battle the moment you see the intricately crafted white-steel structure, which is nestled into the boundaries of three main Cleveland streets. You can see the inside concourses through the exposed support arms that connect like spider webs to steel buckles, matching the lattice work design of many bridges in the area. The vertical light standards, which tower 200 feet above street level, look like big, white smokestacks, modeled after the factories in Cleveland's industrial zone. Brick, stone and granite also help The Jake blend with its downtown surroundings, a white-steel rim adds a crowning effect and a huge, bronze statue of pitching great Bob Feller guards the Indians Square entrance, adding a nostalgic touch.

Ironically, you can experience the park's signature feature without ever passing through a gate. A large section of the Gateway Plaza entrance across from Gund Arena is closed off only by a wrought-iron fence, allowing visitors a panoramic view of the lush green grass field set 18 feet below street level. Two-thirds of the park is exposed from this unusual sightline over the left field corner, which commands at least a momentary pause for any self-respecting fan—

ballpark regulars and employees as well as occasional visitors.

The ballpark designers sprinkled big helpings of "old" elements throughout Jacobs Field like a cook might garnish his gourmet meal. Concourses are decorated with giant photographs of great Indians players and championship celebrations, the field is assymetrical with wall irregularities that obviously can affect play and everything seems intimate and close, a vast departure from the feel of the Indians' former home—cavernous Cleveland Stadium.

JACOBS FIELD (1994-)

Jacobs Field, named for Richard E. Jacobs, who with his late brother, David, bought the Indians in 1986, is a symbol not only of the team's rebirth but of the city's rebirth as well.

It is coupled with Gund Arena, home of the NBA's Cavaliers, to form a sports complex in downtown Cleveland, a complex that has helped spark economic growth and urban renewal.

The Jake is almost everything its predecessor, Municipal Stadium, was not. Where Municipal Stadium was huge and imposing and rarely filled, the Jake is quaint and intimate and almost always filled.

First game: April 4, 1994, an 11-inning come-from-behind 4-3 Indians victory. The stadium's first hit was a home run, by Seattle's Eric Anthony.

■ Site of two World Series (1995 and 1997)
■ Site of one All-Star Game (1997)

You start your visual tour of Jacobs with the "mini-Green Monster," a 19-foot Fenway Park-like wall that runs from the left field foul pole to center field, at which point it angles away and drops to 8 feet. The wall, which houses an out-of-town scoreboard, fronts a Wrigley Field-like bleacher section and the largest free-standing scoreboard in baseball—a 120-foot-high, 220-foot-wide blitzkrieg of visual effects and advertisements with a giant scripted "Indians" logo on top.

The scoreboard, a Mark McGwire moonshot from home plate, commands most of the left field view, but it doesn't detract from the openness of center field and the left field line—windows to the downtown skyline. Lefthanded hitters take aim at a triple-decked grandstand that rises steeply in right and fans from foul pole to foul pole can watch action

The left field scoreboard with the 'Indians' sign on top provides an inviting home run target—that few will ever reach.

from any of four levels—including luxury boxes and suites.

An oddity of The Jake's assymetrical configuration is that both foul lines measure 325 feet and straightaway center field (405) is not the park's deepest point. The spot where the little monster connects to the shorter wall in left-center is 410 feet from the plate and provides one of three angles that can result in erratically bouncing balls.

That center field angle marks The Jake's "Back Yard"—a four-tiered, tree and shrub-lined picnic area that offers a panoramic view of the field over the shorter fence. It also overlooks the Indians' bullpen, which is raised above field level for better sightlines—both in and out.

Such nuances only add to the charm of Jacobs Field, which opened to the baseball world in 1994 as a ballpark throwback modeled in the retro image of Baltimore's Camden Yards. The Jake matched up nicely in beauty and intimate detail, but it could not rival the signature-feature warehouse, which became a natural extension of the Camden Yards complex. So Jacobs makes up for that shortcoming with creativity.

Visitors to Camden Yards come away with a feeling of earthy, old-ballpark charm. Jacobs provides a sense of old—but with all the amenities and comforts of home. The Jake appeals to the family, but it's flashy enough for the young. The music has been carefully choreographed to fit all customers, the electronics are friendly to all eyes and park employees have undergone many hours of Disney training, the better to reach out and touch customers on any level.

But The Jake's greatest appeal might be its complete disassociation from

The overview (left page) shows Cleveland's skyline hulking over Jacobs Field and Gund Arena, home of the Cavaliers. The Jake is all about fans (above, right) and there has been plenty to cheer since the park's 1994 opening.

Cleveland Stadium, the Indians' uninviting, impersonal home for six decades. Jacobs Field (capacity 43,863) is everything the Stadium (74,483) was not—clean, new, vibrant, intimate, noisy and always filled to the brim. It's also filled with expectations, the kind that come from winning teams. Jacobs Field already has played host to six World Series games (more than Cleveland Stadium during its lifetime) and an All-Star Game and its teams ended the millennium with two

pennants and five straight Central Division titles.

Adding to the ballpark flavor are Chris Miltner, the singing beer man (go ahead, ask him what time it is), bleacherite John Adams, the mad drummer, and the Indians' flashy white, red-trimmed uniforms that sparkle under the brightest lights in baseball. The players—shortstop Omar Vizquel, second baseman Roberto Alomar, first baseman Jim Thome—fit nicely into a glittering, festive atmosphere that has become one of the best in baseball.

Coors Field

Rockies become second team to boast two 30-30 players in same season: Ellis Burks (left), Bichette, 1996

Rockies and opponent combine for a record 303 home runs at Coors Field, 1999

Dodger Hideo Nomo pitches first no-hitter in stadium history, Sept. 17, 1996

A.L. 13, N.L. 8 in highest-scoring All-Star Game in history, July 7, 1998

Offensive Rockies boast three 40-homer m
in 1996, '97; four 100-RBI men 1996, '97, '9

DANTE BICHETTE, original Rockie and career leader in most offensive categories

Bichette's three-run 14th-inning homer gives Rockies dramatic 11-9 win over Mets in first game at Coors, April 26, 1995

They call it mountain baseball, the kind where home runs zoom up, up and away through the thin air and scores climb up, up and over the limit of our wildest imagination. Coors Field is a launching pad cleverly disguised as a cozy ballpark. You go there to experience its innocence and charm; you leave with a sense of its offensive and unforgiving personality. Coors is a Mile High paradise—with a nasty edge.

The paradise part was planned—choreographed down to Coors Field's most minute details before it opened as new home of the Rockies in April 1995. Not only was baseball's

Andres Galarraga becomes fourth player in history to hit home runs in three consecutive innings, June 25, 1995

Mark McGwire launches ball 510 feet during home run contest prior to 1998 All-Star Game

Andres Galarraga, The Big Cat: 1996 N.L. home run champ, 1996, '97 RBI champ, 1993 batting champ

Trailing 9-2 after 6½ innings, Rockies score 11 in seventh and hold on for 13-12 win over Padres, July 12, 1996

Colorado hitters take aim at Rockpile

1997 home run champ Walker wins consecutive batting titles in '98, '99

Walker wins percentage triple crown in 1999— .379 average, .710 slugging, .458 on-base

1997 MVP LARRY WALKER: First player to top 400 total bases since Hank Aaron in 1959

Pitcher/pinch-hitter Lance Painter strikes out with bases loaded in ninth as wild-card Rockies drop first postseason game in franchise history to Braves, Oct. 3, 1995

newest retro ballpark an architectural masterpiece of red brick, Colorado sandstone and exposed green girders, it was the magic wand that transformed an old, decaying section of Denver into a vibrant urban village and entertainment center.

The nasty edge was a byproduct of a simple scientific fact: A ball hit in the thin mountain air of Denver will travel 10 percent farther than the same ball hit at sea level. Beautiful new Coors Field was a dark, ugly nightmare for pitchers, a statistics-skewing anomaly for baseball and a career-enhancing blessing for 98-pound-weakling second basemen and shortstops.

This split personality is what gives Coors Field a special niche among such retro contemporaries as Camden Yards, Jacobs Field, The Ballpark in Arlington and Safeco Field. No other park has made such a dramatic impact on both its community and the game. You can feel the buzz of a suddenly active Denver downtown, you can see the explosion of restaurants, nightclubs, shops, art galleries and lofts in LoDo (lower downtown), the warehouse district where Coors is located, and you can calculate the inflated home runs, batting averages and run totals that are redefining the historical perspectives of our national pastime.

The first thing you notice about Coors Field is how it blends into the neighborhood—a warehouse kind of look enhanced by the red-brick facade and low-key design. The main entrance, topped by a distinctive clock tower, rekindles memories of Brooklyn's Ebbets Field and every detail suggests old. Coors Field's height is not overpowering (thanks to the sunken field inside), its coloring is not distinctive to the area and only the light towers and signs reveal its true identity to the casual passer-by.

The Denver skyline towers over the home plate grandstands of Coors Field like a protective mother and the rugged Rocky Mountains provide a scenic backdrop for fans in the first-base-side upper deck and right field stands. Spectacular sunsets over the Rockies are well worth the price of admission, but so are the many quaint, fan-friendly nuances that

Coors Field occupies a significant area of LoDo in full view of the Denver skyline.

give Coors an early-century ballpark feel.

The most captivating is a huge state-of-the-art scoreboard that rises out of the single-deck, open left field bleachers, piggybacking a steel-framed light standard that towers well above the playing field. The latticed light stanchions, designed to reflect LoDo's railroad heritage, also rise periodically from the grandstand rim that circles the park from center field clockwise to the left field foul pole.

Circling the lower-level perimeter of the park is a wide concourse that invites fans to take a leisurely stroll past a playground, a huge mural, baseball's only on-

COORS FIELD (1995-)

Without a commitment for a major league team, plans for a baseball-only facility preceded the awarding of an expansion franchise. So when on June 10, 1991 it was announced that Denver would be the site of an expansion franchise, a new stadium was already in the works.

In 1993 and 1994, before Coors Field was ready, the Rockies toiled in Mile High Stadium, a facility that had seen baseball action with the Class AAA Denver Bears and Denver Zephyrs.

Tickets to Coors Field are a hot commodity, so you take what you can get. But, if you have a choice, try to land a seat in section 330, where the view of the field and the proximity to all of the amenities is unrivaled.

First game: April 26, 1995. Dante Bichette settled a fittingly offensive display in the stadium opener, hitting a three-run homer in the 14th to lead Colorado over the Mets, 11-9.

■ Site of no World Series
■ Site of one All-Star Game (1998)

A steel-framed, state-of-the-art scoreboard is the signature feature of Coors Field, rising proudly from the top of the left field bleachers.

short fences and a confined playing area. Not so. Coors Field is spacious, with lines measuring 347 feet and 350, power alleys 390 and 375 and a 415-foot center field that isn't even the deepest point of the park. That honor goes to a right-center field jag that measures 424.

The combination of thin air and spacious field has made Coors Field a tough place for shellshocked pitchers. "I pitched there my second start of the year and for five starts after that I had brain damage," said Expos righthander Jim Bullinger in 1996. That's understandable. Balls

site micro brewery and distinctive concession stands—without ever losing sight of the field. The coup de grace—a feature no other ballpark can duplicate—is a single row of purple seats (upper deck, row 20) that snakes around the grandstand and marks 5,280 feet, or one mile above sea level.

Rising above the center field backdrop is Coors Field's famous bleacher section—the 2,300-seat Rockpile, which admits children and seniors for the unbeatable price of $1 and everybody else for $4. To the right field side of the backdrop is a water spectacular (set within a tree-and-rock-covered mountain scene), side-by-side elevated bullpens and a long manual scoreboard that serves as a big section of the right field fence, raising its height from 8 to 14 feet.

All of this is backdrop for a sparkling grass field (a perfect centerpiece for the park's green hue) with quirky dimensions. A common perception is that Coors Field is a bandbox, a place where lack of outfield speed is neutralized by

leave Coors like rockets and fall in front of deep-playing outfielders, creating softball-like scores. The Rockies, built offensively around such former and current power hitters as Andres Galarraga, Ellis Burks, Vinny Castilla, Dante Bichette, Larry Walker and Todd Helton, produced four 30-homer men in four of Coors Field's first five seasons and they broke the single-season team home run record in 1996 (271) and 1999 (303). The faces change, but the results stay the same. Rockies hitters are consistently near the top of baseball's offensive charts while their pitchers struggle to lower confidence-shattering and career-threatening ERAs.

Baseball at Coors might not be artistic, but it is exciting. And it comes with crisp mountain air and intimacy, despite the near-capacity crowds of 50,000-plus who routinely pack the ballpark. The seats are close to the field, views are unobstructed and there are usually fireworks during every game—the bat-on-ball type that keep Coors Field on a Rocky Mountain high.

A sunset over the Rockies (above) is as good as it gets, unless you're an aficionado of Mountain Oysters. The purple seats that circle the upper deck (far right) let fans know they are 5,280 feet above sea level.

 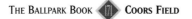

Pro Player
Stadium

Also known as Joe Robbie Stadium (1993-1996)

You can get intimidated by its Teal Monster, lost in its Bermuda Triangle, deflated by its size and overwhelmed by its championship-filled history. Pro Player Stadium doesn't waste any time worrying about frivolous notions like charm and intimacy. This is an imposing concrete-and-steel football edifice that doubles as a diamond in the rough. Young and macho, it already has been the proud championship stage for three Super Bowls and a home-field arena for one of the most unlikely World Series winners in baseball history.

Giants' Barry Bonds hits 400th career homer, becomes first member of 400-400 club, Aug. 23, 1998

Where Mark McGwire hit homer 56, 57, 58, 59 over two games en rout to record 70-home season, Sept. 1, 2, 19(

The Teal Monster

First no-hitter in franchise history: Al Leiter beats Rockies 11-0, May 11, 1996

Marlins record 8-4 interleague win over Devil Rays in first battle of Florida-based teams at Pro Player Stadium, June 24, 1998

Bobby Bonilla hits two-out, two-strike, bottom-of-the-ninth grand slam to give Marlins dramatic 9-6 win over Rockies, Sept. 16, 1997

JEFF CONINE: Career leader in many offensive categories

5-year-old Marlins become youngest World Series champs when Edgar Renteria delivers Game 7-ending single in 11th inning, Oct. 26, 1997

Livan Hernandez strikes out 15 in riveting 2-1 Game 5 NLCS win over Braves, Oct. 12, 1997

Kevin Brown: 17-11, 1.89 ERA in outstanding 1996 season

The Bermuda Triangle

Edgar Renteria's bases-loaded, ninth-inning single gives wild-card Marlins 2-1 Division Series win over Giants in franchise's first postseason game, Sept. 30, 1997

Alex Fernandez, making comeback from rotator-cuff surgery, posts emotional 98-pitch complete-game win over Rockies and punctuates effort with home run, Aug. 6, 1999

Good start: Expansion Marlins down Dodgers 6-3 in Joe Robbie debut, April 5, 1993

Where Robb Nen blew away hitters for four-plus seasons while compiling 108 saves

GARY SHEFFIELD: hit 42 homers, drove in 120 runs in 1996

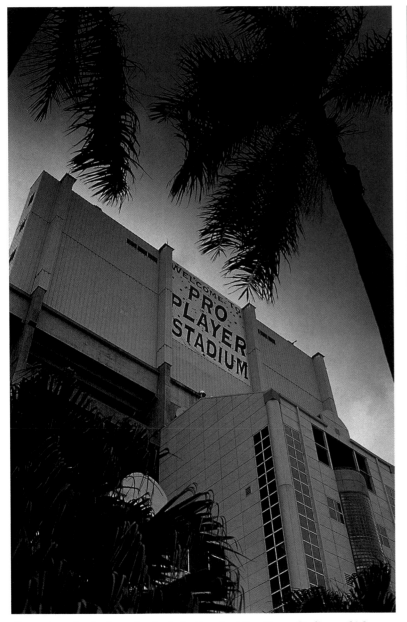

Concrete and palm trees dominate the facade at Pro Player Stadium, which successfully blends baseball into a football-first arena.

PRO PLAYER STADIUM (1993-)

Known as Joe Robbie Stadium (1993-1996)

Home of the Florida Marlins since their inception in 1993, Pro Player Stadium's origins begin as far back as 1984. It was in '84 that Miami Dolphins owner Joe Robbie announced plans to build a new stadium, with the tentative name of Dolphin Stadium.

In April of 1987, before any game had been played in the stadium, it was officially renamed Joe Robbie Stadium. In August of that year, an NFL exhibition game christened the facility.

In 1996, naming rights were granted to Pro Player, a division of Fruit of the Loom, for a period of 10 years. Alas, the Marlins don't plan to see the end of that deal: There are plans for a new Marlins ballpark, to be built in downtown Miami, with an April 2003 targeted opening day.

First game: April 5, 1993. Though major league exhibition baseball came in 1988, regular-season baseball didn't arrive until '93. In that '93 debut, veteran Charlie Hough pitched the Marlins to a 6-3 victory over the Dodgers.

■ Site of one World Series (1997)

■ Site of no All-Star Games

Make no mistake: Pro Player is first and foremost a football stadium, opened in 1987 when Joe Robbie constructed a $115-million, fully enclosed, open-air facility for his Miami Dolphins—funded entirely by private money and located on a 160-acre tract midway between Fort Lauderdale and Miami. When Dolphin Stadium (soon to be known as Joe Robbie Stadium) played host to its first regular-season NFL game, baseball was still six years from becoming a South Florida reality. The expansion Marlins eventually turned Miami into a four-sport city, but Pro Player never loses that sense of football, even though it converts into an attractive baseball field—with personality.

It's the size. The stadium's 75,000-plus seats are rocking during football season, mostly empty for baseball, creating a cavernous, hollow sensation that is enhanced by the blaring sounds of a huge JumboTron board designed to entertain capacity crowds. The outfield upper-deck seats are covered by a blue tarp through most of baseball season to compensate, but the effect is minimal.

The best feature of Pro Player is an assymetrical, natural-grass field that offers enough quirks and surprises to make baseball life interesting. The first thing that captures your eye is a left field barrier that ranges in height from 25 to 30 feet—a so-called Teal Monster that eats up potential home runs. The wall itself is an unremarkable 8 feet, but an uneven out-of-town manual scoreboard tops the fence and extends from just short of the left field corner well into left-center field. A clock sits on top of the scoreboard and seems to pull balls toward it like a magnet.

Just beyond the scoreboard in left-center the fence jogs seriously forward, creating a notch, 434 feet from home plate, called the Bermuda Triangle—a place where balls can disappear and emerge again as triples or inside-the-park home runs. The left field foul pole is 330 feet, straightaway center is 410 and the right field pole is 345, with bleachers covering the entire right field area and the huge video board perched high on the stadium's outer rim. The field's green grass is framed by a sea of orange seats and blue and teal trim, colors that become more vivid with every empty seat.

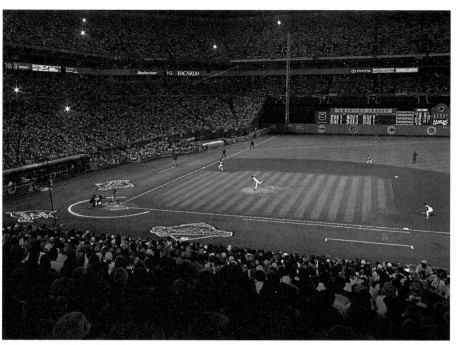

The upper decks at Pro Player were uncovered and filled to the brim in the 1997 World Series, when the 5-year-old Marlins completed their surprising championship run.

Pro Player Stadium. After the Series, Huizenga conducted a shocking player firesale that gave his depleted roster the look of a hopeless expansion team.

Your first thought when you see Pro Player is "expansive"—a monolith surrounded by acres of parking lots and numerous palm trees. Two swirling ramps extend from each corner and lead fans to their seats. Three statues greet you at the main entrance—Robbie, former Dolphins coach Don Shula and the immortal Casey, from Casey at the Bat fame.

An outside attraction called Sports Town features interactive games, food stands, bars and souvenir kiosks under huge tents off the stadium's south perimeter, but Pro Player doesn't have the mall culture you get at newer parks. Inside sightlines are set up for football, as is the lighting, which makes the home plate area dark and pitcher-friendly. When you go to Pro Player, be sure to take an umbrella because it probably will rain—16 delays in 1999. If you go to an afternoon game in the summer, prepare to sweat.

After topping 67,000 in each of the four 1997 World Series games, the depleted Marlins have watched attendance slip drastically and the stadium often feels empty and antiseptic. The one recent exception was September 1 and 2, 1998, when Mark McGwire brought his home run-hitting parade to town and the stadium was packed.

McGwire hit four home runs in two games, two of which landed on the big center field backdrop tarp. The lingering memory for a national television audience was of several teenagers diving onto the tarp and scrambling after a Super Bowl-caliber baseball souvenir.

That was not a problem in 1993, when the first-year Marlins drew more than 3 million fans. They were the creation of H. Wayne Huizenga, who purchased 50 percent of Joe Robbie Stadium in 1990 and became the point man for bringing major league baseball to South Florida. This was a state-of-the-art facility that featured more than 200 luxury suites and a breakthrough special level of "club seats" that provided extra amenities for deep-pocketed patrons—the perfect lure for baseball's bottom-line oriented expansion committee.

Huizenga, who would become the facility's sole owner in 1994 and sell naming rights to Pro Player in 1996, made baseball modifications and began building a free agency-enhanced roster that could contend for a championship. By 1997, the 5-year-old Marlins, led by Gary Sheffield, Moises Alou, Kevin Brown, Alex Fernandez, Bobby Bonilla and Alex Fernandez, won a wild-card playoff berth and became the youngest team to win a World Series when Edgar Renteria delivered an 11th-inning single to beat the Indians in Game 7 at

Bank One Ballpark

Bank One Ballpark does not exactly blend into its Phoenix surroundings. It doesn't even try. BOB creates its own skyline, a monstrous entertainment oasis located strategically in the Valley of the Sun. Inside this 21.9-acre facility exists a veritable Disneyland of baseball where you can go to play, swim, dream, watch, browse, shop, eat, drink and be merry—free from life's worries and the blistering Arizona heat.

Make no mistake: Bank One is not a dome. It sometimes looks and feels like a dome, but that slatted white top is really a retractable roof, a technological cap that can be put on and removed in a five-minute blur. What Bank One lacks in aesthetic

Folding panels double as advertisements and open-air windows

Where Mark McGwire's 510-foot batting practice home run bounced through open window in 1999

National television audience watches Andy Benes and Diamondbacks end franchise-opening five-game losing streak with 3-2 victory over Giants, April 5, 1998

MATT WILLIAMS:
.303, 35 homers, 142 RBIs
in 1999—Diamondbacks'
first division
championship season

Johnson records 11 strikeouts and raises season total to 364—fourth best all-time—as West Division-champion Diamondbacks record 98th win en route to 100, Sept. 30, 1999

176

Kelly Stinnett (right) hits game-tying two-run homer in 16th and Dante Powell (left) singles home winning run in 7-6 win over Dodgers — a 5-hour, 14-minute marathon, April 13, 1999

Cardinals righthander Jose Jimenez not only outduels Johnson, he pitches no-hitter and posts 1-0 win with only run scoring in ninth inning, June 25, 1999

ard-hitting Rockies overpower expansion Diamondbacks 9-2 in first game at new ballpark, March 31, 1998

Where Cubs first baseman Mark Grace made a 1998 splash, literally, when he became first player to hit home run into swimming pool

RANDY JOHNSON: Arizona's first Cy Young winner posted 17-9 record, 2.48 ERA in dominating 1999 campaign

Only park with dirt track from pitching mound to home plate

merit, it makes up for with utilitarian practicality. Every Diamondbacks fan understands that without that roof, summer baseball would not exist in Arizona.

Like the retractable-roofed SkyDome in Toronto, Bank One is an entertainment complex with baseball as its centerpiece. But unlike SkyDome, Bank One is sensitive to the detail and nuances that give the stadium a baseball personality beyond its bells and whistles. It's the only air-conditioned retractable-roof sports facility in the world with a natural grass playing surface and you can't go there without getting a heavy dose of baseball history, no matter where you sit, walk or look.

Bank One can overpower you. It's huge, big enough to fit the nearby America West Arena (home of the NBA's Suns and NHL's Coyotes) inside its 1.3 million square feet—eight times. A traditional red-brick facade combines with green structural steel to give

Bank One Ballpark is a huge entertainment complex that creates its own skyline.

BANK ONE BALLPARK (1998-)

With its perpetually clear blue skies and warm temperatures, Arizona has long been an ideal baseball destination, especially for spring training and fall instruction. But when it came to bona fide major league baseball, the 162-game, round-the-summer variety that was eventually committed to Phoenix in 1995, stadium designers and planners had to deal with one less-than-ideal factor—the weather, namely the searing desert heat.

And they handled it with two tried-and-true methods for beating the heat—air-conditioning and a swimming pool. A strip of dirt that runs from pitcher's mound to home plate is the third distinctive characteristic of Bank One Ballpark (a name determined by corporate sponsorship). Bank One, more casually called The BOB, has a state-of-the-art cooling system that can drop the temperature 30 degrees in three hours and a sliding roof that opens and closes in five minutes.

If that's not enough ambience, there's the pool, located outside the right-center field wall, built to replicate an "upscale Arizona backyard."

Yes, you're always comfortable at The BOB.

First game: March 31, 1998. Arizona's first franchise hit, run, RBI and home run came on a blow by Travis Lee, but the D-backs lost to Colorado, 9-2.

■ Site of no World Series
■ Site of no All-Star Games

the building design elements in keeping with its warehouse surroundings and outside walkways buzz with activity before and after games, highlighted by the Leinenkugel's Ballyard Brewery in the plaza along Fourth Street.

The roof dominates the inside, whether open or shut. Most games are played with roof closed after the first week of May because of stifling heat, but the top remains open most days so sunshine can feed the natural turf. Only about three hours is needed to cool the facility before games and fans often stay after the final out to watch the roof silently slide open, revealing a whole new universe beyond.

With roof in place, its steel girders give you the feel of a giant airplane hangar. And your first panoramic view reveals an advertising blitz that almost knocks you over—there's nothing subliminal about Bank One's ties to its many sponsors. But other visual effects help ease that pain and baseball takes care of the rest.

Your eyes are drawn quickly to a giant center field scoreboard with one of baseball's most active JumboTrons. On each side of the board are massive square panels that open and close—advertisements one minute, open-air windows the next. It was through one of these panels that Mark McGwire bounced a prolific batting practice blast estimated at 510 feet. Additional scoreboards are perched high above the stands down both lines and fans are treated to running pitch counts and Randy Johnson strikeout totals. The most distinctive field feature is a dirt track from the mound to home plate, reminiscent of pre-20th century baseball.

Most of the 49,075 seats are located in foul territory, forcing a five-level grandstand to rise steeply into the baseball stratosphere. The trick at Bank One is securing seats in one of the three lower levels between first and third base, where you're close to the field and can actually get a cozy-ballpark feel. But with such hitters as Matt Williams, Travis Lee and Luis Gonzalez taking advantage of the second-highest elevation (approximately 1,100 feet) in baseball, you're bound to get plenty of action no matter where you sit.

A glove might be in order in bleacher sections located behind the left and right field fences. The bleachers wrap around unusual bullpens that angle behind the foul poles toward the main lower-deck grandstand, meaning balls hit into them can be either home runs or long fouls. The field is oddly assymetrical—330 feet to left, 407 to center and 334 to right, with the deepest points in right-center and left-center (413) where 71/2-foot left and right field fences angle away from a 25-foot center field barrier.

One of Bank One's charms is the variety of ways in which baseball can be viewed. The most novel is from a swimming pool/hot tub area that can be rented for parties beyond the right-center field wall—an inviting 415-foot home run splash from home plate. Others include a tiered picnic area behind the center field wall, beer gardens that overlook the field, a restaurant down the left field line, a stadium club down the right field line and from the main concourse, which circles the lower deck without losing sight of the action.

That concourse offers a variety of shops, concessions and even a playground—as well as a progressive dose of baseball history. The Cox Clubhouse is like a mini-Hall of Fame with displays on loan from Cooperstown and as you circle the park you're besieged by interesting photographs, glass-encased memorabilia, a graphic sports timeline and videos—monitors everywhere offering glimpses of baseball's past. Fans are greeted at the main entrance by a terra cotta rotunda floor display honoring the state of Arizona.

The Bank One package was enough to lure 3.6 million fans to games in the Diamondbacks' 1998 debut season and more than 3 million in 1999—when the free agency-built team rose from the expansion ashes to claim a National League West Division title. With Bank One Ballpark providing a long-term backdrop, baseball should occupy center stage in Phoenix for years to come.

The interior is dominated by the roof (below), but one of Bank One's special features is the swimming pool (right) that allows fans to enjoy a game in real comfort.

Tropicana Field

One of four rings—or catwalks—that circle field area, providing support for roof

Where outdoor-loving Tampa fans can spend a day at The Beach and watch baseball, too

It's the self-billed "Ballpark of the 21st Century," a technologically enhanced playground with a distinctive surf-and-sand personality. Tropicana Field is downright proud of the cutting-edge amenities and entertainment options it serves up with its baseball. Where else can you combine pitch counts and batting averages with a beach, a shopping mall, a cigar bar, a bank, a travel agency, a climbing wall and more food groups than you ever knew existed?

The Devil Rays boast that their stadium has "nearly 290 points of sale" around its wide, visitor-friendly concourses. It also has one of the

FRED McGRIFF: 32 homers, 104 RBIs in Tampa Bay's second American League season

What went up didn't come down for Jose Canseco in May 2, 1999, game vs. Tigers—ball landed on "B" ring catwalk and Canseco was credited with double

Where Jose Canseco hit his franchise-record 34th home run onto the roof of the Batter's Eye Restaurant, Sept. 28, 1999

McGriff drives in four runs and Rolando Arrojo (left) pitches six innings as Devil Rays record franchise's first win with 11-8 decision over Tigers, April 1, 1998

Jogs in left-center, right-center field fences create erratic bounces

Two-run, 14th-inning home run by light-hitting Kevin Stocker gives first-year Devil Rays 6-5 win over Indians and two-game series sweep, May 12, 1998

WADE BOGGS:
Veteran third baseman brought Hall of Fame air to Devil Rays' franchise-beginning lineup

Boggs becomes baseball's 23rd 3,000-hit player, and first to reach milestone with home run, off Indians lefty Chris Haney, Aug. 7, 1999 oddest-looking domes ever constructed—a Teflon-coated fiberglass cap that slants at a 6.5-degree angle. That slant makes Tropicana, the world's largest cable-supported dome, look like a tilting spaceship ready to shoot into the stratosphere. If it does, nobody inside will ever be bored.

Come early, stay late because there is never a dearth of things to see or do. Your Tropicana experience begins spectacularly with a walk toward the main entrance along a 900-foot, tropical-theme ceramic mosaic walkway—1,849,091 brightly colored tiles depicting the sun, sea and beach. The walk is enhanced by a sound system delivering play-by-play of great baseball moments and Devil Rays games as well as music and theatrical lighting.

Catwalks, fence jogs and a center field restaurant make Tropicana interesting, as does a slanted dome (top photo) that gives it a spaceship-like look.

The main entrance, an elaborate and ornate eight-story rotunda patterned after the one that greeted visitors for almost a half century at Brooklyn's Ebbets Field, is merely an appetizer for what lies beyond. You step out of the rotunda onto Center Field Street—a bustling retail area featuring the Batter's Eye Restaurant, Cuesta-Rey Cigar Bar, the Budweiser Brew House and an assortment of other shops and business establishments. The Taste of Tampa Bay food court offers samplings of the area's most popular cuisine.

The barrage of food, shops, gimmicks and conveniences never stops as you circle the concourses—or even after you step into the field area. High over the left field fence, covering most of the second deck, is The Beach—a 1,339-seat section featuring palm trees, pina coladas, ushers in Hawaiian shirts, a spa, a restaurant and drinks at the Tiki Bar. The hitter's backdrop in center field is the backside of the Batter's Eye Restaurant, with diners hidden by tinted windows that allow them to view action while they eat. Special seats behind the plate come armed with touch video screens that allow you to sample views and replays from various camera angles.

And then there's baseball, which supposedly is the facility's major attraction—if not its only focus. When you get past all the distractions, this really is not a bad place to watch a game. Seats are close (only 50 feet from plate to backstop), you're out of the Florida heat and rain and the field is well lit, brighter than any other roof-covered park. And it has some funny little quirks that make baseball life interesting.

The surface is AstroTurf 12, which is dense, soft and fast. Balls shoot the gaps quickly and are prone to strange bounces, thanks to a sharp backward angle in the left-center field fence—a dropoff to the park's deepest point at 410 feet—and a lesser angle in right-center (404). The lines are an inviting 315 (left) and 322 (right) and the basepaths are all dirt, a departure from the base-cutout design employed by most other domes. Bullpens, once located in home run territory beyond the left and right field fences, now are located in foul territory down both lines.

But the granddaddy of quirks is a product of the cable design—four rings, or catwalks, that circle the roof and help keep it in place. Two of the rings are high and well out of play. Two others are reachable with batted balls and can affect the game. The lowest is a potential foul ball obstacle, the second actually crosses fair territory in the outfield. Catwalks, used only for maintenance purposes, have been hit a handful of times and one Jose Canseco drive actually landed on the second catwalk and never came

Tropicana was in a festive mood when the Devil Rays and Red Sox prepared for battle in the 1999 home opener.

TROPICANA FIELD (1998-)

Also known as Florida Suncoast Dome (1990-1993)
and the ThunderDome (1993-1996)

Opened in 1990 as the Florida Suncoast Dome, it took eight years for the stadium to host its own major league baseball team.

After three years as the home of the NHL's Tampa Bay Lightning, the facility was closed for 17 months to be configured for baseball.

Of the domed facilities in use in baseball today, it's the only one that features turf and all-dirt basepaths, instead of the dirt cutouts around the bases. Another unique feature: After Devil Rays victories, the dome is lit up orange (Tropicana orange) to signify the win.

First game: March 31, 1998. Before almost 60,000 fans, the Tigers ruined the Devil Rays' debut, 11-6.

■ Site of no World Series
■ Site of no All-Star Games

down, resulting in a double.

Such an occurrence probably was never envisioned when the 1.1-million-square-foot facility, built for baseball, opened in 1990 as the Florida Suncoast Dome—not as you would expect in trendy, progressive Tampa, but in nearby St. Petersburg, a quiet haven. The translucent roof, which is lighted orange after a Devil Rays home victory, was slanted to decrease construction costs and the amount of air that requires climate control. The apex of the dome, which sits 6 feet above sea level, measures 225 feet above second base and declines to 85 feet at the center field wall.

Tampa/St. Petersburg officials hoped the facility would attract a major league team, but that didn't happen through its first eight years. Various sports events were staged there and the NHL's Tampa Bay Lightning played their home games there for three years (1993-96, when it was called ThunderDome), but baseball didn't arrive until 1998 in the form of an expansion team that would win only 63 games and draw 2.5-million fans.

The Devil Rays have come a long way in a short time. A power lineup now includes names like Canseco, Vinny Castilla, Greg Vaughn and Fred McGriff—and baseball is threatening to claim a much bigger piece of Tropicana's multi-attraction pie. But one thing is unlikely to change inside the coral-gray structure with green-tinted glass: The game will share the spotlight, but it won't own it.

Gone, But Not Forgotten

ome have been gone for decades—League Park, Braves Field, the Polo Grounds, Ebbets Field, Crosley, Shibe, Forbes; others have just departed—Tiger Stadium, Candlestick, the Astrodome and the Kingdome.

Nearly all were classics, places of the heart and longtime stages for baseball magic. But some are immortalized only by a few remnants scattered about, marking their place in the game's long history, while others have been razed without much thought given to permanence.

No matter. Their permanence is in the memories that baseball fans continue to cherish. They might be gone, but they're not forgotten.

Arlington Stadium

Also known as Turnpike Stadium (1965-1971)

Where 18-year-old Texas high school pitching sensation David Clyde won his major league debut, June 27, 1973

Arlington Stadium never played host to a postseason game in its 22-year existence

Rangers surrendered A.L.-record 13 runs in ninth inning, Sept. 14, 1978

Where 46-year-old Ryan pummeled Chicago's Robin Ventura, who charged mound after being hit by pitch, Aug. 4, 1993

Toby Harrah: Texas' palindromic infield fixture from 1972-78

Catcher JIM SUNDBERG won six Gold Gloves from 1974-83

For 22 years, it was the hottest sports ticket in town—literally. Baseball was served at Arlington Stadium with a complementary sauna and a guaranteed tan. You had to appreciate the open friendliness and down-home simplicity of the best little ballhouse in North Texas, but you also had to curse its refusal to hide from the oppressive summer heat.

Unlike Houston's air-conditioned Astrodome, Arlington Stadium was not a venue for the faint of heart. It was uncovered and vulnerable, an erector-set facility that dared to challenge the scorching Texas sun. If the 100-plus-degree heat didn't get you, the inelegant teams that competed there would. It wasn't easy to be a Rangers

Rangers become third team in 55 years to produce three 200-hit men in same season—Rafael Palmeiro (203), Ruben Sierra (203), Julio Franco (201) in 1991

A perfect ending: California's Mike Witt retires all 27 Rangers he faces in season-closing 1-0 victory, Sept. 30, 1984

Fergie Jenkins earned 1974 Comeback Player of the Year honors during his 25-12, 225-strikeout, 2.83-ERA season

Training ground for Juan Gonzalez (right) and Ivan Rodriguez (left), the next generation Rangers

Ryan makes Rickey Henderson 5,000th career strikeout victim, Aug. 22, 1989 . . . On May 1, 1991, at age 44, Ryan celebrates "Arlington Appreciation Night" by beating Blue Jays with seventh no-hitter

Where big Frank Howard thrilled Texas fans with long first-inning homer in Rangers' first game at Arlington Stadium, April 21, 1972

Bill Stein sets A.L. record with seventh straight pinch hit, May 25, 1981

Dave Nelson steals show on Aug. 30, 1974, when he swipes second, third and home in one inning

NOLAN RYAN: The Rangers' first Hall of Famer completed his 27-year career here

Jeff Burroughs: 25 homers, 118 RBIs, .301 average in MVP 1974 season

Buddy Bell becomes first A.L. player to collect 200 hits without batting .300, 1979

Yankees first baseman Don Mattingly homers in his record-tying eighth straight game, July 18, 1987

Larry Parrish belts third grand slam in one week, July 10, 1982 fan, but it was hard not to like Arlington Stadium.

Located in an entertainment strip of suburban Arlington next to the Six Flags amusement park, it was a former minor league facility that attempted to introduce two divergent Texas cities to major league society. A few miles to the east was Dallas, cosmopolitan and glitzy—fans armed with cell phones and beepers. A few miles to the west was Fort Worth, blue collar and basic—fans who took life seriously. This was a baseball melting pot, a no-frills stadium with a simple charm behind its plain, patchwork exterior.

Much of that charm was a byproduct of Arlington's humble roots. It opened in 1965 as Turnpike Stadium, the 10,600-seat home of the Class AA Texas League's Spurs on the Dallas-Fort Worth Turnpike. It was constructed with an eye toward expansion, the first of which took place in 1970 and raised seating capacity to 21,000. When the former Senators were moved from Washington to Arlington before the 1972 season, emergency construction lifted capacity to 35,694 and gave the stadium the basic look it would retain throughout its history.

The renamed Arlington Stadium was a basic single-deck structure with a make-it-up-as-we-go architectural design. Set in a natural bowl that dropped the playing surface 40 feet below street level, it featured a leveled grandstand behind home plate, high-rising seats down both lines and fair-territory bleachers that extended from foul pole to foul pole. A special "plaza" deck, built atop the stands behind the plate in 1978, raised capacity to 41,284 and captured the essence of a

makeshift construction that resulted in peculiar nooks and crannies as well as unexpected open-air windows to the outside world.

If Arlington wasn't the most sightline-friendly ballpark in the majors, it had to be close. It also was the hottest, with little shade to compensate. More than a third of its seats were in the expansive outfield bleachers—sun-blistered aluminum benches that dispensed their heat to general admission fans. From mid-May to September 1, the Rangers were forced to play all their games at night, with temperatures seldom getting out of the 90s.

The left field bleachers were topped by a distinctive 200-by-60-foot scoreboard, a piece of which was shaped like the state of Texas. The field, with lush green grass that somehow withstood daily assaults from the sun, featured hitter-friendly 330-400-330 symmetrical dimensions, but swirling winds blowing over the center field fence made life easy for pitchers.

That changed after the 1983 season, when the Rangers removed the scoreboard and topped the outfield rim with a 30-foot wall that stretched from foul pole to foul pole. Not only did the barrier block the winds and make life tougher for pitchers, it gave the park a whole new personality. Five state-of-the-art video and scoreboards were spaced along the wall, separated by huge advertising billboards. On one, the Marlboro Man gazed down with apparent disinterest from his right-center field perch.

That disinterest might have stemmed from Rangers teams that only occasionally contended for division

ARLINGTON STADIUM (1972-1993)

Also known as Turnpike Stadium (1965-1971)

Dedicated on April 23, 1965, 10,600-seat Turnpike Stadium (a nod to its location on the Dallas-Fort Worth Turnpike, which today is Interstate 30) would be the nucleus of the Texas Rangers' first home on land just northwest of the team's current home, The Ballpark in Arlington.

After American League owners voted in September 1971 to allow the transfer of the Washington Senators to Texas, an expanse of bleacher and outfield seats running from foul line to foul line was added in order to meet A.L. seating requirements, taking capacity from 21,000 to 35,694.

Rechristened Arlington Stadium, the expansion and renovation before the '72 season included the addition of one of the stadium's most distinctive characteristics—a 200-foot-by-60-foot scoreboard behind the left field stands that included a 60-by-60 area shaped like the state of Texas.

One of the stadium's most enduring moments corresponded with its first sellout—June 27, 1973, when Texas high school sensation David Clyde made his major league debut against the Twins. But if you stand outside The Ballpark in Arlington today, you will quickly know which native Texan made the biggest impact on Arlington Stadium and Rangers fans. Look northwest from Nolan Ryan Expressway and you can almost see a ghost of the old stadium and hear fans stomping their feet on the metal outfield bleachers as the future Hall of Famer, at age 44, pitches his seventh no-hitter (May 1, 1991) against the Blue Jays.

First game: April 21, 1972. The Rangers, with their scheduled April 6 home opener canceled by a players' strike, defeated the California Angels, 7-6, before 20,105 as Dick Bosman got the victory and Frank Howard hit a first-inning home run. Managed by Ted Williams, the Rangers would win four straight at home before suffering their first Arlington Stadium loss. But they went on to finish that inaugural season 54-100, last in the A.L. West, 38 1/2 games behind the division-champion Oakland A's.

Final game: October 3, 1993. Gary Gaetti's two-run homer off Tom Henke paced the Royals' 4-1 victory. Juan Gonzalez made the last out for the Rangers, who finished 906-844 (.518) in 22 seasons at Arlington Stadium.

■ Site of no World Series
■ Site of no All-Star Games

titles in the stadium's life-span. Players like Toby Harrah, Buddy Bell, Jeff Burroughs, Richie Zisk and Ferguson Jenkins were fan favorites, but the Rangers always competed in the massive shadow of Texas' first sports love—almighty football. From August through the remainder of the season, a Dallas Cowboys score relayed by the public address announcer generated bigger cheers than anything on the baseball field.

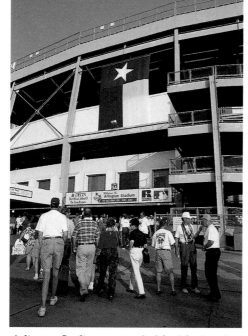

That changed in 1989, when the Rangers acquired aging Nolan Ryan, a tried-and-true Texan who became the most popular player in franchise history. Arlington Stadium, seldom packed, was filled to capacity every time he pitched—and the atmosphere was electric. The P.A. announcer would implore fans in the outfield bleachers to "scooch together" and a huge Ryan photograph greeted visitors, right alongside the Texas flag, at the main entrance.

Sights and sounds were important to Arlington fans. They still remember the right field temperature board, the sound of roller coasters and other rides from nearby Six Flags, superfan Zonk behind the first base dugout, Lone Ranger clips on the video board and Dot Races—an Arlington invention, according to some Texans. But nothing stirred emotions more than the first musical notes of "Cotton-Eyed Joe," a stadium staple during the seventh-inning stretch.

Sun beaten and worn beyond its years, Arlington Stadium gave way to a modern new facility after the 1993 season. Ironically, the Rangers won their first division championship and brought postseason play to North Texas only three years later.

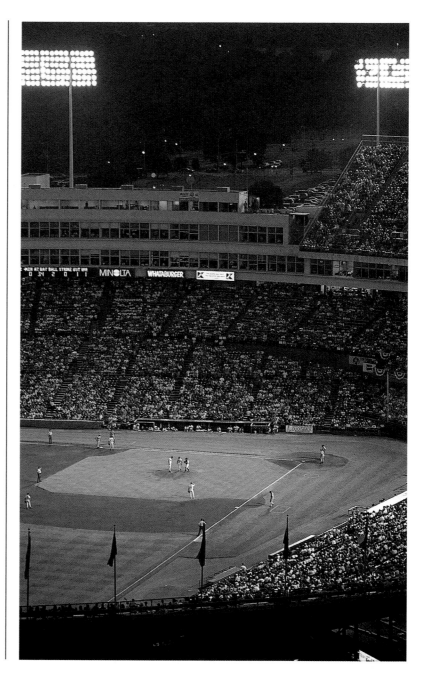

Arlington Stadium was packed (right) when the Rangers staged a special day for favorite son, Nolan Ryan, in September 1993. The Texas state flag greeted visitors at the facility's main entrance (above).

Fulton County Stadium

Also known as
Atlanta Stadium (1966-1975)

They called it "The Launching Pad," a place where teams could go to inflate their home run and victory totals. But Fulton County Stadium was so much more than a ballpark stereotype. It was Atlanta's ticket into the big leagues, baseball's doorway to the deep South and the stage on which Hank Aaron achieved baseball immortality. Round, symmetrical, multi-purpose and plain in many ways, Fulton County Stadium also was a venue of special significance and history.

You sometimes struggled to get that sense of significance over the

Francisco Cabrera's two-out, ninth-inning pinch single beats Pittsburgh and gives Braves their second straight pennant, Oct. 14, 1992

Braves set modern record by winning first 13 games in 1982 en route to West Division crown

Aaron's 715th

Where Chief Noc-A-Homa pitched his tepee

Braves clinch third straight West Division title with final-day victory, Oct. 3, 1993

PHIL NIEKRO:
Knucksie won 268 games for Braves and threw Atlanta's first no-hitter, Aug. 5, 1973

Bob Horner hits four homers on July 6, 1986, but Braves still lose to Expos

Braves pitchers Larry McWilliams and Gene Garber stop
Pete Rose's 44-game hitting streak, Aug. 1, 1978

Tom Glavine, Mark
Wohlers stop Indians on
Game 6 one-hitter, Oct. 28,
1995—Braves' first World
Series crown since 1957

Cy Young heaven: Braves (left to
right) Tom Glavine (1), John Smoltz
(1) and Greg Maddux (3) dominate
over 6-year span, 1991-96

San Diego's Nate Colbert clubs five homers and
drives in 13 runs in doubleheader, Aug. 1, 1972

Pirates' slugger Willie Stargell spoils Braves' Atlanta
debut with 13th-inning homer, April 12, 1966

Launching pad for many milestone home runs: Aaron's 500th . . .
July 14, 1968; 600th . . . April 27, 1971; 700th . . . July 21, 1973; 715th
. . . April 8, 1974; Willie McCovey's 500th . . . June 30, 1978

The Braves' 40-homer 1973 triumvirate:
Dave Johnson 43, Darrell Evans 41, Aaron 40

Aaron thrills Atlanta
Stadium crowd with homer
in N.L.'s 10-inning All-Star
win, July 25, 1972

Where 46-year-old
Hoyt Wilhelm pitched
in 1,000th career
game, May 10, 1970

Dale Murphy hits two
homers, drives in six in
sixth inning of 10-1 win
over Giants, July 27, 1989

Center fielder Dale Murphy:
Consecutive MVPs in '82, '83

HANK AARON:
Baseball's all-time
home run king

years because of the Braves' consistent losing and some bizarre promotions designed to attract fans to the 52,710-seat facility. But you never lost the sense of history, enhanced by the stadium's location a mile south of midtown Atlanta, in the shadow of Georgia's state Capitol building. By itself, the white, bowl-like structure was nondescript. In the bright Georgia sunshine, it glowed majestically against Atlanta's modern skyline.

It was all a matter of perspective. And there were many ways of looking at Fulton County Stadium.

You could circle the stadium's exterior and experience the sights and sounds of the open-backed concourses and runways, stopping periodically to admire statues of Aaron in home run form, Phil Niekro floating a knuckleball homeward and Atlanta-born Ty Cobb, the Georgia Peach, sliding spikes-first into baseball history. Or you could step inside and experience the explosion of color, starting with the green grass field and the rich, red, eye-popping Georgia dirt.

The color rose around you, courtesy of multi-tinted seats in triple-tiered stands that circled the field. The lower level gave way to a narrow press and club level and an expansive upper tier that climbed precipitously to a white-rim overhang. Horizontal light standards balanced perilously from the rim, threatening to drop on unwary patrons below, and a multi-paneled scoreboard provided need-to-know information from the rim in straightaway center. A giant Calliope added a strange backdrop to the atmosphere of the ballpark.

The field was symmetrically perfect with lots of foul territory down both lines. Pop fouls into the stands at other parks were easy outs here. It didn't take long to figure out this was a hitter's park, and the home run was the weapon of choice.

"It was a fun place to play," recalled former center fielder Dale Murphy, the National League's MVP in 1982 and '83. "The ball carried great. Good light, could always see the ball. It's always been a great place to hit."

The home run-haven reputation was enhanced by the city's elevation—1,057 feet above sea level, the major leagues' highest until Colorado began play. Balls shot out of the park and the Braves celebrated their home runs with a war dance by Chief Noc-A-Homa, who maintained his tepee for many years in the left or center field stands. The Braves built a power lineup around Aaron, who would take the art of home run hitting into uncharted territory.

It was hard to sit anywhere in the park without thinking about Atlanta's No. 44, baseball's all-time home run king. His presence overshadowed the team's meager accomplishments for many years; his aura hung over the place like a thick cloud after retirement. A "715" circle just over the left field wall marked the spot of Aaron's record-breaking homer on the night of April 8, 1974—a shot into what was then the Braves' bullpen. It was not only the most momentous moment in Fulton County Stadium history, it was one of the great moments in baseball's glorious past.

FULTON COUNTY STADIUM (1966-1996)

Also known as Atlanta Stadium (1966-1975)

The story of the stadium's origin began in 1961, when Ivan Allen Jr., in a campaign for mayor, said he would build a modern sports stadium.

When he was elected, his next challenge was to find a team to play in his prospective park, thereby giving him the chance to acquire land and money.

The first target was Charlie Finley's Kansas City Athletics. When Finley was told to stay put, talks with the Milwaukee Braves heated up.

In the spring of 1964, less than a month after an announcement that a team was interested in moving to Atlanta, ground was broken on the new stadium.

It wasn't until the fall of '64 that the Braves announced an official move to Atlanta and it wasn't until '66 that the team began play in Atlanta. In the interim, Atlanta Stadium, as it was known until 1976, was the home of the Crackers, a Braves farm team.

The former stadium site, now a parking lot, sits in the shadows of Atlanta's new baseball facility, Turner Field.

First game: April 12, 1966. The Pirates' Matty Alou was the first batter and Felipe Alou was the Braves' first batter. (In the final game at the stadium in 1996, Montreal's Moises Alou would be the final regular-season batter). Hank Aaron stole the first base. Pittsburgh won in 13 innings, 3-2.

Final game: October 24, 1996. In the fifth game of the World Series, the Yankees shut down the Braves — and the stadium — with a 1-0 victory.

■ Site of four World Series (1991, '92, '95 and '96)
■ Site of one All-Star Game (1972)

But Aaron's accomplishments often were offset by the erratic play of Braves teams that posted non-winning records in 18 of their first 25 Atlanta seasons and the questionable antics of a fan-hungry owner. After the early excitement of major league base-ball, the stadium often took on a ghost-town atmosphere with fewer than 2,000 fans once turning out to watch Nolan Ryan pitch.

In retrospect, the stadium really was nothing more than a means to get Atlanta to its 1990s end—a job it performed admirably. It was a symbol of hope in 1965 when it opened its gates to the International League's Atlanta Crackers as a pre-lude to stunning announcements that the Braves would move operations from Milwaukee to Atlanta and the NFL would award the city an expansion franchise (the Falcons) for the 1966 season.

By the time Ted Turner took control of the team in 1976, attendance had dwindled so much that he insti-gated a line of crazy promotions — "Wedlock and Headlock Night," fans racing on ostriches, a local disc jock-ey diving into a huge ice cream sun-dae and even a wet T-shirt contest. But all Turner had to show for his efforts through the 1980s were two division titles and consistently-low attendance figures.

Fulton County Stadium was a multi-purpose facility that ushered Braves baseball into a new era of prosperity. It gave way to Turner Field, which in 1996 could be seen under construction right across the street (below).

Everything changed in 1990, thanks to the efforts of new general man-ager John Schuerholz and new manager Bobby Cox, who transformed the Braves into the "team of the '90s." One of the first things they did was rip up the turf, long considered the worst in baseball, resurface the field and hire a crack groundskeeping crew. Other amenities were added, as was an outstanding pitching staff featuring Greg Maddux, Tom Glavine, John Smoltz and Steve Avery and a lineup with Fred McGriff, David Justice, Chipper Jones and Javy Lopez. The Braves began collecting division titles, N.L. pen-nants and a 1995 World Series cham-pionship—their first since 1957.

When Fulton County Stadium played host to its final major league season in 1996, it was more alive, fans were chanting and per-forming tomahawk chops and base-ball life was suddenly good for Turner and actress wife Jane Fonda, who were visible ballpark regulars in their box near the first base dugout.

Ironically, when the Braves moved across the parking lot to Turner Field in 1997, they said goodbye to a baseball facility that was much better than the one that had put Atlanta on the major league map 31 years earlier.

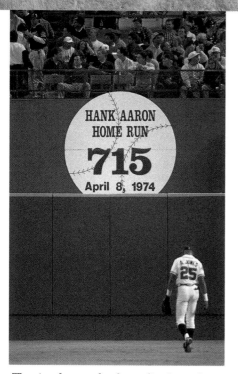

The view from under the stadium's overhang was steep and spectacular (right). Sights at Fulton County ranged from superfans (below) to a circle beyond the left field fence marking Aaron's record home run.

A disappointed fan raises his tomahawks in salute to Fulton County Stadium after a Game 5 loss to the Yankees in the 1996 World Series—the park's grand finale.

Memorial Stadium

Cal Ripken J
MVP in 1983,

Frustrated O's open 1988 season 0-21

L ike a Dave McNally fastball, Memorial Stadium kind of snuck up on you. At first glance, it wasn't impressive architecturally, it didn't assault your emotions and it didn't fill you with anticipation. But, oh, that perfectly manicured, emerald-green grass field!

This wasn't heaven; it was Baltimore. Memorial Stadium, broken down to its most common denominator, was about as close as baseball could get to the pastoral Field of Dreams portrayed so eloquently on the movie screens. It was impossible to resist its grass, the foul pole-to-foul pole openness of its outfield and the stately green trees that did double sentry over the back of the field and the residential neighborhood beyond.

Brooks Robinson frustrates Reds by making numerous spectacular plays throughout 1970 World Series . . . Pitcher Dave McNally rocks Cincinnati with grand slam in Game 3

Senators' Ton
Cheney strike
out 21 Orioles
16-inning gam
Sept. 12, 196

Four 20-game winners in 1971: Jim Palmer, Dave McNally, Pat Dobson and Mike Cuellar

BROOKS ROBINSON:
Caretaker of A.L. third base
Gold Glove for 16 years

Orioles lose 1983 Series opener 2-1 when Scott McGregor serves up eighth-inning homer to Phillies' Garry Maddox after waiting for completion of TV interview with President Ronald Reagan

Mike Cuellar stops New York on six hits in Game 1 of World Series—the O's last win vs. the Miracle Mets, Oct. 11, 1969

Target for fan favorite Boog Powell, who pounded 303 Oriole homers

Six Cy Youngs in 12-year span: Mike Cuellar 1969; Jim Palmer (right) 1973, '75, '76; Mike Flanagan 1979; Steve Stone 1980

Frank Robinson's homer wins fourth and final game of 1966 World Series 1-0

Indians slugger Rocky Colavito hits four consecutive home runs vs. Orioles, June 10, 1959

Steve Barber, Stu Miller combine for no-hitter, but Tigers score twice in ninth on walks, wild pitch and error for 2-1 win, April 30, 1967

Sammy Stewart sets big-league debut record by striking out seven straight batters, Sept. 1, 1978

Frank Robinson hits homer No. 500, Sept. 13, 1971 . . . Baltimore-born Tigers star Al Kaline doubles for 3,000th hit, Sept. 24, 1974

Where Orioles lefty Billy O'Dell retired final nine hitters he faced in All-Star Game, preserving 4-3 A.L. win, July 8, 1958

Feisty Earl Weaver (left) managed Orioles to four pennants and one Series championship in 17 years . . . Jim Palmer won 268 games over 19-year career

FRANK ROBINSON:
1966 MVP and Triple Crown winner

That's what Memorial was all about—baseball for the senses. You went there for the smells, the sounds and the visual simplicity of the game as it was meant to be played. The memories were a bonus, locked into the essence of the ballpark like a soul is to the body.

How could you look at the venerable ground around third base and not see Brooks Robinson diving left, then right, throwing from his knees or from beyond the foul line? That was the mound of Jim Palmer, Mike Cuellar, Mike Flanagan and Steve Stone, Cy Young winners all, and the home plate dirt kicked, tossed and spit upon by the always-feisty Earl Weaver. First base belonged to Eddie Murray, shortstop to Mark Belanger and Cal Ripken, center field to Paul Blair. Frank Robinson was to the left field bleachers what Boog Powell was to the bleachers in right.

Memorial Stadium's considerable aura was well concealed by a plain, reddish-brown and tan brick facade that surrounded a horseshoe-shaped facility. It looked like a big museum set awkwardly in the midst of family neighborhoods just north of downtown Baltimore. Only a careful inspection and towering light standards revealed its true identity as a ballpark.

Still, your first greeting stirred somber emotion rather than excitement—an inscription etched into the concrete facade above the main entrance that read: "Time Can Never Dim the Honor of Their Deeds," a tribute to Baltimore veterans who died in both World Wars and the Korean War. Your baseball senses began perking up on the walk from the gate through easy-to-negotiate corridors lined with concessionaires hawking their wares.

The inside was a revelation. You just never expected the rush of green, white and brown, no matter how many games you attended there. Only after you had settled into the intimacy of the park did you realize you had been duped—this was really a good-sized facility (53,371 capacity when it closed to baseball), big enough to double as home of the NFL's Colts for 30 years, with a three-level

grandstand that rose steeply from foul pole-to-foul pole behind home plate.

Enhancing the open feel was an upper deck without a roof—baseball's first open-air topside when the stadium was opened to major league baseball and the relocated St. Louis Browns in 1954. The grandstands gave way to single-deck bleachers that extended at an angle into left-center and right-center field before giving way to a scoreboard (left-center), video board (right-center) and the tree-surrounded (dead center) flagpole.

Because of the field's unusual shape (two crescents that came together at points behind home plate and in center field), you never got a sense of the park's symmetry. Dimensions changed drastically over the years as Memorial Stadium, a rebuilt version of old Municipal Stadium at the same site, became more comfortable with its baseball ties. Memorial's 1954 debut season was played with a green concrete wall that curved sharply away from the 309-foot foul poles toward a makeshift wire fence in center that was a distant 450 feet from home plate.

"To play that outfield right, you needed five outfielders," said former Oriole Gil Coan.

That changed when an inner fence was constructed from right field to left, leaving the foul poles intact but gradually reducing center field to a more reachable 405 feet. To its final day, fans in the corners were right on top of the field and balls hitting the angled corner walls bounced sharply toward center instead of back to the infield.

Memorial Stadium, while retaining an "old" feel, was not averse to modern tastes and technology. The scoreboard and video board were state-of-the-art, the sound system was outstanding and the food of choice, crab cakes, ranked high among ballpark delicacies. Baseball also was state-of-the-art, thanks to pitching-loaded Orioles teams that finished an incredible 612 games over .500 in a 24-year stretch from 1960 to '83 while winning six American League pennants and three World Series.

MEMORIAL STADIUM (1954-1991)

It was a football stadium, known as Venable Stadium, Metropolitan Stadium and Babe Ruth Stadium before major league baseball arrived in 1954. Major renovations on the stadium began in 1949 and continued until just before the '54 season, when the St. Louis Browns relocated to Baltimore.

Its name was an honorable tribute to Baltimore veterans who died in both World Wars and the Korean War.

In the spring of 2000, demolition of the stadium, on 33rd Street north of downtown, is scheduled to begin.

First game: April 15, 1954. Vice President Richard M. Nixon threw out the first pitch and major league baseball returned to Baltimore with a 3-1 Orioles win over the White Sox.

Final game: October 6, 1991. A 7-1 Tigers win took a backseat to postgame festivities that saw almost 100 former Orioles take the field and say their final tearful goodbyes to the stadium.

■ Site of six World Series (1966, '69, '70, '71 '79, '83)
■ Site of one All-Star Game (1958)

Opening day at Memorial in 1960 provided a good view of the 309-foot right field corner with fans right on top of the action.

Memorial featured an unusual shape, a scoreboard topped by the 'Gunther Beer' sign and a distant center field fence when it opened for major league play in 1954.

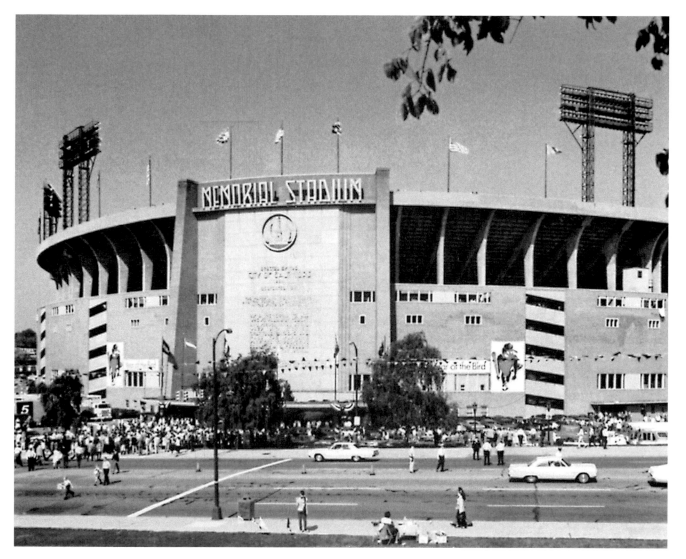

Memorial Stadium's tan-brick facade gave the facility a museum look. Greeting visitors was a giant inscription over the building's main entrance that paid tribute to veterans who died in both World Wars and the Korean War.

Robinson's 450-foot home run off Luis Tiant made history as the only ball to leave Memorial Stadium.

Memorial-style baseball also was about bugle-induced "Charge!" calls, ushers dressed in orange jackets, Wild Bill Hagy standing on the dugout, inciting the crowd by contorting his body to spell out "Orioles," tomato vines climbing the wall up the third base line and the national anthem, during which fans screamed out "O" when the song reached its "O say does that star spangled banner yet wave" crescendo.

Memorial Stadium reached its crescendo in 1991, after 38 seasons, when the Orioles moved to a beautiful new ballpark facility in a downtown Baltimore area near the Inner Harbor. The team might be gone, but the memories will hang forever over the East 33rd Street site—like a towering fly ball in the blue sky of a crisp summer afternoon at Baltimore's first real ballpark.

Over the years, Memorial Stadium became known as a homey stadium with a ballpark feel. That perception was enhanced by signature sights and traditions that gave it a distinctive flavor.

A "Gunther" beer scoreboard sign was a fixture for many years, as was the "HERE" flag that flew above the left field bleachers, marking the spot where, in 1966, Frank

Braues Field

Braves finish 38-115, 61½ games behind Cubs in futile 1935 season

Bob Elliott hits three-run homer, Braves beat Giants 3-2 and clinch first N.L. pennant since 1914, Sept. 26, 1948

Shortstop Rabbit Maranville (right) made his belt-buckle catches here . . . Casey Stengel clowned his way through six managerial seasons

JOHNNY SAIN:
Four-time 20-game winner led Braves to 1948 pennant

Red Sox used more spacious Br Field as home base during 1915 1916 World Series

Red Sox lefty Babe Ruth wins 14-inning pitching duel vs. Brooklyn in Game 2 of 1916 World Series

Paul Waner collects hit No. 3,000, June 19, 1942

Tommy Holmes hit in 37 straight games in 1945

I
t was a curious antique, a dead ball-era survivor that never quite made the transition to modern baseball. Braves Field was a huge, luxurious palace when it opened in 1915, an outdated, oft-renovated dinosaur when it closed 38 years later. From beginning to end, it was a house of pain for fans and players of the National League Braves.

Braves Field was a victim of bad timing and ownership without vision. The last of the early-century steel-and-concrete ballparks opened the season after

1948 slogan: "Spahn (left) and Sain (right) and two days of rain"

Braves, Dodgers play to 2-2 tie in 23-inning game called by darkness, June 27, 1939

Jim Tobin hits three homers and pitches Braves to 6-5 win over Cubs, May 13, 1942 . . . no-hits Dodgers, ices 2-0 win with home run, April 27, 1944

Braves' Joe Oeschger and Brooklyn's [Leo]n Cadore wage Herculean pitching [ba]ttle that ends in 1-1 tie after major [lea]gue-record 26 innings, May 1, 1920

Thirtysomething rookies Jim Turner and Lou Fette post their 20th wins on consecutive days, Oct. 2, 3, 1937

Where Augie Galan's disputed homer hit old foul pole during N.L.'s first All-Star Game win in 1936

Umpire rules Phil Masi safe on controversial pickoff play, helping Sain outduel Bob Feller 1-0 in Game 1 of 1948 World Series

Jury Box was home for about 2,000 bleacherites

Where Ernie Padgett turned baseball's fourth unassisted triple play, Oct. 6, 1923

Catcher Hank Gowdy left team to enlist as first major leaguer in World War I

Dodgers clinch 1952 N.L. pennant in final game at Braves Field

Where Dutch Leonard and Ernie Shore pitched Red Sox to consecutive 2-1 wins in Games 3 and 4 of 1915 Series

WALLY BERGER hit rookie-record 38 homers in 1930, 199 in eight seasons with Braves

Lester Bell hits three homers into special section of seats in front of left field fence, just misses fourth, June 2, 1928 the Miracle Braves had captured the hearts of Boston fans with their mad rush to a World Series championship and a few years before Babe Ruth would change the course of baseball with his booming bat. Most of Braves Field's existence was spent in a losing funk while the American League's Red Sox thrived at Fenway Park, only a few blocks away.

Braves Field, in deference to owner James Gaffney's love of inside-the-park home runs, spent the first third of its existence promoting nineteenth-century baseball while the rest of the nation was stricken with home run fever. Early Braves Field, featuring 402-foot foul lines and an unreachable 550-foot center field barrier, was billed as "the largest baseball park in the world," an assessment endorsed by pitchers who were further aided by Boston's notorious East wind. "One thing is sure," Ty Cobb declared at first glance. "Nobody is ever going to hit a ball over those fences."

Cobb wasn't far off. Of the 38 home runs hit at Braves Field in 1921, 34 stayed inside the park. The Giants hit four in one game. It wasn't until 1925, the park's 11th season, that a ball hit by Giants catcher Frank Snyder finally cleared the cement left field wall.

Because of those cavernous dimensions and expansive foul territory, Braves Field never enjoyed the sense of intimacy you found in other ballparks of that era. But it wasn't without subtle charms.

A view over the left field fence revealed the Charles River, sometimes filled with the shells of Harvard racing crews, and a railroad yard that gave the park its distinctive smell. Visitors to Braves Field could arrive on the Commonwealth Avenue trolley, which would swing inside the park's main facade and drop them off right at

their gate. But the park's signature feature was the "Jury Box," a fair-territory bleacher section that seated about 2,000 and formed the outer right field boundary.

At first, the right field foul pole connected to the Jury Box and its front wall was the target for lefthanded home run hitters. But later renovations, which came fast and furious after the 1927 season, shifted the foul line away from the Jury Box and cut into a right field pavilion, part of which went from foul territory to fair.

The park was actually divided into four sections—a roofed, single-deck grandstand that curved behind the plate and extended down the lines well past first and third base, two uncovered sections that extended to the foul poles, and the Jury Box. The first scoreboard was ground level on the left field fence. Later versions were elevated atop the wall.

The 40,000-seat ballpark was far less ornate than many of its contemporaries, although a distinctive stucco facade housed the team's business offices and featured arched gateways through which fans could pass into the facility. After 1927, they never knew what they might find.

That was the season management broke down and added bleacher sections in front of the left and center field walls, reducing home run distance by about 70 feet. But opponents feasted on the new dimensions and the bleachers were gone

BRAVES FIELD (1915-1952)

Before they were the Braves, they were the Red Stockings, the Beaneaters, the Doves (named for George and John Dovey, brothers who owned the team from 1907-1910) and the Rustlers (for former owner William Hepburn Russell).

And before they played in Braves Field, they played in South End Grounds and Congress Street Grounds.

In 1912, that all changed. James Gaffney, who had connections to New York's Tammany Hall politicians, acquired the team. Tammany Hall politicians were often called "braves" because its named is derived from an Indian chief named Tamanen.

Hence, the Braves — and Braves Field — were born. (Until 1936, when they were called the Bees, mostly because the new team president, John Quinn, wanted to erase the vestiges of a spectacularly unsuccessful history. In 1941, they went back to being the Braves.)

Boston University purchased the field in the 1950s. Nickerson Field, the school's football facility, is laid out on the grounds, and a plaque to commemorate Braves Field stands at the Gaffney Street entrance.

First game: August 18, 1915. With Hall of Famer Rabbit Maranville driving in the field's first run, the Braves downed the Cardinals, 3-1.

Final game: September 21, 1952. Brooklyn beat the Braves, 8-2, in a game no one knew would be the Braves' last in Boston. It wasn't until the spring of '53 that the team announced its immediate relocation to Milwaukee.

■ Site of three World Series (1915, '16 and '48)
■ Site of one All-Star Game (1936)

by late season. From that point on, the park underwent almost annual (some claimed daily) renovation before settling on its final look in 1947—337 feet down the left field line, 390 to center and 319 to right with a 25-foot wooden inner left field fence that was covered by double-decked rows of advertising. A right field inner fence was 4-foot high with a 6-foot screen. The 10-foot outer wall remained as an unnecessary backdrop.

One thing that never changed was Boston's inability to field competitive teams. After second and third-place finishes in 1915 and '16, the Braves forged losing records in 27 of the next 36 seasons with only one pennant—1948—to ease their frustration. Life at Braves Field, despite such capable players as Wally Berger, Tommy Holmes, Rabbit Maranville, Warren Spahn, Johnny Sain and Shanty Hogan, sometimes resembled a comedy act directed by such ringmasters as Judge Emil Fuchs, who doubled one memorable season as the team's owner and manager, and Casey Stengel. The Braves even changed their name to "Bees" from 1936-41, but camouflage tactics proved ineffective.

It all added up to sagging attendance and the shocking 1953 announcement that Braves Field, final home park of the immortal Ruth (1935), would lose its team to Milwaukee. In retrospect, it's not insignificant that of the eight World Series games contested at Braves Field, five were played by the 1915 and '16 Red Sox.

The 'Jury Box' bleacher section in right field (above) seated about 2,000 fans, many of whom would stand in line outside the main entrance (below) for tickets.

Ebbets Field

Where Hilda Chester clanged her cowbell for many years

Ebbets Field was co-host to N.L.'s first two pennant playoffs—Dodgers lost to Cardinals in 1946, Giants in 1951

Two four-homer games: Dodgers' Gil Hodges (left) in 1950, Braves' Joe Adcock in 1954

Where Phillies' Dick Sisler hit his pennant-winning three-run homer on final day of 1950

Babe Herman (above), Dazzy Vance and Chick Fewster all end up on third base after Herman's double, resulting in a double play for Braves, Aug. 15, 1926

Dem Bums won 9 pennants, 6 in 10-year stretch from 1947-56, but only 1 World Series—1955 vs. hated Yankees

Dodgers collect 10 hits, 15 runs in first-inning rampage vs. Reds, May 21, 1952

I t was, in the truest sense, a ballpark—a cozy, friendly little place where you could forget your troubles, inhale a few hot dogs and peanuts and cheer on your beloved Dodgers—boisterously and with passion, like hard-living Brooklyn fans attacked everything in life.

It was a gaudy, colorful, wonderfully-misshapen arena where everything seemed out of sync, balls bounced out of control and you not only learned to expect the unexpected, you counted on it.

It was a shrine in the Borough of Churches, where you could go to

JACKIE ROBINSON:
Second baseman broke baseball's color barrier in 1947, ignited Dodgers' offense over next decade en route to Hall of Fame

Home of three-time MVP catcher Roy Campanella (right), 1951, '53, '55; inaugural Cy Young winner Don Newcombe, 1956

Dazzy Vance:
28 wins,
2.16 ERA, 30
complete games,
262 strikeouts
in 1924

Cardinals' Jim
Bottomley hits two
homers, drives in
single-game-record
12 runs vs. Dodgers,
Sept. 16, 1924

Center
fielder Duke
Snider hit
40-homer
plateau in
five straight
seasons,
1953-57

Uncle Robbie
(Wilbert Robinson)
was master of
Dodgers universe for
18 seasons, 1914-31

Where Cookie Lavagetto's game-winning
double bounced off the concave right field
wall in Game 4 of 1947 World Series, ruining
no-hit bid by Yankee Bill Bevens

Dodgers and Reds
play 19-inning
scoreless tie,
Sept. 11, 1946

Abe Stark's
'Win a Suit' sign

Where Yankee second baseman Billy
Martin made World Series-saving
catch of Jackie Robinson popup in
seventh inning of 1952 Game 7 classic

Cincinnati lefty Johnny
Vander Meer posts
unprecedented second
straight no-hitter in first
Brooklyn night game,
June 15, 1938

Where bird
flew out of
Casey Stengel's
cap in 1918

Where catcher Mickey
Owen missed connections
with third strike in Game
4 of 1941 World Series,
setting stage for Yankees'
winning rally

Cardinals pitchers
Dizzy and Paul Dean
post double-shutout
doubleheader win—
Dizzy a 3-hitter,
Paul a no-hitter,
Sept. 21, 1934

Clem Labine
outduels Bob Turley
in 10-inning thriller,
keeps Dodgers alive
in Game 6 of 1956
World Series

PEE WEE REESE:
Clutch-hitting
shortstop was heart
of Dodgers pennant-
winning teams
in 1940s and '50s

Brooklyn

chastised the "Gints", an alien force from somewhere across the East River. "Ya bum, ya" was a daily admonition, not necessarily restricted to Dodgers opponents.

"All I knew about Brooklyn was that it was some strange, outer world. When they told me I'd been traded to Brooklyn (in 1939), I didn't know what on God's great earth to expect," recalled outfielder Dixie Walker, who went on to lasting Brooklyn fame as "The People's Cherce."

The fans were only part of the zany atmosphere of a ballpark that stretches the imagination of anybody unfortunate enough not to have attended a game there. There were critics who called Ebbets Field a ratty architectural disaster, but history cherishes it as an aesthetic treasure. It was non-conformist in every sense, with nuances and physical oddities that affected the way the game was played. It was a stadium overflowing with personality.

Part of it came from the close proximity of the seats to the field, especially around dugouts that seemed to blend into the stands. You could almost reach out and touch some-

worship players named Leo, Newk, Dazzy, Dixie, Babe, Campy, Jackie, Pee Wee and the Duke. It was where Hilda Chester clanged her cowbell and Shorty's Sym-Phony Band stayed out of tune for two decades.

Ebbets Field was charming and charismatic—equal parts madhouse and magic kingdom, a rickety baseball palace where pennants were won, dreams were shattered and your emotions were stretched to the limits of ecstasy and disappointment.

The charm of Ebbets started and ended with its fans—the most raucous, colorful, knowledgeable zealots ever to unite their passions in a common cause. You couldn't empower the Dodgers without talking the talk—a distinctive dialect in which you "moidered dem bums," cheered for "Boit" Shotton and

one in uniform—a closeness that created a special bond with the Dodgers and an irritating dialogue with opponents. "You were so close to the field, sitting anywhere in that old park, that you could hear the players talking to each other," said Red Patterson, a former Dodgers vice president.

The personality started with an ornate rotunda inside the main entrance and extended to the field itself, which must have been constructed by somebody with a sense of humor. The right field wall was a concave nightmare, mastered by Walker and Carl Furillo but a confusing puzzle to most opposing outfielders. Shots off the wall, which sloped inward from the top and bottom, bounced around the field like a billiard ball coming off a cushion. The wall was an inviting 297 feet down the line, but it was topped by a 20-foot fence that protected the

The front entrance of Ebbets Field *was a busy place before* *a game in July 1949.*

Big, gaudy, colorful advertisements played a part in creating the sometimes-crazy atmosphere at Ebbets Field.

The Schaefer Beer and Abe Stark signs were scoreboard staples (below) and familiar sights to regulars sitting in double-deck stands behind home plate.

windows of businesses along Bedford Avenue.

The right field wall was divided by a giant scoreboard that jutted onto the playing field—another nightmare for outfielders. And the left field wall, backed by a double-decked grandstand occupied by the rowdiest bleacherites in baseball, made two angled cuts away from the plate before meeting the concave wall in deepest right-center field.

At first glance, Ebbets was a shock to your nervous system. You could become mesmerized by the colorful and gaudy signs that added character to a park that already had more than its fair share. The most prominent signs were on the scoreboard—a full-length strip across the bottom sponsored by Abe Stark, who challenged players to "Hit Sign, Win Suit," and a Schaefer Beer sign in which the "h" and "e" in the word Schaefer could be illuminated to designate a hit or error.

It was easy to become overwhelmed by the personality of Ebbets Field, where several legendary fans gained as much renown as the players they rooted for. The cowbell-toting Hilda was a noisy fixture for years in the left-center field bleachers and the five-piece Sym-Phony band seemed to be everywhere, irritating the opposition with their musical antics while saluting their Dodgers heroes. Hilda, who could bellow an "eatcha heart out, ya bum" put-down that could be heard throughout the park, was an intimidating obstacle for Giants fans who might venture into enemy territory.

Charles Ebbets might have suspected life would be different at Ebbets Field when his Dodgers played their first game at the new park in 1913, but not before bleacher ticketholders were kept waiting outside the gate because someone had forgotten the key, and the dedication march to the center field flagpole was delayed because somebody had forgotten the flag.

Things would only get wilder and crazier. What more perfect setting for Casey Stengel's tip-of-the-hat gesture to heckling Dodger fans, releasing a live bird that flew away to freedom? Where else could the Daffiness Boys of Wilbert Robinson have received such loving affection in the 1920s? Where else could you find a singing newsboy who would regale you with Dodger tales, the tone of his melodies reflecting the team's successes and failures?

Babe Herman, who made it perfectly clear to anybody who would listen that he never was hit on the head by a fly ball, did slide into third once, only to find teammates Dazzy Vance and Chick Fewster already there. Herman's bases-loaded double turned into a double play. Umpire George Magerkurth became a famous Brooklyn figure only because he was floored by an irate fan, who held him down and pummeled away near home plate. Hungry fans, upset at not being able to purchase tickets for a critical game against the Giants in 1924, used a dismantled telephone pole to batter in the gate and flowed into the already-packed stadium.

This was the proper setting for yellow baseballs, a milkman/batting practice pitcher and a dropped third strike that cost the Dodgers an important World Series victory. Where else could Johnny Vander Meer have mustered the strength to pitch his second straight no-hitter—in the first night game ever played at Ebbets Field? What park, with its incredible melting pot of patrons, was more fitting for the great sociological experiment—Jackie Robinson's 1947 breaking of baseball's color barrier? Cookie Lavagetto's 1947 double off the right field wall still bounces through the soul of Brooklyn, a vivid, happy memory of one of baseball's greatest World Series moments.

There were plenty of World Series moments in the 1940s and '50s, when Brooklyn fans watched their Dodgers win seven pennants—but only one

EBBETS FIELD (1913-1957)

Baseball in Brooklyn was played by teams with a variety of names and in a variety of places before there came the Dodgers and Ebbets Field.

They were the Wonders, Bridegrooms and Superbas and they played in Eastern Park (where "Dodgers" originated from the name Trolley Dodgers, fans who had to dodge trolleys to get to the park) and Washington Park.

In 1912, Brooklyn owner Charles Ebbets secured the final parcel of a 4½-acre tract in Brooklyn's Flatbush neighborhood. By 1913, on the blighted tract of land — bordered by Bedford Avenue, Sullivan Street, Franklin Avenue and Montgomery Street — the new stadium was ready.

Sportswriters are credited with encouraging the naming of the park in Ebbets' honor.

After the Dodgers moved west for the '58 season, Ebbets Field stood another two years. Demolition began in 1960; today, the Ebbets Field Apartments mark the site.

First game: April 9, 1913. The Philadelphia Phillies made a first-inning run hold up in a 1-0 victory over the Superbas. (In the park's first exhibition game, on April 5, Brooklyn center fielder Casey Stengel had the Superbas' first hit, an inside-the-park homer.)

Final game: September 24, 1957. Before just 6,702 fans, most of them stunned by the team's announced departure for Los Angeles, the Dodgers shut out Pittsburgh, 2-0.

■ Site of nine World Series (1916, '20, '41, '47, '49, '52, '53, '55 and '56)
■ Site of one All-Star Game (1949)

championship. Twenty-eight World Series games were played at Ebbets, 14 victories and 14 defeats. But, thanks primarily to the talented Yankees, "next year" didn't arrive until 1955, two years before Ebbets Field played host to its final major league game.

All the color, 45 years worth of fascinating memories, all the special ties between players and fans—the heart and soul of Brooklyn baseball—were tainted in 1957 by the Dodgers' announcement they would move to Los Angeles for the 1958 season. It was like a stake in the heart of a city that had invested more than it could afford in a relationship gone bad.

The divorce became official on February 23, 1960, when a demolition crew began dismantling Ebbets Field, effectively removing the last vestige of a special team in a special place at a special time.

Ebbets Field, tucked snugly in the heart of Brooklyn (left), offered an interesting view from beyond its right-center field fence across Bedford Avenue (below bottom). The park's visitor's bullpen, located down the left field line (below top), was a frequent October work area for the cross-town New York Yankees.

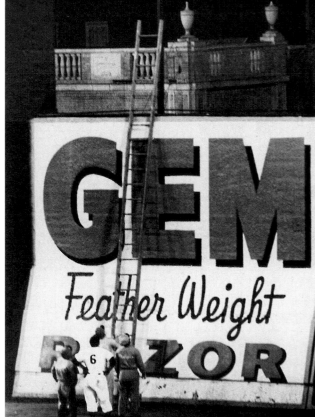

Superfan Hilda Chester (above) kept things rocking at Ebbets with her ever-present cowbell. A worker (right) climbs over the right field wall to get a ball that stuck in the screen. This ground-rule double, hit by St Louis star Stan Musial, typified the craziness that happened a lot at Ebbets.

Comiskey Park

Park where "Black Sox" lost
three times to Reds during
infamous 1919 World Series

Eddie Collins, Shoeless Joe
Jackson and Happy Felsch get
three hits apiece in 8-5 Game
win that sets stage for 1917 Wor
Series championship

NELLIE FOX
played in record
798 straight games
at second base
during 14 seasons
with Sox

Left fielder Al Smith gets famous
beer shower following Dodger
homer by Charlie Neal in Game 2
of '59 World Series

Cubs used Comiskey as their
"home park" during 1918 World
Series loss to Red Sox

The first thing you
noticed about old
Comiskey Park was its
imposing brick facade,
an all-white, weather-beaten,
decaying mirror that reflected the
tough South Side neighborhoods
surrounding it. It was hard to
imagine this worn-down, street-
wise structure as the former
"Baseball Palace of the World,"
but neither could you escape the
Comiskey spell—a powerful sense
of baseball history that drew
you around its perimeter like
an awestruck tourist.

Where
seven-time
stolen base
champion
Luis Aparicio
performed
defensive
magic and
served as
catalyst for
Go-Go Sox
from 1956-62

214

Site of Bill Veeck's "Disco Demolition" promotion, which causes near riot and results in forfeit to Tigers, July 12, 1979

Bill Veeck: Master showman and king of exploding scoreboards

Fred Lynn hits first grand slam in All-Star Game history as A.L. rolls in classic's 50th anniversary contest, July 6, 1983

Harold Baines ends 8-hour, 25-inning battle vs. Brewers with home run, May 9, 1984

he first All-Star Game was layed here, July 6, 1933 . . . d Schoendienst decides 1950 -Star classic with home run in 14th inning

Ted Kluszewski muscles up for two homers during 11-0 Game 1 win in '59 Series . . . Dodger Chuck Essegian sets record with second pinch-hit homer in Game 6

1990, final season at old Comiskey: Carlton Fisk (left) sets record for career homers by catcher and Bobby Thigpen posts record 57 saves

ikee pitcher Andy Hawkins itches no-hitter—loses to Vhite Sox 4-0, July 1, 1990

LUKE APPLING: White Sox career leader in games, runs, hits, doubles, total bases and RBIs

Bewildered Orioles end ason-opening-record 21-game losing streak with 9-0 win, April 29, 1988

Where Mike Squires made brief appearances as the first big-league lefty catcher in 22 years, May 4, 7, 1980

Cleveland's Larry Doby breaks A.L. racial barrier as pinch hitter, July 5, 1947 . . . Minnie Minoso breaks White Sox racial barrier and hits home run in first plate appearance, May 1, 1951

COMISKEY PARK

HOME OF THE WHITE SOX.

This was the creation of Charles Comiskey, the Old Roman who opened his modern-day Colosseum in 1910. This was "Home of the White Sox" for 81 years, the stomping ground of Big Ed Walsh, Ted Lyons, Eddie Collins, Nellie Fox, Luke Appling, Luis Aparicio, Minnie Minoso, Carlton Fisk and, of course, Shoeless Joe Jackson. This was where working-class Chicago, blue-collar Chicago, came to watch serious baseball, not the cuddly Cubbies version played on the city's North Side. This was a social melting pot of macho, burly, rowdy fans who could set aside differences and unite in a common cause for a few hours on a Sunday afternoon.

A first visit to the baseball fortress at 35th Street and Shields Avenue was sure to provide instant gratification. Comiskey from the outside, with 12 distinctive ticket booths forming a semi-circular shield at the main entrance, was imposing. But the feeling inside was personal and inviting. The green seats formed a bond with the grass field below, the grandstand roof hovered overhead like a protective mother and the scoreboard, Comiskey's "Monster," dominated the center field view, ready to explode at a moment's notice.

It was hard to take your eyes off that huge, wonderfully colorful scoreboard—the most distinctive of Comiskey's features for three decades. Baseball's first exploding scoreboard, introduced by former owner Bill Veeck in 1960, released a strange cacophony of sounds ranging from foghorns and a cavalry-charge bugle to crashing trains and a circus calliope when celebrating a White Sox home run. The board, which filled the open center field area above the bleachers (the only area not enclosed

COMISKEY PARK (1910-1990)

It opened in 1910, a predecessor of Wrigley Field, Tiger Stadium, Fenway Park and Yankee Stadium, but Comiskey Park never enjoyed the reputations those parks attained.

But when Charles Comiskey built it, it was ahead of its time. A replacement for 39th Street Grounds, Comiskey is said to have built the new park as a more comfortable place for fans, as a safer place for players and, with steel instead of wood construction, a more fire-resistant structure.

Its enduring features were its upper-deck grandstand, which was extended into the outfield in 1926-27, and its electronic scoreboard that debuted in 1951. But years of relative neglect eventually doomed the park.

Today, new Comiskey sits adjacent to the old ballpark site. New Comiskey's third-base concourse provides an overlook to the old site, now a parking lot. What's left on the parking lot is an outline of old Comiskey's basepaths.

First game: July 1, 1910. Even with Big Ed Walsh on the hill, the White Sox lost to the St. Louis Browns, 2-0.

Final game: September 30, 1990. The White Sox record their 3,024th regular-season win (vs. 2,926 losses) in Comiskey, a 2-1 victory over Seattle.

■ Site of four World Series (1917, '18, '19 and '59)
■ Site of three All-Star Games (1933, '50 and '83)

One of Comiskey Park's signature features was its grandstand roof, which was imposing whether you viewed it from above or below.

by the grandstand roof), changed size, shape and color over the years, but its "Disneyland" theatrics never failed to delight fans and draw the wrath of opposing players and coaches.

Once you pried your eyes away from the scoreboard, Comiskey became a menagerie of sights, sounds and baseball memories. The view from behind home plate was dramatic, even if the left field roof did block out a spectacular downtown Chicago skyline. Portals in the lower left field grandstands let in light and diminished the feeling of enclosure. A catwalk allowed fans to pass to and from the upper left and right field grandstands behind the scoreboard and retired numbers of special White Sox players

were featured on the right field wall. A ground-level picnic area in left field provided a marvelous view of batting practice—and a respite from the biting north wind off Lake Michigan that sometimes turned Comiskey into a spring or summer icebox.

How could anyone possibly hit a ball over the double-decked roof, in either right or left? Well, it happened 44 times, including shots by Babe Ruth, Lou Gehrig, Jimmie Foxx and Ted Williams that were temporarily immortalized by signs across the face of the upper deck. Foxx and Hank Greenberg were among the magnificent seven to reach the original center field bleachers, before the White Sox put up a distance-shortening center field fence in the 1980s.

Home runs, no matter how long, were always of interest in Comiskey,

From its early days right on through the Bill Veeck era, Comiskey has always been known for its scoreboards. The early board (far left) had its Longines clock and Veeck's later versions had pyrotechnic displays (above) and a sound system to match.

Promotions were a Bill Veeck specialty, including this 1959 surprise in which little spacemen showed up to capture Luis Aparicio and Nellie Fox.

one of baseball's biggest ballparks over the years. When the stadium was opened with a grandstand roof that wrapped behind home plate from first base to third, the lines measured 362 feet and it was 420 to dead center. When the grandstands were extended in 1927, the lines shortened to 352 but center field moved back to 440—a distance that an inner fence cut to 402 from 1986 through Comiskey's final 1990 season.

"It was a great park, big, a fair park," Appling recalled before Comiskey closed its gates for the final time. "There were no gimmes in right field or left field with a short fence, and center field was so big you could put in another field."

In the quirky, oddly-shaped world of early-century baseball, Charles Comiskey emerged as a champion of symmetry, a principle that was never sacrificed through the park's many renovations. Neither was Comiskey's place in history, which was not always achieved through conventional methods.

The park was the home of one championship team and the site of four World Series, one of which was played there by the Cubs, not the White Sox, in 1918 and another that turned into the most infamous scandal in baseball history—Cincinnati's 1919 win over the "Black Sox." Only the Go-Go Sox of Aparicio and Fox in 1959 reached a World Series over the park's last seven decades.

Comiskey's "palace of baseball" reputation was underscored in 1933 when it was chosen to play host to the first All-Star Game, an honor punctuated by Ruth's game-deciding home run. It was the site of the only opening day no-hitter in history, the debut of the American League's first black player and numerous Negro League World Series. This is where Veeck kept everybody on edge with his crazy promotions and the 1983 White Sox "won ugly" and captured a West Division title.

Comiskey Park entered the 1990 season as the oldest major league park still in use, two years older than Tiger Stadium and Fenway Park. Still stately and regal despite a crumbling, creaky facade, the park passed on its legacy—and the White Sox—to new Comiskey Park, a state-of-the-art facility built right across the street. The new pride of Chicago's South Side.

Old Comiskey Park lasted through the 1990 season before giving way to new Comiskey, which was built right across the street (right).

Crosley Field

Also known as Redland Field (1912-1934)

It was an oasis in the middle of a brick and smokestack-filled desert, a bright green carpet covering a small piece of Cincinnati's drab, deteriorating West End. Crosley Field was a colorful Mecca in a sometimes-gray world, a place of renewal and rejuvenation. Life was simple there—the baseball was entertaining, the heroes were friendly and everybody had fun, no bad times permitted.

It was hard not to love the simplicity and intimacy that oozed from every nook and cranny of this odd-shaped structure. Crosley was cozy, tightly carved into the

Dodgers' Leo Durocher circles bases on bunt in wild 1938 All-Star Game

Johnny Vander Meer overpower Boston Bees, the first of his recor two straight no-hitters, June 11, 19

Reds' Jim Maloney, Astros' Don Wilson fire no-hitters on consecutive days, April 30, May 1, 1969

Where Grady Hatton's pop fly fel among three Braves, robbing John Sain of perfect game, July 12, 194

Where Dutch Ruether (right), Slim Sallee won first two games of 1919 World Series, with a little help from scheming White Sox

TED KLUSZEWSKI:
Big Klu topped 100 RBIs four straight seasons (1953-56)

Mel Ott's ninth-inning homer helps Giants' Carl Hubbell win record 24th straight game, May 27, 1937

Bucky Walters fires shutout, hits homer in key Game 6 win over Tigers in 1940 World Series

Where Ernie Lombardi "snoozed" in Game 4 of 1939 World Series

Where 15-year-old Joe Nuxhall made h league debut, June 10, 1944

Giants hit five home runs in 12-run ninth inning, beat Reds 14-0, Aug. 23, 1961

Mill Creek flood buries Crosley Field in 1937

Slight incline in ront of wall makes e interesting for left fielders

MVP Central from 1938-40: Ernie Lombardi (above), Bucky Walters, Frank McCormick

Ewell "The Whip" Blackwell (right), two outs short of second straight no-hitter, surrenders ninth-inning single to Brooklyn's Eddie Stanky, June 22, 1947

Former site of the old laundry, an inviting target for righthanded power hitters

Site of Larry MacPhail's great experiment: The first major league night game, May 24, 1935

47-year-old Satchel Paige becomes oldest pitcher in All-Star Game history, July 14, 1953

Giants 1, Reds 0 in 21 innings—Bob Lee walks home winning run, Sept. 1, 1967

Jim Maloney throws 10-inning no-hitter vs. Mets, loses in 11th on Johnny Lewis' home run, June 14, 1965

Key parts for Big Red Machine (Rose, Bench, Perez) were assembled in final years at Crosley

1961 MVP FRANK ROBINSON hit 324 of his 586 career homers in a Reds uniform

Hank Aaron singles for 3,000th hit, May 17, 1970

framework of the angled streets that surrounded it, and you quickly learned to make visual associations with the landmarks that gave it a special personality.

A laundry, the Superior Towel & Linen Service, covered much of the left field wall on York Street, providing an inviting target for righthanded power hitters until the area was cleared after the 1960 season to make room for parking. Buildings marked "Merchants Paper" and "Lackner Neon Signs" stood sentry over the center and right-center field walls on Western Avenue. Billboards dotted the right-center field skyline, hawking attractions and products like Coney Island, Hudepohl Beer ("Get moody with Hudy"), Shillito's department stores, Young & Bertke sheet metal company, Coca-Cola and Petri wine.

You did not go to Crosley Field to watch baseball. You went to experience it. It was about smells, sights and sounds—peanuts, bratwurst, red hots and beer or lemonade; the buzz that filtered through the park at the sight of players trekking to and from their clubhouse, right through the third base stands; pregame activities and promotions with fans, alongside players, on the field; superfan Harry Thobe, dressed in customary white suit with red tie, doing a victory jig; Smitty's Band, Ronnie Dale's organ music, public-address announcer Paul Sommerkamp's voice; and, of course, park idiosyncracies like the terrace, the Sun Deck and Goat Run.

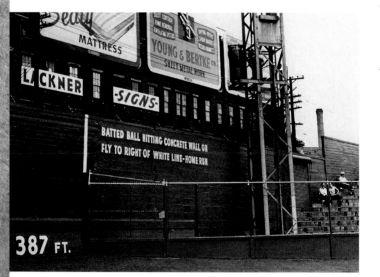

The white line and explanation served as a center field ground rule during the late 1940s at Crosley Field. It was made necessary because of the unusual way in which the wire right field bleacher fence connected to the center field wall.

Old-timers still like to tell about Babe Ruth's first experience with the terrace, an incline that started 20 feet in front of the left field fence and gradually sloped upward until it reached a four-foot grade at the wall. The aging Ruth, playing left field in 1935 for the Boston Braves, fell on his face while chasing a fly ball on the terrace, got up and grimly walked off the field, refusing to return. Ruth wasn't alone. Even Reds players, familiar with the incline, hated the deformity, which was caused by an underground stream.

The Sun Deck was a colorful name for the right field bleachers that were

Crosley was in all of its cozy glory and dressed to the hilt for the 1953 All-Star Game (left). Trolley lines marked Crosley's corner at Findlay Street and Western Avenue (right).

backed by the intersection of Western Avenue and Findlay Street. The bleachers intersected at a point with the center field fence, necessitating a white line to the right of which a hand-painted ground rule pronounced, "Batted Ball Hitting Concrete Wall on Fly to Right of White Line—Home Run."

Big Ted Kluszewski tested the line more than once. So did Vada Pinson and righthanded power hitters like Ernie Lombardi, Frank McCormick, Gus Bell, Wally Post and Frank Robinson. But the righthanders were more likely to take aim at the laundry and a small sign, perched above the roof in left-center field, which challenged hitters to "Hit this sign and get a Siebler suit free." Post was the unofficial suit champion with 11 hits.

To be a Reds fan required patience and an ability to accept change. Between its 1912 christening as Redland Field and its 1970 farewell as Crosley, no park underwent more renovations—most of them after Powel Crosley purchased the team in 1934. Its roofed double-decked grandstand was extended from two-thirds of the way down both lines to the left and right field corners, portable seats were installed, removed, re-installed and removed in various areas of the park, home plate was relocated twice, a right field screen went up and down several times and a state-of-the-art scoreboard, with a 7-foot, 10-inch Longines clock perched on top, replaced the old ground-level board in 1957.

Through the constant makeovers, Crosley retained its irregular dimensions.

After 1938, the left field foul pole measured 328 feet, center was a friendly 383 and the right field line was a whopping 366, except for two periods when seats were installed in front of the Sun Deck bleachers, cutting the distance to 342. The so-called "Goat Run" was expected to aid the muscular, sleeveless Kluszewski, but his booming line drives seldom took advantage of the fly ball-friendly seats.

CROSLEY FIELD 1912-1970

Also known as Redland Field (1912-1934)

Its original name was Redland Field, a last-minute name substitution made by team president Garry Herrman, who had apparently been leaning toward calling the field League Park. The name Redland recognized the traditional color of Cincinnati baseball teams. Previously, the corner of Findlay and Western had been the home of Redland's predecessors, League Park (1884-1901) and the Palace of the Fans (1902-11).

In 1934, the name was changed to Crosley Field, after new owner Powel Crosley Jr., a Cincinnati businessman who made his money in home appliances and a radio empire.

Today, a number of businesses occupy the Findlay and Western site, just a mile and a half from Cinergy Field. There is, however, a "New Crosley Field" for those who want to experience the old ballpark. The re-creation, complete with actual artifacts from old Crosley, is in Blue Ash, a town northeast of downtown Cincinnati.

First game: April 11, 1912. After spotting the Cubs a 5-0 lead, the Reds rallied with six in the fourth inning and eventually won, 10-6.

Final game: June 24, 1970. Lee May and Johnny Bench hit back-to-back homers in the eighth as the Reds rallied to beat the Giants, 5-4. Bobby Bonds' groundout closed the doors at Crosley after 4,543 games.

■ Site of four World Series (1919, '39, '40 and '61)
■ Site of two All-Star Games (1938 and 1953)

The great Mill Creek flood of 1937 turned Crosley into a giant swimming pool (far left). Superfan Harry Thobe, dressed in customary white with umbrella and megaphone (left), was a Crosley Field fixture for many years.

Two Crosley trademarks (left): the left field incline and the laundry beyond the left field fence. The overview (above) shows a packed Crosley with temporary seats in front of the outfield walls on opening day in 1937.

Over its 58-year run, Crosley was the home of four pennant-winning teams and two World Series champions—the last in 1940 under Bill McKechnie. It also was the factory where Reds management began piecing together the Big Red Machine that would grind opponents into submission in the 1970s—after the team's move to new Riverfront Stadium.

But Crosley might be better remembered for the zaniness and innovations that created indelible memories. This was the park where the first acts of World Series scandal unfolded, courtesy of the 1919 Chicago White Sox. This is where Larry MacPhail staged the first night game in major league history, Johnny Vander Meer pitched the first of his consecutive no-hitters and The Whip, Ewell Blackwell, barely missed duplicating Vander Meer's feat nine years later. A woman once batted in a major league game here and a 15-year-old lefthander threw his first big-league pitch from Crosley's mound. The magic of Crosley Field was never demonstrated more emphatically than in 1937, when it disappeared —beneath the flood waters of nearby Mill Creek.

When Crosley Field disappeared for good from the major leagues on June 24, 1970, a near-capacity crowd of 28,027 turned out to bid a final, sometimes-tearful farewell. They left with the pleasant memory of consecutive Johnny Bench and Lee May home runs that produced a 5-4 victory over the Giants.

League Park

Also known as Dunn Field (1920-1927)

Highlanders' Tom Hughes loses no-hitter with one out in 10th, drops 5-0 decision in 11, Aug. 30, 1910

Johnny Burnett gets nine of Cleveland's record 33 hits in 18-inning 18-17 loss to A's, July 10, 1932

A's slugger Jimmie Foxx hit three homers here in famous 18-17 game

Player-manag[er] Lou Boudreau['s] office was her[e] from 1942-46

NAPOLEON LAJOIE:
Indians were called "Cleveland Naps" from 1903-14 because of popular second baseman Nap Lajoie, a .338 career hitter

Area blanketed by third basemen Bill Bradley, Larry Gardner, Willie Kamm and Ken Keltner from 1901-46

Lajoie gets 3,000th career hit vs. Yankees, Sept. 27, 1914

Senators steal eight bases in first inning of July 19, 1915 game

Tris Speaker gets 3,000th hit off Washington's Tom Zachary, May 17, 1925

I t was an oddly-shaped, funny-looking little relic, squeezed tightly into a working-class neighborhood near downtown Cleveland. League Park was a delightful sports playground that tried hard to be cozy and quaint. But it also was a house of insanity, a place where baseball was contorted to fit into the most illogical dimensions ever conceived.

"Wall Ball" is what they called it in Cleveland. And, indeed, most of League Park's mystique emanated from a 40-foot combination concrete-and-wire

From 1932-46, League Park shared the Indians with massive Cleveland Stadium

Ossie Vitt's Crybabies finish one game behind Tigers in 1940 pennant race

Ted Williams belted a monster shot here; Babe Ruth hit a 460-foot shot here

Third baseman Joe Sewell: 4 strikeouts in 578 official at-bats in 1929
Pitcher Jim Bagby: 31-12, 2.89 ERA in 1920

Home of Bill Wambsganss, who pulled off unassisted triple play in Game 5 of 1920 World Series, and pitcher Elmer Smith, who hit first World Series grand slam in same contest

Where Yankee great Babe Ruth hit his 500th career homer, Aug. 11, 1929

Where Addie Joss pitched his perfect game, outdueling Chicago ace Ed Walsh, Oct. 2, 1908

Stan Coveleski nails down only League Park World Series crown with 3-0 Game 7 win over Brooklyn, Oct. 12, 1920

17-year-old rookie Bob Feller strikes out 17 A's in two-hit victory, Sept. 13, 1936

TRIS SPEAKER:
The Grey Eagle patroled center field with Hall of Fame grace from 1916-26

Cozy dugouts put players shoulder-to-shoulder with opinionated fans right field barrier that stood an inviting 290 feet from home plate, a distance mandated by the natural boundary of Lexington Avenue. With the left field line measuring 375 feet and straightaway center a whopping 460 (later 420), the playing field had a peculiar rectangular shape unmatched by any other park.

Babe Ruth, Lou Gehrig and other lefthanded American League sluggers were delighted to see their fly balls turn into 300-foot home runs, but line drives were another matter. The 20-foot concrete right field wall was topped by a 20-foot screen from the corner to the center field scoreboard. The chicken-wire screen was supported by a series of vertical steel beams that created their own special problems.

Line drives hitting the lower wall bounded like a shot past outfielders. Balls hitting the screen could do one of three things: drop straight down; get stuck in the wiring, a ground-rule double; or hit a beam and shoot in any direction, depending on the angle. You never knew what to expect. Balls could deflect all the way to left field—or back to the infield. The fence, much like the Green Monster at Boston's Fenway Park, also turned potential extra-base hits into outs at second—or long singles.

Everything at League Park revolved around the wall. Lefties drooled, righthanders changed their batting stroke, every fielder kept a wary eye on balls hit to right and fans screamed with delight at the strange occurrences they would witness. But the biggest beneficiaries were the kids—packs who, unable to afford a ticket, would position themselves on Lexington Avenue, hoping to pick off a batting-practice ball or home run they could turn in for a free pass.

It was that way from 1910, when the original League Park, which had stood at East 66th Street and Lexington since 1891, was remodeled from a wood-based field into a steel-and-concrete ballpark. Eventually, the field would feature a roofed, double-decked grandstand from the right field foul pole to just short of the left field pole, where a section of single-deck stands wrapped into left and met a narrow section of bleachers fronted by a 10-foot barrier—3 feet of concrete, 7 feet of screen. The big green scoreboard, which was updated by kids hanging numbers on nails, was not flush with the ground, allowing balls to occasionally disappear underneath.

One of League Park's stranger quirks was the positioning of bullpens, which

LEAGUE PARK (1910-1946)

Also known as Dunn Field (1920-1927)

Built at Lexington and East 66th because of that site's proximity to streetcar lines, League Park—its official name was National League Park—was nestled into a neighborhood that had served as home for the Cleveland Spiders as far back as 1891.

In 1910, League Park was rebuilt from a wood-based park into a steel-and-concrete structure that would serve as the Indians' home until 1946.

Standing on the site today, about three miles east of Jacobs Field, is a city playground.

First game: April 21, 1910. Detroit shut out the Indians, 5-0.
Final game: Sept. 21, 1946. The same Tigers defeated the same Indians, 5-3.
■ Site of one World Series (1920)
■ Site of no All-Star Games

were crammed into the corners and hidden from view to many spectators by special stands that angled in an arc from the pavilions just behind third base until they almost touched the foul lines. When fair balls rolled into the left field bullpen, outfielders would have to throw over the stands to get the ball to the infield.

Summer afternoons at League Park (Dunn Field from 1920-27) were fun and relaxing—gates open at noon, batting practice, the smell of hot dogs on the grill, smiling players interacting with kids and anticipation of a 3:30 game, after which kids would be allowed to run the bases. Conversely, the pace around the brick-based exterior was furious, kids jockeying for position to chase balls, fighting for knothole spots and battling for wildcat vantage points from the Dunham School fire escape or the roof of the Andrews Storage Company, a dangerous climb.

No matter where you were positioned, you felt like part of the action—mes-merized by the sweet swing of Shoeless Joe Jackson, caught up in the passion of Stan Coveleski and Jim Bagby, looking over Earl Averill's shoulder, shuddering at the crack of a Bob Feller fastball. You had to love Joe Sewell's appreciation for foul balls into the stands and the 1920 World Series-champion Indians. You had to mourn the premature demise of Addie Joss and Ray Chapman. But most of all, you had to admire the incredible ability of Tris Speaker, positioned almost on the edge of the infield, to cover all 460 feet of center field.

League Park played host to Indians baseball for 36 wonderful years, the final 14 as co-host with new, larger Cleveland Municipal Stadium—Sunday, holiday and night games (League never had lights) at Municipal, the rest of the schedule at League Park, which never had a permanent seating capacity over 22,000. Owner Bill Veeck moved the team permanently to Municipal Stadium in 1947.

The overview shows an almost-rectangular field with covered grandstands and a right field fence topped by a screen with steel support posts.

Municipal
Stadium

Also known as Cleveland Stadium and Cleveland Municipal Stadium

Carlos Baerga homers from both sides of plate in same inning—a baseball first—vs. Yankees, April 8, 1993

Joe DiMaggio's 56-game hitting streak ends, thanks in part to two fine defensive plays by third baseman Ken Keltner, July 17, 1941

30-year-old Tigers rookie Floyd Giebell shuts out Feller, Indians to clinch A.L. pennant, Sept. 27, 1940

Frank Robinson, making debut as Indians player/manager, homers in first at-bat , April 8, 1975

Tigers shortstop Cesar Gutierrez goes 7-for-7 in 12-inning win over Indians, June 21, 1970

Indians hit four consecutive homers off Angels' Paul Foytack, July 31, 1963 (Woodie Held, Pedro Ramos, Tito Francona, Larry Brown)

Beer Night promotion goes awry and Indians forfeit game to Rangers, June 4, 1974

LOU BOUDREAU
A.L. MVP Lou Boudreau led Indians to 1948 World Series championship

Y ou have to admire its perseverance, a tired, old concrete-and-steel edifice that stood up to a depression, a burning river, economic turmoil, bad baseball and the ill winds that blow relentlessly off Lake Erie. Cleveland Municipal Stadium was a tough old bird, massive, imposing and scarred from years of neglect and abuse. It also was a proud remnant of a bygone era, when ballparks were measured as much by size and function as by charm and charisma.

Imposing had given way to clunky and awkward by 1993, when the stadium finally closed its gates to baseball after more than six decades. But through most of its existence,

Where Bill Veeck (center, holding hat) literally "buried the pennant" after Indians fell out of 1949 title chase

Pitchers (from left) Bob Lemon, Early Wynn, Mike Garcia and Feller help Indians post 111 wins, capture 1954 A.L. pennant

Boston lefty Matt Young pitches no-hitter, but Indians ruin his day by posting 2-1 victory, April 12, 1992

Len Barker pitches a perfect game on a blustery night vs. Blue Jays, May 15, 1981

Where Red Sox slugger Ted Williams hit his 500th career home run off Wynn Hawkins, June 17, 1960

Senators reliever Dean Stone won '54 All-Star Game, an 11-9 A.L. victory, without retiring a batter when he caught Red Schoendienst trying to steal home

Where Senators shortstop Ron Hansen turned eighth unassisted triple play in major league history, July 30, 1968

Where Negro Leagues legend Satchel Paige took the mound in Game 5 of the 1948 World Series, breaking baseball's postseason color barrier

Montreal catcher Gary Carter homers twice in N.L.'s 1981 All-Star Game win before record crowd of 72,086

Where Herb Score was hit in the eye by Gil McDougald's line drive, May 7, 1957

Luis Tiant strikes out 19 in 10-inning game, July 3, 1968

BOB FELLER
Rapid Robert struck out 348 in 1946, led A.L. in strikeouts seven times and won 20 games six times

Where Vic Power stole home twice in a game vs. Tigers, Aug. 14, 1958

CLEVELAND MUNICIPAL STADIUM (1932-1993)

Also known as Cleveland Stadium and Municipal Stadium

Borne partly out of the limited seating capacity of League Park, Cleveland Municipal Stadium was just the opposite. It was huge (74,483) and forboding, a massive structure that looked all the more massive when its seats were not filled.

True to its hulking reputation, the distinctive feature of the stadium was its deep center field. No batter ever reached the center field bleachers; the closest, it was said, was Jose Canseco, who hit the facing of the bleachers in left center.

The stadium was demolished in 1996. Fittingly, a new stadium — Cleveland Browns Stadium, home of the NFL's Browns — sits on the site.

First game: July 31, 1932. In a game in which six future Hall of Famers participated — Connie Mack, Lefty Grove, Mickey Cochrane, Jimmie Foxx, Al Simmons and Earl Averill — the Philadelphia Athletics beat the Indians, 1-0.

Final game: October 3, 1993. It opened with a shutout and ended the same; Chicago White Sox 4, Cleveland 0.

■ Site of two World Series (1948, '54)
■ Site of four All-Star Games (1935, '54, '63 and '81)

Municipal Stadium was big and tough, a monument to old-style, iron-belt baseball.

it had been a perfect match for a tough, no-frills, factory-dominated city in the middle of America's iron belt. It was huge, unpretentious and lacking in the physical quirks and nuances that gave other early-era ballparks personality. It was, in the truest sense, a stadium—a downtown sports arena that survived 62 years of erratic lakefront weather without a lot of love or tender care.

You noticed quickly that Cleveland Stadium had not been pampered like Fenway Park or showered with Wrigley Field-like affection. This was a hulking, horseshoe-shaped fortress with a nondescript sandstone facade and protruding buildings that served as business and ticket offices. On a clear summer afternoon, with the sun glistening off Lake Erie, it looked like a big, beached white whale. The first sign of baseball life was an elevated welcome sign featuring a smiling, toothy Chief Wahoo, bat cocked and ready to smack a long one into the unpaved parking lot.

The smile was misguided. The inside concourses were dingy, damp, concrete walkways and corridors that circled and branched endlessly to points unknown. Bathrooms were tiny, concession stands were small and boxes were stacked in corners like the remainders of a past life stored in someone's attic. The first sense of a grand stadium with a historic aura did not come until you reached the field area.

It was hard to get past that first, overwhelming feeling of huge. A double-decked, roofed grandstand filled with small, wooden seats rose up around you like a protective shield, giving you a sense of enclosure. But any claustrophobic fears were quickly relieved by the open center field, through which upper-deck fans on the right field side could get an angled view of the lake.

At this open end were a big scoreboard and some of the most famous bleacher seats in sports—the infamous Dawg Pound section that tormented football opponents of the Cleveland Browns. For baseball, these bleachers were in dead center field, 470 feet from home plate, a target no batted ball ever reached. The seats in the back row of the bleachers were farther away from home plate than any other seats in baseball and the scoreboard, more than 500 feet from fans behind the plate, was hard to see and a very basic blend of information and scores.

To really appreciate Cleveland Stadium, you have to recognize it as a child of the Great Depression. Baseball's first municipally-owned park was built as an attempt to attract the 1932 Olympic Games, but that failed and Cleveland was left with an 80,000-seat multi-sports facility that was more conducive to football than baseball. When the Indians played their first game there in 1932, 76,979 fans—more than had ever witnessed a major league game—filed through the gates and everybody marveled at the incredible structure.

"The stadium is perfect," said commissioner Kenesaw Mountain Landis. "It is the only baseball park I know where the spectator can see clearly from any seat. This is perfection."

Landis apparently did not tour the higher altitudes of Cleveland Stadium, where steel girders obstructed the view of many fans. Nor did he anticipate the hollow, empty feeling of a stadium with only 12,000 seats filled. The Indians quickly grasped that problem and spent the next decade and a half jockeying games between Cleveland Stadium and tiny League Park—Sunday, holiday and night games in the larger, more-expensive-to-operate facility.

The original dimensions of the symmetrical field were imposing—470 feet to center, 463 in the power alleys and 322 down both lines. But owner Bill Veeck installed a foul line-to-foul line inner fence in 1947 that cut the center field distance to 410 and the power alleys to 385. The distances were tailored over the years to Indians talent and the area between the fence and the bleachers was used for standing-room, a garden and eventually a family picnic grounds.

An easy first impression was that this building was much more fit for football, a perception perpetuated by Cleveland's long love affair with the Browns. Football games, often played in blizzard-like conditions with a nasty wind whipping off Lake Erie, were always packed. Baseball games, particularly through the lean 1960s, '70s and '80s, were not. The 12,000 or so vocal baseball fans were like lost souls, free to roam from section to section in search of the perfect seat.

It wasn't that way during the 1940s and '50s, when the Indians claimed the stadium's only two pennants and one World Series championship (1948). But economic hard times and weak teams hurt the Indians and lack of upkeep and renovation doomed the stadium, which was sarcastically dubbed "The Mistake by the Lake."

For many years, a smiling Chief Wahoo (right) greeted visitors at Gate A. In later years, a bat-swinging Wahoo was perched on the other side of the stadium.

In retrospect, that's harsh. While the stadium might have been lacking in physically distinctive features, it was easy to get lost in its history—the distinctive Bob Feller windup, the ghosts of Early Wynn, Mike Garcia, Bob Lemon and Feller, who pitched the Indians to an incredible 111 wins in 1954. Names like Doby, Rosen, Colavito, Easter, Averill, Wertz, Trosky, Thornton and, of course, Boudreau assaulted the brain like the rhythmic pounding of superfan John Adams' excited drumbeats. Football memories of Graham, Groza, Lavelli, Brown, Kelly, Sipe and Kosar dangled chillingly from imaginary rafters. Joe DiMaggio, it was said, was still looking in 1993 for that hit to extend his record streak to 57 games.

There's no denying Cleveland Stadium lived most of its life as a haggard, worn-down super-structure from the 1930s—a charmless albatross to disbelieving visitors. But it's also hard to deny Cleveland fans their special moments. There is, after all, no place like home.

A standing-room crowd of 78,431 jammed Cleveland Stadium (left) in May 1948 and eager fans lined up later that year (below) for World Series tickets. Five years later, a new scoreboard (right) divided the center field bleachers and the Cleveland Symphony Orchestra entertained in relative obscurity.

Tiger Stadium

Also known as Navin Field (1912-1937);
Briggs Stadium (1938-1960)

Senators' Frank Howard hits ball over left field roof—his 10th home run in six-game span, May 18, 1968

Cecil Fielder becomes first Tiger to hit ball over left field roof, Aug. 25, 1990 . . . second to hit 50 homers in season, 51 in 1990

Lefty closer Willie Hernandez: MVP, Cy Young double in 1984

Where irate fans showered Cardinal Joe Medwick with garbage in Game 7 of 1934 World Series

AL KALINE, a 10-time Gold Glove-winning right fielder, collected 11 hits while leading Tigers to 1968 World Series title

Pitcher Tommy Bridges pulls off Houdini-like escape after surrendering leadoff ninth-inning triple to Chicago's Stan Hack in Game 6 of 1935 World Series . . . Mickey Cochrane scores winning run in bottom of inning

Tigers (Frank Tanana) outduel Blue Jays (Jimmy Key) 1-0 to complete season-ending sweep and win East Division title, Oct. 4, 1987

ou felt that tingle, a sense of anticipation and incredible history, well before you reached The Corner, the intersection of time, space and baseball at Michigan and Trumbull. It was a good feeling, a response to the sweet Siren's song emanating from inside the great white castle that stood majestically on Detroit's own little corner of the world. This was Tiger Stadium, the house of Cobb and Crawford, Gehringer and Greenberg, Kaline and Kell, Trammell and Whitaker—and all the other friendly ghosts of baseball past.

At first glance, Tiger Stadium was

Home of Charley Gehringer (left) and Hank Greenberg . . . Big Hank made 1938 run at baseball history with 58 homers

Denny McLain becomes first 30-game winner since 1934 when Tigers rally to beat A's in ninth, Sept. 14, 1968

Kirk Gibson hits two Game 5 homers, Tigers close out Padres in 1984 World Series.

Where Babe Ruth crushed "626-foot" homer in 1926, a ball that rolled all the way to Brooklyn Street before upper-deck grandstand was added

Tigers were 3,764-3,090-19 over 88 memorable seasons here with 6 A.L. pennants, 4 World Series titles

Boston's Ted Williams wins 1941 All-Star Game with three-run, ninth-inning home run

Reggie Jackson's titanic blast spices up 1971 All-Star Game

Where Yankee Lou Gehrig ended his iron man streak at 2,130 games, May 2, 1939

Where Johnny Neun turned unassisted triple play vs. Indians, May 31, 1927

Home of longest-running keystone combination in baseball history—shortstop Alan Trammell, second baseman Lou Whitaker, 1977-95

Where Mark "The Bird" Fidrych talked to ball and groomed mound in a captivating 1976 season

TY COBB:
The Georgia Peach compiled an all-time best .367 average, won record 12 batting titles and amassed 4,191 hits

Roger Clemens matches his single-game record in 20-strikeout effort vs. Tigers, Sept. 18, 1996 a shock to the system, an explosion of white in an otherwise dark and dingy working-class neighborhood. It was a jewel, guarded by vulture-like light standards that seemed ready to pounce from their rooftop perch and polished by the distinctive sounds of baseball, especially the buzz of milling fans and

The 'No Visitors' sign was a laughing matter for many years, but Tiger Stadium's cramped clubhouse facilities were not.

the pleas of enthusiastic vendors. Its secrets were well hidden, with only specks of peeling paint and other hard-to-spot blemishes revealing a hint of the truth.

There were no secrets inside this aging fortress. From the hard streets of Detroit you stepped into an old-fashioned, throwback ballpark, not all that different from how it looked—and smelled—a half century earlier. Bodies packed into extremely narrow concourses of yellow tile; layers of peeling paint, exposed wires and pipes; old telephone booths, tiny concession stands; a century's worth of hot dog, sausage, beer and peanut fumes literally dripping from the walls and melting your memory. A postcard from the past.

"Walking from the old train station, I thought the park looked like an

impressive battleship," said Hall of Fame right fielder Al Kaline, recalling his first sighting of Tiger Stadium as an 18-year-old rookie. "But then inside, walking through the aisles and seeing the green, green grass and the thousands of seats around, and more than anything feeling the peacefulness, it seemed almost magical. On that day I was awestruck. Today, 46 years later, I find myself still humbled and overwhelmed."

Such was the almost-mystical power of Tiger Stadium, which opened in 1912 in Detroit's historic haymarket district amid news the Titanic had sunk. The steel-and-concrete facility, known then as Navin Field in honor of owner Frank Navin, continued the baseball tradition that had existed at Michigan and Trumbull since 1896 (Bennett Park) and began an 87-year run of its own that would "humble and overwhelm" players and fans through its emotional final game in

TIGER STADIUM (1912-1999)

Also known as Navin Field (1912-1937), Briggs Stadium (1938-1960)

Tracing the history of baseball in Detroit has always been easy. Find the corner of Michigan and Trumbull; that's where the action always was.

Built on the site of an old haymarket, the playing field was called Bennett Park from 1896 to 1911. In 1912, an expansion of stands and a reconfiguration of the playing field—home plate moved in from right field—also brought a new name, Navin Field. That marked the beginning of 87 years of baseball in the facility.

The status of Tiger Stadium is much-debated. Today, the stadium stands, albeit baseball-less but still worth a visit, about a mile west of Detroit's new stadium, Comerica Park.

First game: April 20, 1912. An 11-inning Tigers win, 6-5, over Cleveland that featured, fittingly, a steal of home by Ty Cobb.

Final game: September 27, 1999. In an emotional farewell, an 8-2 win over the Royals was highlighted by a mammoth eighth-inning grand slam by Rob Fick.

■ Site of six World Series (1934, '35, '40, '45, '68 and '84)
■ Site of three All-Star Games (1941, '51 and '71)

Saturday night fireworks displays were a regular feature of Tiger Stadium's final major league baseball season.

Tiger Stadium, known as Briggs Stadium from 1938-60, was within hailing distance of the Detroit skyline (right).

Bennett Park (above), also located at Michigan and Trumbull, was Tiger Stadium's predecessor.

Baseball was always front and center at Tiger Stadium, but bleacher fans could always find time for a cotton candy break (below).

1999.

The real beauty of Tiger Stadium might have been its resistance to change. After a 1938 renovation in which new owner Walter Briggs installed an upper grandstand that completely enclosed the park and a grandstand roof that enclosed everything except straightaway center field, the park remained structurally unaltered for more than six decades. It was during a 1930s renovation that the right field fence was moved in 42 feet and the upper deck was widened 10 feet at both its top and bottom, creating the stadium's signature feature and the most famous overhang in baseball history.

Everything about the inside of Tiger Stadium was quirky, starting with the sense of intimacy and coziness that literally slapped you in the face. Part of it was the enclosed roof overhead that gave the field a bandbox feel; part of it were seats so close to the field that you yearned to reach out and touch someone. When seated behind the plate, every popup, every ball hit toward right looked like a challenge for the inviting upper-deck porch that could suck harmless fly balls into home run heaven.

The right field line was only 325 feet away, 15 feet shorter than a left field line that also looked closer than it really was. Pitchers who could get hitters to drive balls toward the center field bleachers enjoyed a 440-foot margin of error. The center field fence was fronted by a 125-foot flagpole, the tallest fair-territory obstacle in any stadium, and the open bleachers were topped by a huge scoreboard for many years, video and replay boards in their waning seasons.

The best seats in baseball could be found at Tiger Stadium. So could the worst seats, thanks to obstructed views created by support pillars. But you always had

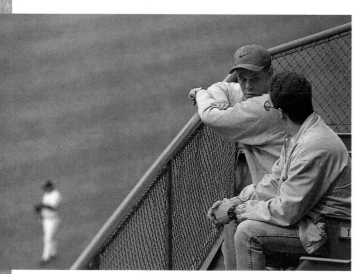

The park's signature feature was an overhang that suspended fans over the right fielder.

a sense of involvement, whether suspended over the right fielder in the front row of the overhang, seated within conversation distance of the players in the dugout or catching a few sun rays in the center field bleachers. Tiger Stadium's seats were cramped and uncomfortable and the narrow aisles were not conducive to between-innings traffic, but it was hard not to like the view they afforded.

That wasn't true for the players, who were confined to the smallest dugouts and bullpens in the major leagues. Dugout ceilings were low and seats were angled awkwardly, forcing players to jump up quickly when balls hit to left disappeared from view. Bam! Instant headache! Relief pitchers were even more limited visually, relegated to life in sunken, caged bullpens (the Submarines) in foul territory down both lines.

But Tiger Stadium was as much about tradition as it was sights and sounds. There,

high on the roof in right-center field, was the light standard transformer that Reggie Jackson hit with his prolific 1971 All-Star Game blast. There, perched high on the facade just below the right field roof, were the four Tigers retired numbers (Kaline, Greenberg, Gehringer, Hal Newhouser), four World Series championship banners (1935, '45, '68, '84) and the No. 42 logo honoring Jackie Robinson. There, on the same facade in foul territory, were the names of 12 Tigers Hall of Famers.

Tiger Stadium was charm and character, stark white uniforms with the olde English "D" on the breast, Ernie Harwell at the mike, Mickey Cochrane diving into the dugout after a foul pop, the best dirt in baseball, Kaline playing a corner carom, Willie Horton glaring at the pitcher, foul balls out of the stadium, opening day snowstorms, home runs over the roof and dark green seats that, unfortunately, were changed to orange and blue during a sprucing-up craze. Twenty-nine home runs cleared the right field roof, but only four cleared the roof in left—Harmon Killebrew in 1962, Frank Howard in 1968, Cecil Fielder in 1990 and Mark McGwire in 1997.

Tiger Stadium was not perfect, as fans and players would attest. Support beams obstructed views and low dugout ceilings (below) resulted in many headaches.

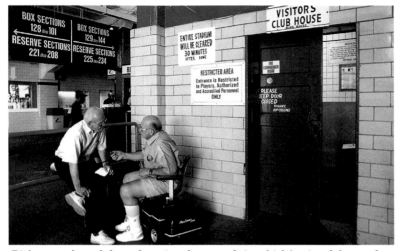

Right up to the end, fans of varying shapes and sizes (right) enjoyed the wonders of Tiger Stadium. So did longtime radio voice Ernie Harwell (above left).

Old timers might remember leather-lunged Patsy O'Toole and his memorable chant of "Boy, oh boy, oh boy!" More recent fans might recall Herbie (the Hoofer) Redmond, the boogieing groundskeeper, or Mark (the Bird) Fidrych, the groundskeeping pitcher. For years, players and team officials chuckled over a sign on the visiting clubhouse door that proclaimed, "Visitors Club House"—"Positively No Visitors Allowed"—"By Order of Joe Cronin, Pres."

Over the decades, Tiger Stadium survived the fiery rampages of Ty Cobb, two World Wars, a depression, some bad baseball, a fire, three name changes (Navin Field to Briggs Stadium in 1938 to Tiger Stadium in 1961), 37 years as home of the NFL's Lions, two World Series losses, 17 seasons with Sparky Anderson and years of premature talk about the Tigers moving to a new facility. That finally came to pass as the millennium came to a close and the curtain dropped on one of baseball's two oldest stadiums—a distinction Tiger Stadium shared with Fenway Park.

Harwell best captured the sense of loss, the feeling of regret, with this reflection that appeared in Detroit's 1999 media guide:

"For almost 40 years, I've spent as much time at the corner of Michigan and Trumbull as I have at home. I've been elated, dejected, thrilled and disappointed. I've sweltered through the summer heat and I've frozen in the spring and fall. Yet, in sickness or in health, it has been my home, my refuge.

"Tiger Stadium was a dear friend. I mourn its passing."

The Astrodome

Judge Roy Hofheinz created "Eighth Wonder of the World" complete with $2 million exploding scoreboard, air-conditioning and baseball's first artificial turf

Phillies' Mike Schmid hits ball off speaker, turning sure homer into one of longest singles ever hit, June 10, 1974

Mets lefty Jesse Orosco strikes out Kevin Bass to end 16-inning NLCS Game 6 classic, Oct. 15, 1986

Where Nolan Ryan recorded fifth career no-hitter, Sept. 26, 1981 . . . 4,000th career strikeout, July 11, 1985

First indoor and AstroTurf All-Star Game: Willie Mays scores only run for N.L. win in 1968 classic

Toy Cannon Jimmy Wynn hit 223 homers here . . . Second baseman Joe Morgan began Hall of Fame career here

JEFF BAGWELL:
The brawn behind Astros' Killer B's
(Biggio, Derek Bell)

Millions of visitors marveled at her grandeur and millions more were mesmerized by tales of her majesty and mystique. During her prime, Houston's Astrodome was the grandest lady in all of sports, the queen of a universe beyond anyone's imagination. During her twilight years, she served as a stately reminder of what can be achieved when vision and dreams are stretched beyond the boundaries.

You never lost that sense of elegance and vision over the Astrodome's 35-year reign as home of the Houston Astros. Whether

Mets' broadcaster Lindsey Nelson calls Mets-Astros game from gondola 208 feet directly above second base, April 28, 1965

Bagwell hits two homers in one inning, three in game—a 16-4 win over Dodgers, June 24, 1994

1980, '86 West champs; 1997, '98, '99 Central champs—but no pennant

Game called due to "rain-in" June 15, 1976. Players made it to Dome, but umps, fans and stadium personnel were unable to make it through flooded Houston

Where Giants' Willie Mays hit 500th career home run, Sept. 13, 1965

Error by Mets shortstop Al Weis lets in winning run, ending 24-inning 1-0 marathon, April 15, 1968

Randy Johnson shuts out Phillies on five hits in first Houston start as Bagwell homers twice, Aug. 7, 1998

Fireballer J.R. Richard suffers stroke while playing catch during workout, July 30, 1980 . . . Manager Larry Dierker suffers seizure during June 13, 1999 game vs. Padres

Cesar Cedeno (above) performed defensive magic here for 12 seasons. . . Jose Cruz did the same for 13

Braves beat Astros 7-5 in Game 4 of 1999 Division Series—final game at Astrodome

Houston native Roger Clemens claims MVP honors in 3-2 A.L. All-Star win, July 15, 1986

Where Phillies' Pete Rose bowled over catcher Bruce Bochy and scored winning run in 10th inning of Game 4 in 1980 NLCS

Mike Scott pitches no-hitter vs. Giants as Astros clinch West Division title in spectacular fashion, Sept. 25, 1986

Second baseman CRAIG BIGGIO jump starts the offense

stepping into this futuristic wonderland in 1965 or paying your last respects in 1999, you always came away with a feeling of immensity and history—the sense that this huge, overwhelming, multi-purpose structure was the first of its kind and that the innovations that sprang from it would continue to have an impact on the sports world long after playing host to its final event.

The Astrodome was never about charm, charisma or beauty, characteristics long associated with America's ballparks. It was about that Texas-like appetite for big, powerful and extravagant. Conceived, pushed and coddled to completion by Astros owner Judge Roy Hofheinz in 1965 as an antidote to the oppressive Texas heat, the structure became the most incredible sports facility ever constructed— the so-called Eighth Wonder of the World.

Indeed, the Astrodome will forever be credited as the inspiration for the new craze of sports arenas that gripped the country in the 1970s and '80s. It provided undeniable proof that baseball could be played indoors, it introduced AstroTurf,

a synthetic playing surface that changed the way the game was played, it showed the viability of multi-purpose facilities in today's economic world and it gave credence to the idea that comfort, luxury and other extravagances could be part of the ballpark experience.

Extravagance was the name of the game when the Astrodome was unveiled in 1965 as the world's first covered stadium. It seemed to glow, like a crown jewel, set all by itself in the open fields of south Houston, surrounded only by an expansive parking lot—a 9 1/2-acre fantasy island. The structure was immense, a feeling that really struck home when you stepped inside.

The dome literally exploded overhead, like a cascading fireworks display. The dome's panels were held in place by steel-framed supports that worked their way skyward toward the 208-foot apex—a dynamic, intricately-patterned puzzle for the eye. It was an architectural marvel that never escaped attention, no matter how many times you attended games there.

Animated video characters (top), extravagant suites (center) and vacuuming astronauts were part of the experience when the Astrodome (right) was unveiled in 1965.

In the late 1960s, visitors from all over the world flocked to Houston to get a first-hand look at baseball's Eighth Wonder of the World.

Neither could you escape the eye-blinking vividness of the multi-colored seats, spread over six decks, and a 474-foot scoreboard that wrapped around much of the perimeter above the outfield. The board displayed information as well as animated cartoons, the most amazing of which celebrated an Astros home run with snorting bulls and a six-gun battle between two cowboys over the length of the board. The scoreboard remained an Astrodome landmark until it

The incredible ceiling, speakers dangling from above, waves of seats circling the AstroTurf field: This upper-deck view shows the Astrodome in all of its glory.

was dismantled after the 1988 season and replaced by more state-of-the-art video boards.

"All the comforts of home," as advertised, was not an Astrodome illusion. Cushioned seats looked down on a carpeted field that was designed for baseball. The facility was air-conditioned, escalators transported fans, skylights and floodlights simulated the brightness of a clear, sunny afternoon and there was enough plumbing in place for 40,000 fans to wash their hands simultaneously. The only suffering here was during an Astros' loss.

Hofheinz's vision of a "spectator's paradise", free from the heat, cold, wind, rain and mosquitoes that affect games and comfort levels at other major league parks, was a critical success—an architectural breakthrough that soon would be copied by other cities, but never with the classy vision that went into the Astrodome. It also was Hofheinz's vision to use real grass, but the transparent

ceiling panels created such a horrible glare during afternoon games that the panels had to be covered by a translucent acrylic coating. With the sun blocked out, the grass died, thus creating a necessity for AstroTurf.

Over the years, the Astrodome was a good place to watch baseball, even with a few quirky ground rules dictated by the oddities of indoor baseball. Incredulous fans during a 1974 game watched Philadelphia third baseman Mike Schmidt hit what appeared to be a prodigious home run, only to see the ball carom off a speaker and drop into short left-center field for a single. There was even a rule that declared pigeons in play, just in case one might be struck by a batted ball.

The Astros, a 3-year-old expansion team when the Astrodome was built, shared the facility with the National Football League's Oilers for 29 seasons, but no team was more closely associated with a stadium. Early Houston clubs, playing in one of baseball's most difficult home run parks, were turf teams that relied

The Astrodome was less than three weeks old when Lindsey Nelson and producer Joel Nixon broadcast a game for the Mets from the gondola (above) suspended from the apex of the dome over second base.

on speed, defense and pitching. It wasn't until 1980 that a team led by Jose Cruz, Cesar Cedeno, Phil Niekro and J.R. Richard won the Astros' first division title and sustained success did not arrive until the Jeff Bagwell, Craig Biggio-led teams of the late 1990s.

Astrodome patrons have never witnessed a World Series, but the facility has drawn other major events like a magnet. Billy Graham crusaded there and Judy Garland, the Supremes, Elvis Presley and the Rolling Stones made people dance. This is where Muhammad Ali introduced his Ali Shuffle, Billie Jean King overwhelmed Bobby Riggs and Elvin Hayes outdueled UCLA and Lew Alcindor. Movie scenes have been filmed at the Astrodome, as have scenes from a Final Four and a Republican National Convention.

It seemed only fitting that the Astros' final game of the millennium and the final baseball game at the Astrodome would come in postseason play. The Braves' 7-5 Division Series win on October 9, 1999, dropped the curtain on the most heralded, most talked about and most innovative sports arena ever to grace the earth.

THE ASTRODOME (1965-1999)

It was officially named the Harris County Domed Stadium, but it always and forever will be the Astrodome, a symbol of not just the city's future but of the nation's future as well.

Having been awarded an expansion franchise in 1960, major league baseball began in Houston in 1962. In April of that year, the Colt .45s opened play in Colt Stadium. As the nation soared into space, and to honor Houston's ground control role, the Colt .45s were renamed the Astros and the stadium became the Astrodome in 1964.

The Astrodome remains standing, a landmark on the south outskirts of the city you can't miss as you drive past on I-610. The city's new baseball stadium will be located downtown, but the new football stadium is being erected on the Astrodome site. Plans for the future of the Astrodome structure are undecided.

First game: April 12, 1965. The Astrodome was officially christened with a 2-0 Phillies victory. Three days before, on April 9, the Astros and Yankees played an exhibition game, with President Lyndon Johnson in attendance, and Mickey Mantle cracked the first home run.

Final game: October 9, 1999. The Astros' bid to bring a World Series to the Astrodome are stymied as the Braves beat Houston, 7-5, in a Division Series game.

■ Site of no World Series
■ Site of two All-Star Games (1968 and 1986)

Metropolitan Stadium

Where seat was painted orange in honor of longest homer in stadium history —Killebrew's 520-footer on June 3, 1967

Orioles sweep Twins in first two ALCS, 1969, '70

Where Eddie Stanky managed Texas Rangers for one game before resigning, June 22, 1977

Killebrew hits 500th career home run vs. Orioles, Aug. 10, 1971

Where Bob Allison (right) made spectacular tumbling catch to help Jim Kaat (left) win Game 2 of 1965 World Series

Killebrew's 1965 All-Star Game home run landed, appropriately in "Killer Country"

It was a visual shock, a multi-decked baseball arena that rose unexpectedly out of an isolated Bloomington cornfield. You couldn't help but smile when you spotted Metropolitan Stadium, which was anything but "metropolitan" when it opened its gates to major league baseball in 1961. Located on a barren 164-acre tract about 15 miles south of Minneapolis, the Met lured you in with its curious patchwork charm and won you over with its folksy, down-home graciousness.

More than anything, the Met was friendly, a sociable,

HARMON KILLEBREW, alias The Killer, holds team career marks for home runs (559), total bases (4,026) and RBIs (1,540)

Bob Allison and Killebrew become first teammates to hit grand slams in same inning, July 18, 1962

MVP shortstop Zoilo Versalles leads Twins to 1965 pennant

Where Ken Landreaux compiled 31-game hitting streak in 1980

Tim Laudner homers in first two major league games, Aug. 28, 29, 1981

Twins pound Athletics with five homers in one inning: Rich Rollins, Zoilo Versalles, Tony Oliva, Don Mincher and Killebrew, June 9, 1966

Mudcat Grant's three-run homer, strong pitching win Game 6 of '65 Series

Where .089-hitting pitcher Mike Cuellar deposited wind-blown grand slam in Game 1 of 1970 ALCS

Where Carew tied record by stealing home for seventh time in season, July 16, 1969

Kansas City's Bert Campaneris becomes second player in baseball history to homer twice in first major league game, July 23, 1964

iere Camilo Pascual (above) 1 Bert Blyleven threw nasty ves at hitters for the better part of 1960s and '70s

Orioles' Jim Gentile hits grand slams in consecutive innings vs. Twins, May 9, 1961

Cesar Tovar plays all nine positions in one game, Sept. 22, 1968

Tony Oliva bats .323, becomes first rookie to win batting championship, 1964

ROD CAREW captured seven A.L. batting titles in 10 years, challenged magic .400 with .388 mark in 1977

A triple-deck grandstand gave way to single-deck bleachers in left field (above). The Met was dressed to kill (left) for the 1965 All-Star Game.

unpretentious ballpark not unlike the personality of Twins teams that called it home for 21 special seasons. It was a hitter's paradise, a home run haven without an attitude. This was the place to go for summer-long fireworks and instant gratification, the perfect spot for baseball with an explosive edge.

At first glance, you had to wonder exactly what the Met's architects had in mind. The park looked like a giant Erector set with a crazy combination of single, double and triple decks that appeared to be squeezed together in a design-as-you-go floor plan. The configuration, while odd, seemed to complement a strange blend of colored brick panels and corrugated metal that gave the exterior a look falling somewhere between charming and tacky.

The stands that wrapped around home plate and the infield were triple-decked and those that continued down the right field line to the foul pole were double-decked, as were the expansive (many claimed ugly) fair-territory stands that stretched from the foul pole to center field. Nestled between the triple-decked grandstand and the left field pole were unusual foul-territory bleachers, single-decked but sectioned with blue chair seats in the lower area and wooden planks in the upper. Fans could enjoy a smaller fair-territory bleacher area in right.

None of the stands was covered, giving the park an open-air feel unlike any other in baseball. On beautiful summer afternoons and evenings, that was a blessing. But when it rained or a gusting wind chilled the Minnesota night air, you might feel differently. Another ballpark oddity was the up-and-down ramps outside the stadium, connected to the back of the grandstands like giant leeches.

This was a between-eras ballpark without the quirky charms of an Ebbets

Field or the natural beauty of a Kauffman Stadium. It was built in 1955 with the hopes of luring a major league team to Minneapolis and it was designed with expansion in mind, an unusual concept at that time. The triple-decked grandstand was in place when the American Association's Minneapolis Millers began play there in 1956, but the second decks were added for the 1961 baseball and football seasons when Calvin Griffith relocated his Washington Senators to Minneapolis and the city was awarded an NFL expansion franchise—the Vikings—raising capacity to 45,919.

No baseball park has been more closely tied to the physical makeup of its teams. And few players have more single-handedly influenced the personality of a stadium than a gentle giant with the unlikely nickname of "Killer." Harmon Killebrew, who packed 210 pounds of muscle into his stocky 6-foot frame, quickly discovered the Met's friendly disposition toward home runs and spent the next 14 years carving his name into baseball's all-time power charts.

It wasn't that Metropolitan Stadium offered short home run distances; balls just shot out of the park, often aided by friendly breezes. The park was a symmetrical 330-412-330 when it opened, an asymmetrical 343-402-330 when it closed after the 1981 season. Distance didn't matter to Killebrew, a Washington holdover who became the centerpiece for an offensive machine and the most popular player in Twins history—a popularity that has not diminished more than a quarter century after his retirement.

The 1961-70 Twins literally powered their way to one A.L. pennant (1965) and two division titles (1969, '70) behind the booming bats of Killebrew, Bob Allison, Jim Lemon, Tony Oliva, Jimmie Hall, Earl Battey, Don Mincher and Rod Carew. No seat in the outfield stands was safe, including the left field second deck that Killebrew once reached with a shot estimated at 520 feet. The power display (the Twins hit 446 homers in 1963 and '64 combined) was so impressive, the Met scoreboard in right-center field began posting home run distances—a baseball first.

That scoreboard was a Metropolitan Stadium staple through most of its existence. The basic, no-frills board, with advertisements across the top and a Longines clock perched above, posted lineups, basic information and out-of-town scores. A rectangular backdrop, centered by a towering flagpole, sat next to the scoreboard in an otherwise open center field area. For many years, bullpens were located in front of the scoreboard.

Layout and intimacy were among the Met's special quirks—as well as the ability to move freely around the park and enjoy an interesting variety of views. You could start in an underground concourse, suddenly find yourself in an open bleacher, cross through a tunnel here, over a runway there. There were so many ways of getting places—in and out, over and around. A chain-link fence formed the 8-foot left field barrier for many years and fans could pass under the elevated stands, stop and get a great field-level view of the action.

By the mid-1970s, the Twins had dropped in the standings and their stadium, poorly maintained, had fallen into disrepair. The Met survived through the 1981 season, after which both the Twins and Vikings moved into Minnesota's new Metrodome—a state-of-the-art facility that could offer comfort and amenities, but never rival its predecessor in intimacy and personality.

METROPOLITAN STADIUM (1961-1981)

Pre-dating Metropolitan Stadium and major league baseball in the Twin Cities were two minor league teams: the Millers, who played in Nicollet Park in Minneapolis, and the Saints, who played in Lexington Park in St. Paul.

The Met opened in 1956, even after a fire in February of that year destroyed part of the stands, as the home of the Millers. (In '57, the Saints moved into brand-new Midway Stadium.)

It wasn't until 1961, after the Senators relocated to Minnesota and were renamed the Twins, that major league baseball debuted at the Met.

Built in a once remote cornfield, the site is now smack in the middle of suburban sprawl. The stadium was torn down in 1985. Today, the famous Mall of America, bound on one side by Killebrew Drive, marks the site.

First game: April 21, 1961. The "new" Washington Senators, an expansion ballclub after the "old" Senators relocated to Minnesota, beat those "old" Senators — now known as the Twins, 5-3.

Final game: September 30, 1981. Only 15,900 attended the closer, a 5-2 loss to the Royals.

■ Site of one World Series (1965)
■ Site of one All-Star Game (1965)

Polo Grounds

254

Rube Marquard beats Brooklyn 2-1 for record 19th straight victory, July 3, 1912

Braves end Giants' record 26-game winning streak, Sept. 30, 1916

Landing spot for Bobby Thomson's 1951 Shot Heard 'Round the World

Visitor's bullpen

At first glance, the Polo Grounds was a baseball illusion—an elongated, horseshoe-shaped arena with a compressed field squeezed into its unorthodox contours. It was awkward, clumsy and disjointed, a 19th century relic with a 20th century soul. It was an ugly house of pain for visitors, a stately cathedral for New York baseball worshipers. You had to look deep to see the soul, but you couldn't miss a powerful aura that cloaked one of the great sports venues in history.

The aura was built around a legacy of success and some of the game's most rabid fans. The Polo Grounds, home for three major league teams over its 73-year history, played host to 14 World Series and five champions

Rawlings-to-Kelly-to Frisch double play (4-3-5) brings stunning Game 8 conclusion to Giants' 1921 World Series win over Yankees in the first Battle of New York

Where Heinie Zimmerman chased Eddie Collins across plate in Game 6 of 1917 World Series—the play that gave White Sox championship

CARL HUBBELL: Five-time 20-game winner used nasty screwball to strike out Ruth, Gehrig, Foxx, Simmons and Cronin consecutively in 1934 All-Star Game

Batter's box where Indians shortstop Ray Chapman was struck by fatal pitch from Carl Mays, Aug. 16, 1920

Giants pennants in 1904, '05, '11, '12, '13, '17, '21, '22, 23', '24, '33, '36, '37, '51, '54
Yankees pennants in 1921, '22

Park where Casey Stengel and Amazin' Mets lost 120 games in 1962

Ott hits 500th career home run, Aug. 1, 1945

Cubs' Mordecai Brown outduels Christy Mathewson 4-2 in one-game pennant-deciding playoff forced by Merkle's boner, Oct. 8, 1908

Where Joe DiMaggio made final putout of 1936 World Series Game 2 and ran up the clubhouse steps

483 feet to clubhouse facade behind Eddie Grant memorial statue

Spot where Dusty Rhodes' 260-foot game-ending home run landed in opener of 1954 World Series

Spot where Willie Mays pulled in Vic Wertz smash during Game 1 of 1954 World Series

Three players reached center field bleachers with home runs— Joe Adcock in 1953, Lou Brock and Hank Aaron in 1962

New York bullpen

Fred Merkle failed to touch second during 1908 game vs. Cubs, costing Giants a pennant

...ere Hubbell shut out Cardinals 1-0 ...n 18-inning thriller, July 2, 1933

The great John McGraw (left) managed Giants to 10 pennants, 3 championships in 30 years

Christy Mathewson (right) shuts out A's for third time in six days, closes out 1905 World Series with 2-0 Game 5 win

MEL OTT: 511 career home runs, six N.L. homer titles over 22-year Giants career

The horseshoe-shaped Polo Grounds and its bathtub-like field configuration stood as a New York baseball landmark through the 1963 season. Yankee Stadium, which was opened in 1923, was located a few fly balls away, on the other side of the Harlem River.

while providing a Hall of Fame arena for Christy Mathewson, Ross Youngs, Fred Lindstrom, Mel Ott, Travis Jackson, Bill Terry, Carl Hubbell and a young Willie Mays, who learned to Say Hey in its expansive center field. Babe Ruth won two home run titles here before building his own house across the Harlem River.

This was the stage where John McGraw choreographed Giants victories for more than three decades and Casey Stengel choreographed Mets losses for two seasons. Three of the most memorable moments in baseball history occurred on these hallowed grounds—Fred Merkle's boner cost the Giants a pennant in 1908, Bobby Thomson's homer won them a pennant in 1951 and Mays' catch helped them reach championship heights in 1954.

To fully appreciate the modern-era Polo Grounds, you must envision a huge bathtub with a baseball diamond crammed inside. The result was an outlandish field with peculiar dimensions and quirks unlike any other in baseball. The double-deck grandstands circled deep behind home plate (one end of the tub) and rounded off, continuing straight along the entire lengths of the structure before making slight curves at the opposite end. With home plate centered against the two curved ends, half of the side grandstands were in foul territory, the other half in fair.

As a result, lefthanded hitters could pull a fly ball down the right field line and watch it drop into the lower-deck grandstands for a 257-foot home run. Righthanders could line a ball over the 17-foot wall 279 feet down the left field line, or they could drop a fly into an upper-deck overhang that reduced the distance closer to 250. But woe to any slugger who failed to pull the ball. As the grandstands continued, they angled deeper away from the batter, reaching 455 feet at the curve in left-center and 449 in right-center.

Both grandstands made the turn and stopped, leaving an opening in dead center field. They were divided by two bleacher sections that in turn were divided by a 60-foot building housing both teams' clubhouses and administrative offices. The clubhouse, decorated in later years by a Chesterfield cigarette sign and topped by a Longines clock and flagpole, was indented from the field, 483 feet from home plate, and twin staircases on both sides led players to and from their dressing quarters.

Teams without a speedy center fielder were in trouble at the Polo Grounds, where balls eluding an outfielder could roll all the way to Yankee Stadium after striking the angled left and right field walls. Adding to the quirky nature of the park were inconsistent fences—17 feet at the left field pole, rising to 18 in left-

The right-center field grandstand (above) was a long way from home plate, as was the park's signature feature, a center field clubhouse that attracted autograph seekers (above right), especially before games vs. the Dodgers. The clubhouse indent only complicated life for outfielders (below right).

center and sloping to 12 where the grandstand met the bleachers—and sunken outfields that allowed managers standing in their dugouts to see only the top half of their fielders.

Standing in front of the clubhouse, in fair territory, was a 5-foot memorial statue of Captain Eddie Grant, a former Giants infielder killed during World War I, and plaques honoring Mathewson, McGraw and Youngs hung on the clubhouse facade. The bleacher seats were fronted by an 8-foot wall (4-foot wall, 4-foot screen) and two dark-green canvas backdrops (20 feet-by-17 feet) topped the corners of the bleachers, 460 feet from the plate. The bullpens, topped by a slanting roof, were located on each of the off-center field curves—the only fair-territory bullpens in baseball.

Nothing could prepare you properly for a game at the Polo Grounds. Seeing was believing and all you could do was shake your head at the extremes to which the park would take you. Pop flies would turn into home runs if placed accurately down one of the lines. A monumental smash to center could wind up in somebody's glove, a long, unfortunate out.

The Polo Grounds, a myriad of ramps and entryways (left), provided a scenic view from Coogan's Bluff (right). The upper-deck facing at the old Polo Grounds (above) was ornately decorated with the coats of arms of all N.L. teams.

Giants reliever Don Liddle understood the park in 1954 when he served up a Game 1 World Series pitch that Cleveland's Vic Wertz drove 460 feet toward the right-center field backdrop, only to see Mays pull it in with an amazing over-the-shoulder catch. In the 10th inning of that same contest, Indians starter Bob Lemon let Dusty Rhodes pull a routine fly ball down the right field line and it dropped into the seats for a 260-foot game-winning home run.

If the cheap home run was a Polo Grounds personality flaw, the center field grand canyon more than compensated. In the ballpark's long history, only three balls reached the distant bleachers—Joe Adcock in 1953 and Lou Brock and Hank Aaron on consecutive days in 1962—and no ball ever struck the clubhouse. The park also was hard on pitchers who had to make the long, ego-deflating walk to the center field clubhouse after being knocked from a game.

The Polo Grounds traces its roots back to 1890, when it was built for a team in the outlaw Players League in the northern half of Coogan's Hollow, a grassy meadow in the shadow of Coogan's Bluff. James J. Coogan, a wealthy landowner and Manhattan borough president, had already leased the southern half of the Hollow to the National League's Giants, where they built Manhattan Field. Broth-

POLO GROUNDS (1891-1957; 1962-63)

It was the third of three parks known as the Polo Grounds. The first — at 110th and Sixth Avenue, built on grounds that were used to play polo, hence the name — lasted from 1883-1888. The second, at 155th and Eighth, was home from 1889 to 1890.

The third Polo Grounds stood at 157th and Eighth Avenue, on what had been known as Brotherhood Park. In 1911, it was destroyed by fire, but after just two months in temporary quarters, it was rebuilt enough for the Giants to return.

By 1912, steel-and-concrete reconstruction was complete; in 1923, after losing the Yankees as tenants, another expansion was completed.

The Giants moved to San Francisco following the 1957 season, and the expansion Mets played in the Polo Grounds until their new facility, Shea Stadium, was ready. In 1964, the Polo Grounds finally met its demise when demolition took down the facility.

First game: April 22, 1891. Boston beat the Giants, 4-3.

Final game: September 18, 1963. Playing before a disappointing crowd of only 1,752, the Mets officially closed the historic park with a 5-1 loss to the Phillies.

■ Site of 14 World Series (1905, '11, '12, '13, '17, '21, '22, '23, '24, '33, '36, '37, '51 and '54)

■ Site of two All-Star Games (1934 and 1942)

This field-level view shows the Polo Grounds the way it must have appeared to box seat patrons around mid-20th century. Note how close the left and right field foul poles must have seemed to hitters.

erhood Park, the Players League facility, was built in an elongated shape so it could squeeze between Manhattan Field and the bluff.

When the Players League collapsed after the 1890 season, John B. Day acquired the larger Brotherhood Park and moved his Giants into their new home, in the north Harlem section of Manhattan on the west side of Eighth Avenue between 157th and 159th streets. Home plate was directly beneath Coogan's bluff and center field looked out toward the Harlem River.

It was in this wooden ballpark, dubbed the Polo Grounds after a former Giants home, that McGraw built his early championship teams, Mathewson recorded four 30-plus-win seasons and Merkle made his costly boner. Stairs led down from the bluff to the Polo Grounds ticket offices (later replaced by inclined ramps) and the outfield was open, so the gentry could watch action from their horse-drawn carriages parked behind a center field rope.

When the Polo Grounds burned to the ground in a 1911 fire, owner John T. Brush rebuilt it as a steel-and-concrete structure with an imposing double-deck, roofed grandstand that stopped at the foul pole in left and extended well past the pole in right. Coats of arms of all the N.L. teams were displayed on the upper grandstand facade, a feature that eventually was removed. The old Polo Grounds configuration was retained, but now there were single-deck stands circling the rest of the structure.

After the 1922 season, a renovation gave the Polo Grounds a 55,000 seating capacity and the basic look it would retain over its final four decades. The grandstands were extended, the bleachers and clubhouse were added and scoreboards were perched on the second-deck facade at the foul lines. The lower stands behind the plate extended out from the upper deck and circled to a point well down both lines. Lights would not be installed until 1940.

Through much of the Polo Grounds' 73-year existence it was a championship mecca for baseball, pro and college football and boxing. During their 67-year Polo Grounds stay, the Giants set the baseball success standard by which generations of franchises would be measured. The American League Yankees were saucy young wannabes while the Giants were winning pennants and championships in the first quarter of the century and the teams even shared the Polo Grounds from 1913 to 1922—and World Series revenues when all 13 games of the 1921 and '22 classics were played there, both Series wins for the Giants.

That dominance would change. But one thing that wouldn't was the loud, crazy, demanding and cocky fans who viewed McGraw's Giants as superior and liked to rub their success in the noses of Brooklyn fans. The Giants-Dodgers rivalry bordered on hatred and the Polo Grounds was a forum for some of the most intense battles ever staged. The rivalry was epitomized by the incredible 1951 N.L. pennant race that ended in a Dodgers-Giants tie and was settled by Thomson's playoff home

run—the Shot Heard 'Round the World.

When the Giants jilted their New York fans for the greener pastures of San Francisco after the 1957 season, baseball cut its ties with the ancient, decaying Polo Grounds for the first time in almost seven decades. The stadium returned to the baseball wars four years later as the temporary home of the expansion New York Mets, but after two Amazin' years (1962 and '63) and 231 losses, the proud old ballpark in the shadow of Coogan's Bluff played host to its final game. It was razed one year later.

The final Giants game at the venerable Polo Grounds in 1957 sent New York fans on a riotous rampage (below). The Giants opened the 1958 campaign in San Francisco.

Shibe Park

Home of A's $100,000 infield: Home Run Baker, Jack Barry, Eddie Collins, Stuffy McInnis

Jimmie Foxx was first player to clear left field grandstand in 1928 . . . Dick Allen (left) hit longest homer over barrier, a shot estimated at 529 feet in 1965

Shibe, renamed Connie Mack Stadium in 1953, was home of A 1909-54, Phillies 1938-70

1950 Whiz Kids win first N.L. pennant since 1915, fall to Yankees in World Series sweep . . . 1964 Phillies lose 10 of fina 12 games in collapse that costs them pennant

Boston's Jim Tabor hits four homers, two of them grand slams, and drives in 11 runs in 17-7 and 18-12 Red Sox doubleheader sweep, July 4, 1939

In first A.L. night game, Indians defeat A's 8-3, May 16, 1939

Where Bobby Doerr hit three-run homer in 1943 All-Star Game

Down 15-4 after 7 1/2 innings, A's rally for 13 runs in eighth and post improbable 17-15 win over stunned Indians, June 15, 1925

ROBIN ROBERTS: Talented righthander recorded six straight 20-win seasons for Phillies, 1950-55

Al Simmons drove in 322 runs over 1929 (165) and '30 (157) campaigns

T o Philadelphia sports fans, it was "the tower." To out-of-town visitors, it was a French Renaissance-style landmark, a dome worthy of any baseball basilica. If you didn't genuflect when you spotted the main entrance of Shibe Park, you at least uttered a little prayer to the timeless spirit and incredible perseverance of the great Connie Mack. This wasn't a church, but it's not hard to understand why most Philadelphians approached it with a sense of veneration and reverence.

Seven American League pennants, one National League pennant and five

Scorecard-waving Connie Mack built and rebuilt teams that won seven A.L. pennants and five championships—1910, '11, '13, '29 and '30—over 50-year managing career

Two Home Run Baker blasts spark A's in 1911 World Series . . . Mule Haas' Game 7 homer helps decide 1929 classic

Eddie Plank (left) fires two-hitter, outduels Christy Mathewson in 1913 Game 5 World Series clincher vs. Giants

Longines clock, 75 feet high

4-3 loss to Giants begins Phillies' major league-record 23-game losing streak, July 29, 1961

Jimmie Foxx's 500th home run, hit fittingly at Shibe, comes in Red Sox uniform, Sept. 24, 1940

Connie Mack's 34-foot "spite fence" was erected in 1935

Where Hack Wilson lost ball in sun, owing Mule Haas to circle bases during 0-run seventh-inning explosion that wiped out 8-0 Cubs lead in Game 4 of 1929 World Series

Dodgers' Jackie Robinson hits dramatic 14th-inning homer to beat Phillies, set stage for 1951 pennant-deciding playoff vs. Giants

Yankees second baseman Tony Lazzeri powers two grand slams, drives in A.L.-record 11 runs in 25-2 rout of A's, May 24, 1936

A's post 24-2 win over team of amateur players recruited by Detroit management to replace striking Tigers, May 18, 1912

Boston's Ted Williams completes .406 1941 season with 6-for-8 doubleheader performance on final day

Park where Yankee Lou Gehrig 32) and Chicago's Pat Seerey (1948) enjoyed four-homer games

here Miracle Braves steamrolled A's first two games of shocking 1914 World Series sweep

Jimmie Foxx: Two-time MVP pounded 302 of his 534 career homers for Athletics, including 58 in 1932

The great LEFTY GROVE was 31-4 in incredible 1931 MVP season

World Series championships were won here. This was where Hall of Famers Eddie Plank, Home Run Baker, Chief Bender, Mickey Cochrane, Jimmie Foxx, Al Simmons, Lefty Grove, Eddie Collins, Robin Roberts, Richie Ashburn and Jim Bunning mastered their craft; where two dynasties were built—and ripped apart. This was a temple and a house divided, a place where fans experienced both winning ecstasy and losing despair while supporting the Athletics for 46 years and the Phillies for 32—16-plus as co-tenants of the North Philadelphia palace at 21st and Lehigh.

To fully appreciate Shibe Park, you first must understand Mack's Philadelphia presence—from 1901 co-founder of the A.L. Athletics franchise with Benjamin Shibe and eventual owner to 50 years as the team's field boss. From his top-of-the-tower office he ruled the business side of the operation; from his dugout office he dictated lineups and strategy with trademark waves of his ever-present scorecard. No one person more singlehandedly determined the look and personality of a ballpark than the gaunt, grim-faced Mack—baseball's last manager in street clothes.

Shibe Park, like Mack, was always stately, even while its teams ran the gamut from great to awful. Opened in 1909 as baseball's first steel-and-concrete facility, it was hailed as a crown jewel, the prototype by which a whole generation of new ballparks would be measured. Pittsburgh quickly countered with Forbes Field, Chicago with Comiskey Park and Wrigley Field, Boston with Fenway Park and Detroit

SHIBE PARK (1909-1970)

Renamed Connie Mack Stadium (1953-1970)

It opened as the home of the Philadelphia Athletics and closed as home of the Phillies. In between it spent a full life as home to both.

Shibe Park, named in honor of Ben Shibe, a baseball manufacturer and principal owner of the Athletics, opened in 1909. For the eight preceding years, the A's had played in Columbia Park, just a mile and a half from the eventual Shibe Park site.

Philadelphia had another facility, Baker Bowl, named for Phillies owner William Baker, where the Phillies played from 1887 through 1938. Baker Bowl suffered a number of grandstand collapses and fires in its lifetime. In 1927, a grandstand collapse forced the Phillies to play 12 games at Shibe. With Baker Bowl in a state of disrepair, the Phillies moved into Shibe in 1938 and shared it with the A's until 1954, when the A's bolted for Kansas City. Baker Bowl was destroyed in the early 1950s.

In 1953, Shibe was renamed Connie Mack Stadium. Mack, the renowned Athletics manager, had rebuffed for years efforts to rename the stadium in his honor. In 1952, while Mack was in Florida, the board of directors renamed it Connie Mack Stadium and it remained that way until its final days in 1970.

In 1976, Connie Mack Stadium was demolished, and the site at 21st and Lehigh sat vacant until 1990, when a church was built there.

First game: April 12, 1909. The Athletics beat the Red Sox, 8-1, with an announced attendance of 30,162 in a stadium with a capacity for 20,000.

Final game: October 1, 1970. Oscar Gamble's 10th-inning single drove home Tim McCarver and the Phillies beat the Expos, 2-1.

■ Site of eight World Series (1910, '11, '13, '14, '29, '30, '31 and '50)
■ Site of two All-Star Games (1943 and '52)

Shibe Park's stately 'tower' (left) stood guard at the intersection of 21st and Lehigh from 1909-70, when the Phillies moved to Veterans Stadium.

with Navin Field. Some could come close, others could match, but none could ever top the energy and dignity Shibe retained throughout its 62-year existence.

"Connie Mack Stadium (its name from 1953-70) had character," Ashburn recalled in a 1975 story for the Philadelphia Evening Bulletin. "It looked like a ballpark. It smelled like a ballpark. It had feeling and a heartbeat, a personality that was all baseball. Players could sit in the clubhouse and see and hear the fans, and you could hear the vendors selling hot dogs and programs. It was a total baseball experience."

That character started with the French-style facade that greeted its first visitors in 1909 and extended inside to the innovative folding chairs, sparkling clean corri-

dors, underground garages, below-grandstand tunnels that allowed players private passage from clubhouses to dugouts and even restrooms with attendants and matrons. A double-deck grandstand wrapped behind home plate to the infield edge on both sides and single-deck bleachers extended down both lines to the foul poles.

There was no fair-territory seating, a feature that would change in 1913 with the addition of bleachers that extended from the left field pole to mid-center field, just short of the flagpole. A 1925 renovation added second decks and a roof to all single-deck seats, giving the park a 33,000-seat capacity and the basic look it would retain for the remainder of its years—three-quarters enclosed and roofed, with only right field open to the outside world.

That, too, would change, but not without a battle of wills and much gnashing of teeth among the owners of houses along 20th Street. Early Shibe featured a 12-foot concrete wall in right field, an 8-foot concrete wall topped by a 4-foot wire screen in left. The 20th Street houses offered perfect rooftop perches for fans, hundreds of whom would pay their 25 cents to house owners, climb to makeshift seats and get a suntan as well as a full view of action over the right field wall.

This practice endured from 1909 until 1935, when Mack finally tired of the free-bies. He erected a 22-foot wall extension—corrugated sheet iron that brought its height to 34 feet and blocked the view of rooftop squatters. Mack's "spite fence," challenged in court by neighborhood residents, endured through the life of Shibe Park, creating a monstrous challenge for left-handed hitters. "Guys like me just couldn't hit home runs there because of that wall," said former A's outfielder Elmer Valo. "It was just too high."

And unpredictable. The corrugated fence had ripples that resulted in tricky bounces and awkward ricochets, forcing outfielders to keep their distance and surround balls they normally would play aggressively. In the mid-1950s, a 12-foot wooden fence was installed 2 feet in front of the steel wall to protect outfielders from getting hurt. Balls hitting the lower fence traveled 329 feet; balls hitting the upper wall 331. In 1956, a giant electric scoreboard purchased from Yankee Stadium was installed in right-center field, making a big stretch of the wall 50 feet high with a dropoff to 34 on either side. A Longines clock, perched atop the board, was 75 feet above the field.

Activity along 20th Street was always fun, even after the high wall was erected. Kids looking for home run balls that could get them free entrance to a game roamed the street, as did an A's employee who would keep overeager fans from scaling the wall. If a house window was broken by a batted ball, a worker would appear within 15 minutes to install a new one.

Shibe was known as a hitter's park and a showcase for prodigious home runs. The original dimensions of 378 feet to left, 515 to center and 340 to right produced lots of extra-base hits and a 90-foot distance from home plate to backstop turned an agile catcher like Cochrane into a fourth outfielder. But the 1925 renovations reduced left field to 334, center to 468 and right to 331, creating inviting targets for sluggers like Jimmie Foxx, who hit 28 balls over the left field roof; Bill Nicholson and Babe Ruth, who hit shots over the 20th Street rooftops onto Opal Street; Ted Williams, who hit a ball that landed in a back yard on 20th Street; and Dick Allen, who hit the only ball to clear the huge right-center field scoreboard.

Shibe was always an intimate ballpark that put fans close to the action and

From 1925 on, Shibe (above right) was three-quarters enclosed, roofed and open to rooftops in right. The scoreboard, installed in 1956, measured 75 feet to the top of the clock and the mound had a distinctive dirt path to the plate.

encouraged relationships with players. It also was one of the best maintained ballparks in baseball with a crack groundskeeping crew that kept the grass green and manicured to perfection. No team enjoyed a field tailored more to the talents of its players. And sound echoed through Shibe like nowhere else, giving pitchers a psychological edge when their routine fastballs popped the catcher's glove like a 100-mph heater.

Nowhere was success more appreciated, especially during those incredible Mack dynasty years of 1910-14 (four pennants, three Series winners) and 1929-31 (three straight pennants, two Series titles). And nowhere was futility more sustained (four winning records in 21 years from 1934-54, after which the A's were sold and moved from Philadelphia to Kansas City). One of the beauties of Shibe was that you could see a baseball game virtually every day or night there from 1938-54, when the A's shared the facility with the N.L. Phillies, who bought the aging park and continued playing there through 1970.

The Phillies' only run at Shibe Park success came in 1950, when the Whiz Kids captured the team's first pennant since 1915 on Dick Sisler's three-run, 10th-inning, final-day home run that produced a 4-1 victory over Brooklyn. But the Phils were swept by the powerful New York Yankees in the World Series.

The sights, sounds and memories of Shibe Park remain vivid more than three decades after its demise. This was the site of the first American League night game in 1939 and the place where heavy-breathing sportswriters worked from their bird's-eye perch under the roof behind home plate—probably the highest press box in baseball. You could get a brew at Kilroy's Bar, check out the memorabilia in the A's Elephant Room or bite into one of the best hot dogs this side of Coney Island.

But you could not enjoy a ballpark beer until 1961, watch Sunday baseball until 1934 or see advertisements until the 1950s, thanks primarily to city laws. There were, however, plenty of obstructed views to choose from and one of baseball's first loudspeaker systems gave Philly fans such memorable P.A. voices as Dave Zinkoff, Sherry O'Brien and Pete Byron.

Philadelphia fans have long been accepted as the boobird champions of baseball and nobody could match the 1930s heckling artistry of the Kessler brothers, Bull and Eddie, who forced their powerful voices and strong opinions on everyone in the park. The brothers would sit on opposite sides of the field and carry on conversations, directing their comments to a home or visiting player of their disaffection.

There were plenty of colorful characters among the 47 million fans who paraded through the turnstiles to watch players who usually matched their enthusiasm—in spirit if not performance. When Connie Mack Stadium closed after the Phillies' 1970 season, the surrounding neighborhood had deteriorated, cracks were showing in the foundation of baseball's oldest ballpark and layers of paint peeled away its aging secrets.

But nobody ever called it drab. A red interior combined with the still-beautiful green grass to give Philly fans a nostalgic sense of baseball, the way it was played for more than six decades.

Rooftop viewing from across 20th Street was common until Connie Mack put up his spite fence in 1935. This photo was shot during the 1914 World Series.

Forbes Field

No foul ball went unchallenged, thanks to 110-foot distance from home plate to backstop

Bill Mazeroski blanketed second base from 1956-72

Where "Greenberg Gardens" fence was erected in 1947, slicing 30 feet off home run distance for newcomer Hank Greenberg

Where Yankees left fielder Yogi Berra watched Bill Mazeroski's ninth-inning homer sail over the fence, giving Pirates 1960 World Series championship

Big Poison and Little Poison: Brothers Paul (right field) and Lloyd (center field) Waner combined for 5,185 hits as Pirates teammates from 1927-40

RALPH KINER:
Two-time 50-homer man powered his way into hearts of Pirates fans from 1946-53

Dale Long hits homer in eighth straight game, May 28, 1956 vs. Dodgers

Phillies' Chuck Klein hits four homers in one game—two on the right field roof, July 10, 1936

Honus Wagner marveled at its architectural grandeur. So did the Waner boys, Big Poison and Little Poison, who especially loved its expansive outfield—the better to chase down long fly balls and drop in well-aimed line drives. Pie Traynor scoffed at its rock-hard infield, Ralph Kiner delighted at its inviting "Garden" and Roberto Clemente found peace and harmony with its chummy right field screen.

For 62 years, Forbes Field inspired that kind of affection. This was baseball's second steel-and-concrete stadium, a quirky palace constructed in the affluent Oakland section of

Where right fielder Roberto Clemente won four batting championships and 10 of his 12 Gold Gloves

Babe Ruth's final three career home runs—including the first to clear Forbes Field's right field roof—come in a May 25, 1935 game for Braves

Rip Sewell baffles Browns slugger George McQuinn with "ephus pitch" in 1944 All-Star Game

Harold Arlin became baseball's first radio broadcaster when he described a Pirates-Phillies game here over station KDKA

Babe Adams shuts out Tigers in Game 7 of 1909 World Series, gives Pirates first championship

Reliever Roy Face wins 17th straight game of season, 22nd over two years, Aug. 30, 1959

Pirates played Reds in baseball's last tripleheader, Oct. 2, 1920

Where Pirates were overpowered by 1927 Yankees in first two games of World Series

HONUS WAGNER: Bow-legged shortstop, an eight-time batting champion, mesmerized fans with his defensive prowess through 1917

Willie Mays triples home winning run in eighth inning of first 1959 All-Star Game

Pie Traynor performed defensive magic at third base from 1920-37

Where Pirates' Glenn Wright (May 7, 1925) and Cubs' Jimmy Cooney (May 30, 1927) turned unassisted triple plays

Landing point of Kiki Cuyler's double, which decided 1925 World Series

Three's a charm: Chief Wilson hit record 36 triples in 1912

Where 37-year-old Walter Johnson made "last stand" in mud and rain during 9-7 Game 7 loss to Pirates in 1925 Series

Pittsburgh near the beautiful and pastoral Schenley Park. Ornate and magnificent at its 1909 opening, quaint and worn down at its 1970 demise, Forbes Field never lost its rough Pittsburgh edge while retaining its ability to charm even the toughest of baseball souls.

Charm has never come easy in the Steel City, where beauty is measured by hard work and results, sports heroes are judged by grit and determination and "powerful" wins out over "attractive" in sports venues. The main entrance to Forbes Field was pure Pittsburgh—a grand, old, imposing, theater-like edifice with ornate carvings and designs, deep vertical windows and a porch roof covering arched doorways.

Everything around Forbes set an imposing tone. Three miles away, on the main-entrance side, was the skyline of downtown Pittsburgh. The University of Pittsburgh bordered the left field grandstands, its massive Cathedral of Learning towering into

the factory smoke-filled stratosphere. Schenley Park offered an attractive diversion over the left field fence; Carnegie Tech commanded a view over the center field wall. Surrounded by such beauty and culture, Forbes Field had to be special.

At first, it was mostly big. The original outfield distances of 360 feet down the left field line, 462 to center and 376 to right made it a perfect fit for baseball's dead-ball era. This was a park that demanded fleet outfielders and rewarded speedy gap hitters. The distance from home plate to the backstop was a whopping 110 feet (later reduced to 75), turning an agile catcher into the equivalent of a fourth outfielder.

The original double-decked grandstand wrapped behind the plate in a U-shaped arc that created the backstop expanse. A roofed mini-third deck—early skyboxes?—topped the grandstand, which extended just beyond first and third base. The park's only bleacher section was in foul territory down the left field line and the entire out-

Beautiful Schenley Park provided a nice backdrop beyond the left field fence at Forbes Field.

field was open, interrupted only by a ground-level, hand-operated scoreboard that was topped by a Longines clock—hit the clock, win a home run.

Amazingly, the park underwent only two major renovations during its lifetime. The big one in 1925 extended the double-decked grandstand down the right field line, around the corner and into fair territory, covering a significant portion of right field. That reduced the foul-line distance from 376 to 300, prompting the Pirates to compensate with a 28-foot screen that extended out to the 375-foot marker in right-center. The second, in 1938, added the major leagues' first elevator, which took passengers to a covered third deck behind home plate—a bird's-eye cove for broadcasters and reporters that would become known as the "Crow's Nest."

While major renovations were infrequent, Forbes became known for its quirky nuances. Like the caged light-tower bases that appeared in left-center, center and right-center fields in 1940, creating wall projections and erratic bounces during games. And the 12-foot red brick left field wall, covered with ivy, that replaced the wooden fence in 1945, keeping the park in tune with the look and feel of Schenley Park behind it.

After acquiring aging slugger Hank Greenberg in 1947, the Pirates strung up a chicken-wire bullpen enclosure in front of that wall, lopping 30 feet off home run distances, and dubbed the area "Greenberg Gardens." Greenberg struggled through his one Pittsburgh season, but the enclosure survived through 1953, renamed "Kiner's Korner."

Into this odd-shaped, sometimes-illogical setting fit much of the Pirates' history—a story of success that included names like Wagner, Clarke, Carey, Waner, Cuyler, Traynor, Mazeroski, Greenberg, Kiner, Clemente and Stargell; a story of colorful, quirky memories that gave Forbes Field a personality beyond it players and their accomplishments. Four pennants and three world championships (1909, '25, '60) attest to the historic and success-oriented bottom line, but you had to stop, look and listen to get

the real flavor of Forbes Field.

In the 1930s, you might have marveled at the powerful (most said annoying) lungs of Bruce "Screech Owl" McAllister, a screaming superfan also known as the "Forbes Field Siren." In the 1940s and '50s, you basked in the colorful descriptions of broadcaster Rosey Rowswell—"doozie marooney" (Pirate extra-base hit); "dipsy doodle" (Pirate strikeout); "oh, my aching back" (a Pirates loss); or his sound effect-aided "Get upstairs Aunt Minnie" home run calls. Green Weenies and Polish babushkas were all the wave of the 1960s.

Physical oddities also spiced up life at 35,000-seat Forbes Field. During World War II, a wooden 32-foot U.S. Marine sergeant stood guard in left field fair territory near the scoreboard. A plaque honoring Forbes Field builder Barney Dreyfuss was a long-

By the 1950s, the main entrance of Forbes Field was a little worn and weather-beaten, but it still was an imposing baseball masterpiece.

FORBES FIELD (1909-1970)

Before Forbes, and before the Pirates, minor league baseball was played in the Pittsburgh area in a number of parks. Among those sites was Exposition Park, the present site of Three Rivers Stadium.

After years of playing in parks with limited capacity and enduring flooding of the Allegheny River, owner Barney Dreyfuss announced in 1908 his plan to build a concrete-and-steel structure, a facility befitting his wont for a first-class team.

Forbes Field, named after John Forbes, a British general in the French and Indian War who captured Fort Duquesne (from which the city of Pittsburgh rose) in 1758, initially seated 25,000 and opened in 1909.

The Forbes Field site today is part of the University of Pittsburgh, just a few miles east and across the Allegheny River from Three Rivers Stadium.

Though it was replaced in 1970, remnants of Forbes Field still exist. Home plate is encased on the Pitt campus; a plaque marks the exact spot of Bill Mazeroski's 1960 World Series-winning homer; a part of the left field wall is displayed in the Allegheny Club at Three Rivers; and just outside the University of Pittsburgh library, a portion of the left-center field wall stands. It's here that on October 13 each year, Pirates fans gather to celebrate Maz's heroic homer.

First game: June 30, 1909. A standing-room only crowd of 30,388 came out to the see the new park, broken in with a 3-2 loss to the Chicago Cubs.

Final game: June 28, 1970. Al Oliver homered and Jim Nelson shut out the Cubs, 3-0.

- ■ Site of four World Series (1909, '25, '27 and '60)
- ■ Site of two All-Star Games (1944 and 1959)

The final game at Forbes in 1970 ended with fans attacking the left field scoreboard (right) in search of souvenirs—only a few yards from where Bill Mazeroski's World Series-winning homer left the park in 1960, a spot marked by a plaque (above left) on what is now the University of Pittsburgh campus. Announcers got a bird's-eye view from their perch high above home plate (above).

time decoration on the right-center field fence and an 18-foot Wagner statue monitored Forbes Field proceedings from Schenley Park, just behind the left field wall, from 1955 to the park's 1970 closing. The rock-hard infield (broadcaster Bob Prince's "alabaster plaster") was a Forbes trademark, a quirk that helped decide the seventh game of the 1960 World Series.

An old, decaying Forbes Field finally gave way to new Three Rivers Stadium midway through the 1970 season, leaving Pittsburgh fans to ponder hundreds of priceless memories and several distinctions unmatched by any other six-decade ballpark—no advertisements ever appeared on Forbes Field's outfield walls and nobody ever pitched a no-hitter from its mound.

Candlestick Park

The 'Stick: Wind, fog, cold and 40 years of memories

Diminutive reliever Stu Miller gets blown off the mound in windy 1961 All-Star Game

Bay Area World Series featuring Giants and A's is interrupted by major earthquake, which causes death and destruction moments before the start of Game 3, Oct. 17, 1989

Astros' Eddie Mathews hits 500th career homer, July 14, 1967

Joe Morgan's dramatic final-day, three-run homer wrecks the pennant hopes of hated Dodgers, Oct. 3, 1982

Where Jack Sanford won his 16th straight game, Sept. 11, 1962

T hey called it "the Hawk," a reverent tribute to the mean-spirited wind that soared over, into, around and through Candlestick Park for four decades, bewildering and frustrating the men who tried to play baseball there. The Hawk was an invisible ghost, a howling, swirling, darting and dancing demon that tortured San Francisco fans, made life miserable for players and stretched the boundaries of everyone's endurance and imagination.

Back-to-back no hitters, Sept. 17-18, 1968; Giants' Gaylord Perry (left) on 17th (1-0), Cardinals' Ray Washburn on 18th (2-0)

WILLIE MCCOVEY:
Giants first baseman 1959-73, 1977-80; 521 career homers, 1,555 RBIs.

All in the family: Bobby Bonds (right) topped 30 homers three times for Giants; son Barry has three 40-plus homer seasons

Mays hit N.L.-record-breaking
512th homer on May 4, 1966 and joined
3,000-hit club on July 18, 1970

Barry Bonds becomes second member
of baseball's 40-40 club, 1996

Where Juan Marichal pitched a one-hitter
in big-league debut, July 19, 1960, and beat
Warren Spahn, 1-0, in a 16-inning game
decided by a Mays homer, July 2, 1963

Braves pitcher Tony
Cloninger becomes first
N.L. player to hit two
grand slams in same game,
July 3, 1966

Where Dodgers manager Tommy
Lasorda stopped to blow kisses to
heckling crowds on his long treks
from visiting clubhouse near right
field corner to the third base dugout

Where Bobby Richardson
caught McCovey's line drive,
ending 1962 World Series

Cancer victim Dave Dravecky
posts inspirational 4-3 win
over Reds in comeback bid,
Aug. 10, 1989

Where Houston's Bob Watson
scored baseball's 1-millionth run,
May 4, 1975

WILLIE MAYS
.302 career average,
660 homers, 3,283
hits, 1,903 RBIs

Where Juan Marichal attacked
Dodgers catcher John Roseboro
with a bat, Aug. 22, 1965

Wind and fog (below left) were consistent problems at Candlestick Park, but there was nothing wrong with the stadium's picturesque setting on Candlestick Point (left).

car bell—one clang for every run.

When the 'Stick opened in 1960 as the permanent home for the transplanted New York Giants, it was anticipated as a baseball showcase and hailed as the "Taj Mahal of games." And at first glance, Candlestick was not so far removed from those expectations when it kicked off a stadium building boom that changed the look of baseball in the 1960s and '70s. It was the first ballpark to be built entirely with reinforced concrete, the first with unobstructed sightlines and the first with radiant heating—a novel idea that, unfortunately, never worked. It also had the biggest, most modern scoreboard in the major leagues.

And throughout its 40-year tenure, you would have been hard-pressed to visit Candlestick and not come away with a sense of personality you'd never find in the cookie-cutter stadiums of Pittsburgh, Cincinnati, Philadelphia and St. Louis. It started with the location.

The 'Stick sat on Candlestick Point, which jutted into the San Francisco Bay and commanded a magnificent view of the harbor and rolling water that, under a warm, clear sky, would be filled with diving birds, white sails and colorful sports boats. You could stand outside the stadium and look down Cardiac Hill to the filling parking lot or to the harbor where yachts and other vessels delivered their passengers to a game.

Inside, Candlestick was a ballpark, not the horrid snake pit of an arena so often portrayed by the national media. You might not feel the tradition of a Yankee Stadium, the charm of a Crosley Field or the personality of a Fenway Park, but you did get the character that was missing from so many parks of its era and a friendly openness that was not lost when Candlestick's open end was enclosed during a 1972 renovation that accommodated the NFL's 49ers and raised baseball seating capacity to

No natural or man-made phenomenon has consistently affected baseball games more than the ill winds of Candlestick—the gusts that blow off the Pacific Ocean and collide with Bay View Hill before fragmenting into swirling, gale-force mini-cyclones that turned pop flies into home runs, foul balls into unexpected outs and competent defenders into bumbling fools. No ballpark in baseball history has been more vilified, more joked about, more cursed and more universally hated, even by the people who call it home.

"My fondest memory of that stadium is the day they tear it down," said former Los Angeles Dodgers outfielder Rick Monday. "When you go there you don't walk inside to see a ballpark, you go inside to see an arena. You expect gladiators to come out; the last one standing is the victor, and the last one standing is always the wind."

But the reality of Candlestick was not just the wind and the bone-jarring cold of a July or August night. It also was a Willie Mays catch, a Juan Marichal leg kick, an Orlando Cepeda gapper, a Gaylord Perry spitter, a Barry Bonds moonshot or the courageous effort of Dave Dravecky. It was Willie McCovey's line drive right at Yankees second baseman Bobby Richardson in Game 7 of the 1962 World Series. It was Tommy Lasorda blowing kisses to the maddening crowd as he made the long death march from the visitor's clubhouse in the right field corner to the third base dugout. It was the sound of a foghorn proclaiming a home run, a cable

58,000. Life was good when you could sit back and enjoy the anticipation of a game against the hated Dodgers on a beautiful sun-drenched afternoon, complete with a grass-covered field, the smell of the ocean and, of course, a world-class Polish sausage.

And then came the Hawk. The wind whipped up at midafternoon and funneled into Candlestick, turning the field into a dust storm and shooting hot dog wrappers through the air like giant snowflakes. Wind currents swirled and whirled unpredictably throughout the stadium, often with an average velocity of 16 mph and occasional gusts up to 60. Balls hit to left and left-center field were knocked down, balls aimed toward right often were lifted right over the fence. Anything in the air became a potential nightmare, including thrown and pitched balls.

Diminutive reliever Stu Miller could attest to the wind currents that literally blew him sideways during mid-delivery in the 1961 All-Star Game, resulting in a balk. Ken Boyer's throw to first during the same contest was blown sideways, result-

Bay View Hill, as seen during the 1961 All-Star Game (left), overlooked the park. No discussio of Candlestick would be complete without the names (left to right) Mays, McCovey and Cepeda.

ing in an error. Former infielder Duane Kuiper tells of a foul pop that catcher Milt May chased to the backstop, gave up on and as he was walking back to the plate, the ball hit him on top of his head. The one-time symmetrical park even changed shape because of the wind as management shortened the left and left-center field fences to help beleaguered right-handed hitters.

The wind usually subsided by 4 or 5 p.m., at which time the fog rolled in and, acting like an air-conditioner, dropped temperatures 10 or more degrees. It wasn't unusual to start a game on a picturesque 75-degree afternoon, suddenly feel the wrath of the wind and then finish in a 55-degree chill. Life at Candlestick was erratic.

The wind problems diminished when the stadium was enclosed, but Candlestick never escaped its ignominious ties to the weather. Games were occasionally delayed by fog, fans bundled themselves in parkas for summer contests and a packed stadium was even rocked and damaged by a major earthquake just moments before Game 3 of the 1989 World Series—one of Candlestick's two fall classics.

But structural damage was repaired, the Giants went on to lose the Bay Area Series to Oakland and the stadium survived for another decade. Candlestick finally closed her gates to baseball after the 1999 season, to the cheers of many and the tears of those who knew her best.

CANDLESTICK PARK (1960-1999)

Renamed 3Com Park at Candlestick Point (1996-1999)

Two seasons after their move from New York to San Francisco, two seasons in which they played in temporary quarters at Seals Stadium, the Giants opened Candlestick for the 1960 season.

Its name, which came from a balloting of fans, was derived from its location, Candlestick Point, which juts into San Francisco Bay.

Contrary to nearly 40 years of mostly negative reaction, Candlestick actually was lauded at its opening for being a pioneer in stadium design. First, it was the first stadium to be built in a non-urban area, a bit of foresight as Americans began their flight to suburbia. Second, it was heralded for a design that featured no view-obstructing pillars.

Candlestick originally featured natural grass and was open in center field. In 1971, it was replaced with artificial turf, which remained until 1979. In 1972, construction to enclose the stadium was completed.

And through it all was the weather — the legendary wind and fog — that locals were always prepared for with layers of clothing and unprepared visitors were always amazed by.

First game: April 12, 1960. A 3-1 Giants win over the Cardinals witnessed by Vice President Richard Nixon.

Final game: September 30, 1999. A 9-4 Giants loss to, appropriately, the rival Dodgers, in inappropriately warm, balmy, ideal weather conditions.

- Site of two World Series (1962 and 1989)
- Site of two All-Star Games (1961 and 1984)

A powerful earthquake brought a temporary end to the 1989 World Series and sent A's players scrambling to find their families (above). The Series continued 12 days later, after repairs were made to the 'Stick (below).

The Kingdome

It was ugly, a stark, gray, dingy circle of cement. Players, coaches, fans, broadcasters—everybody agreed the Kingdome was no work of art. It was a giant mushroom growing in an industrial area just south of downtown Seattle, a wart on the city's otherwise beautiful landscape. Criticized, ridiculed and abhorred, baseball's second domed stadium kept a stiff upper lip near the shore of Puget Sound for 23 sometimes-difficult seasons.

Visually, the Kingdome deserved the abuse. But the essence of the white, wavy-topped facility goes much deeper than appearance. The reality of the Kingdome is that it put Seattle on the major league sports map, served as a launching pad for the careers of Ken Griffey Jr. and Alex

Gaylord Perry beats Yankees 7-3 for 300th career victory, May 6, 1982

Willie Horton's high drive hits speaker, costing him his 300th career homer, June 5, 1979

Where Griffeys, 20-year-old Ken Jr. and 40-year-old K Sr., took field as first father-son duo to play togethe in major league game, Aug. 31, 1990

Mariners beat Angels in one-game playoff, claim first division title in team's 19-year history, Oct. 2, 1995

ALEX RODRIGUEZ: Baseball's first 40-40 shortstop and its first shortstop with back-to-back 40-homer seasons ('98, '99)

Where Dave Parker throws cut dow Jim Rice and Brian Downing, saving d for N.L. in 1979 All-Star Game

Alvin Davis, Mark Langston finish 1-2 in A.L. Rookie of the Year voting, 1984

Mike Blowers becomes 13th player to hit grand slams in consecutive games, May 16, 17, 1993

Catcher Dan Wilson chugs home with inside-the-park grand slam, May 3, 1998

Randy Johnson strikes out 19 White Sox, becomes first to reach that plateau twice in one season, Aug. 8, 1997

Randy Johnson: 18-2, 2.48 ERA, Cy Young in 1995

After retiring first 26 Oakland batters, Brian Holman loses perfect game when Ken Phelps hits home run in eventual 6-1 Mariners win, April 20, 1990

Mike Parrott ends 18-game losing streak, beating Brewers in Rene Lachemann's first game as manager, May 6, 1981

Griffey Jr. ties major league record with homer vs. Minnesota—his eighth straight game with home run, July 28, 1993

Second baseman Harold Reynolds anchored infield for 10 seasons, 1983-92

Griffey Jr. ties record with fifth homer in a postseason series and Mariners bring down Yankees in Game 5 Division Series thriller, Oct. 8, 1995

Where Lenny Randle illegally blew ground ball foul, May 27, 1981

Griffey Jr. slams three-run homer and Mariners thrill sellout crowd with Kingdome-closing 5-2 win over Texas, June 27, 1999

Four ceiling tiles fall prior to game vs. Orioles, forcing Mariners to play remainder of schedule on road, July 19, 1994

Griffey Jr.: First Mariner with back-to-back 50-homer seasons (1997, '98), three straight 140-plus RBI campaigns (1996, '97, '98)

KEN GRIFFEY JR.: Seattle's record book is dominated by Gold Glove center fielder, the A.L.'s 1997 MVP

MARINERS

Rodriguez and combined with the towering Space Needle to make the city a Great Northwest tourist attraction. It was the ugly duckling from which a new-millennium swan (Safeco Field) emerged.

"It's been called ugly by a lot of people through the years, but it will always be beautiful to me," said Dave Niehaus, the Mariners' play-by-play broadcaster since their expansion debut in 1977. "It's been a huge part of my life. I'm going to miss it. Aesthetically? No, I won't miss it. I know people are excited to see it go, but remember, we wouldn't have baseball here at all if it wasn't for the Kingdome."

That's an impressive legacy. The King-dome sprung out of Seattle's need for a major league facility after the city fumbled its first shot at big-league baseball. The expansion Seattle Pilots were whisked away after a difficult 1969 season at tiny Sick's Stadium and it took the promise of a domed, multi-purpose facility to lure professional

THE KINGDOME (1977-1999)

In 1967, American League owners awarded an expansion team to Seattle. The team, known as the Pilots, began play in 1969.

The plan was for the Pilots to play in Sick's Stadium, which opened for play in 1938 as home of Emil George Sick's Pacific Coast League team, until a domed facility could be built.

But the relationship between Seattle officials and the Pilots went bad from the start, and in March of 1970 the Pilots' move to Milwaukee was approved.

In order to re-enter the majors, the city went ahead with building the domed facility. In 1972, after protracted debates over location, a site was selected. By 1977, the stadium — within King County, hence the name — and a new expansion team, the Mariners, were ready.

First game: April 6, 1977. In the first of 98 losses in their expansion year, the Mariners lost to California, 7-0.

Final game: June 27, 1999. Led by Ken Griffey's 377th career home run, the Mariners beat the Rangers, 5-2.

■ Site of no World Series
■ Site of one All-Star Game (1979)

sports back to the city—the expansion Sea-hawks of the NFL arrived in 1976 and the Mariners opened play a year later. The Kingdome, unlike Houston's Astrodome, was a building of function rather than flash.

The outside was plain, hard and gray, with little around it to draw visitors without a baseball agenda. The view of Puget Sound, with boats chugging to and from port, was enchanting, the distant sight of Mount Rainier on a clear summer day spectacular, the twinkling lights from the Seattle skyline embracing. But no attempts were ever made to present the facility itself as anything more than a lump of concrete with a lonely American flag blowing in the salt-water breezes from its apex.

One of the Kingdome's greatest attributes was accessibility—next to Seattle's King Street railroad station, which made baseball trips convenient from Portland, Spokane and Vancouver; a few blocks from the waterfront, making it easy for boaters; walking distance from downtown and only a few miles from the Space Needle. But its greatest weakness was personality.

The dome (250 feet from field level to apex) sprawled over the turf-covered field like a gigantic umbrella, protecting its patrons from the rain and chills of Seattle's inclement weather. Speakers suspended from the ceiling provided grounds-rule nightmares and the Mariners tried to dress things up with banners, bunting and red, white and blue ceiling streamers, but nothing seemed capable of relieving the cavernous, morgue-like atmosphere that plagued the building through much of its tenure.

The field was an assymmetrical 331 feet to left, 405 to center and 312 to right, and the turf was hard and fast, inviting an offensive playing style. A 23-foot wall made life interesting in right and right-center (a mini-Green Monster nicknamed Walla Walla) and

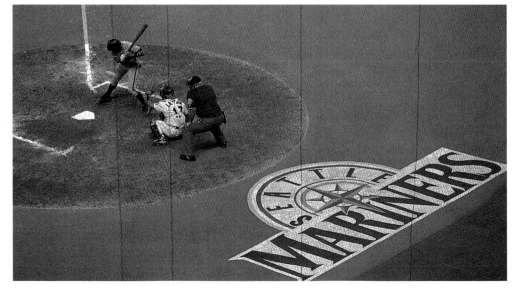

a huge scoreboard dominated the left field view above the third-deck grandstand. An out-of-town board, installed in 1990, flashed scores on the right field wall and a giant tarp covered a portion of the right field upper deck in the early '90s, relieving some of the stadium's normal empty feel.

The 59,856-seat Kingdome did have some distinctive sights and sounds. For several years, outfield dimensions were offered in both feet and fathoms and through most of the 1980s the USS Mariner, a gold ship positioned behind the left-center field fence, would rise up and salute Mariners home runs and victories with a cannon blast. This was the home of Rick Kaminski, one of the best-known peanut vendors in the world, and "Ruuuuuuuupe" —the nickname for popular outfielder Ruppert Jones from 1977-80.

Baseball life in Seattle took its most dramatic turn in 1995 when the Mariners captured their first A.L. West Division championship. That title, which was repeated two years later, ignited a fan fury that transformed the stadium from a tomb into a loud, raucous house of fun, complete with offensive bombers named Griffey, Rodriguez, Jay Buhner and Edgar Martinez and a flame-thrower named Randy Johnson, a k a "The Big Unit."

With that success came some of the personality Mariners officials had always sought. Griffey and A-Rod became national figures. The popular Buhner, alias Bone, attracted his own right field following—a section called the Boneyard. One of the more fascinating Mariners promotions was Buhner Buzz Night, when hundreds of fans would shave their heads (like Buhner) for free admission to the game.

Ironically, the Kingdome was a more fun and happy place when it closed its doors to baseball in mid-1999—a baseball home that was functional, but never really appreciated.

"I really liked it on those days when it was 40 degrees outside and raining," said former first baseman Alvin Davis, who spent eight of his nine major league seasons in Seattle. "For me, the Kingdome is baseball in Seattle. This place is like home to me."

The Kingdome was plain, hard and gray (below), a building of function over flash. It also was a house of pain, a park without a division title until the Mariners broke through in 1995 and 1997 (left).

Sportsman's Park

Also known as Busch Stadium (1953-1966)

I t was home for the Gashouse and Knothole Gangs, a playground for unlikely heroes named Dizzy, Rajah, Pepper, Frankie, Ducky, Enos, Gibby and Stan the Man. This is where the Horse Lady whinnied and a goat was used to trim the outfield grass—some say a little too close for comfort. Sportsman's Park was a sometimes-wacky, always-raucous baseball funhouse—a place of magic where a midget and one-armed outfielder could play with the big boys and the game's most depressed franchise could rise to storybook prominence and win a pennant.

How could you not like Sportsman's Park, where life was never dull and

Cardinals brought 10 pennants, seven championships to Sportsman's Park

Where one-armed outfielder Pete Gray made big-league debut for Browns, April 17, 1945

Landing point for final-day, ninth-inning grand slam by Hank Greenberg that gave Tigers 6-3 win over Browns and 1945 A.L. pennant

MVP Ken Boyer led Cardinals to 1964 pennant; Bob Gibson secured World Series championship with Game 7 win over Yankees

STAN THE MAN MUSIAL: Cardinals' three-time MVP, seven-time batting champ collected 3,630 career hits, fourth all-time

Dean brothers, Dizzy and Paul, combined for 49 wins in 1934

Musial goes crazy: five home runs, nine RBIs in doubleheader vs. Giants, May 2, 1954

Browns' Bobo Holloman fires no-hitter in first major league start, May 6, 1953

286

Where Mike Shannon's 1964 World Series homer bounced off scoreboard

Point where Max West's All-Star Game-deciding home run landed in 1940

Point where one of Babe Ruth's three Game 4 home runs cleared bleachers in 1926 World Series, breaking auto dealer's window across Grand Avenue

A 33-foot screen topped fence fronting right field pavilion

Great defensive shortstop Marty Marion wins 1944 MVP, Cardinals defeat Browns in World Series—the only all-St. Louis fall classic

Chet Laabs homers twice, Browns beat Yankees 5-2 and win only A.L. pennant, Oct. 1, 1944

Browns first baseman George Sisler (below) batted .420 and compiled 41-game hitting streak in 1922; six-time Cardinals batting champ Rogers Hornsby hit .424 in 1924

...sepaths where Enos ...ughter made his Mad Dash ...win seventh game of 1946 ...orld Series

A long line of great Cardinals second basemen: Rogers Hornsby, Frank Frisch, Red Schoendienst, Julian Javier

Where Browns' Bob Cain outdueled Indians star Bob Feller 1-0 in double one-hitter, April 23, 1952

DIZZY DEAN: Colorful righthander clinched 1934 pennant on final day by beating Reds 9-0, recording 30th victory

Tigers 38-year-old player-manager Ty Cobb hits 3 homers, double, 2 singles and drives in 5 runs in 14-8 win over Browns, May 5, 1925

Where Horse Lady Mary Ott drove everybody crazy

...ter's box where Eddie Gaedel, ...ill Veeck's midget, drew walk in surprise appearance vs. Tigers, Aug. 19, 1951

Fans manage Browns in another Veeck promotional stunt, Aug. 24, 1951

The center field corner of Grand and Sullivan (above) braced for the power onslaught of the Babe Ruth, Lou Gehrig-led Yankees during the 1928 World Series. Six years later, Sportsman's (right) played host to a Cardinals-Tigers World Series.

memories of the people who cheered and competed there remain as vibrant as the colorful Budweiser eagle that flapped its wings atop the massive left field scoreboard for more than a decade, as if threatening to carry the ballpark and everybody in it off to baseball heaven? This was a ballpark of the people, where stars were revered, characters often were bigger than life and popularity was as much a measure of personality as success.

In retrospect, it's hard to imagine how Sportsman's Park thrived for 33 years as a house divided—between the American League Browns and the National League Cardinals from 1920-53, the longest ballpark co-habitation in history. The Browns were owners and the Cardinals paid rent for most of that period, but Sportsman's Park will long be remembered for the Cardinals' successes and the Browns' desperate and creative attempts to simply remain solvent.

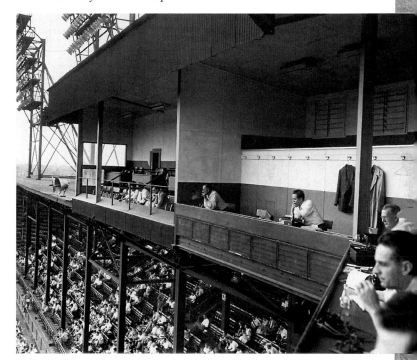

SPORTSMAN'S PARK (1902-1966)

Renamed Busch Stadium (1953-1966)

The origin of Sportsman's Park—the name and stadium site—reach as far back as 1875, when St. Louis' first professional baseball team was called the Browns. That team did not last very long, but two men—Chris Von der Ahe and Al Spink—banded together under an organization known as the Sportsman's Club to re-form the Browns, who played on the corner of Grand and Dodier. Spink was credited with naming the facility Sportsman's Park.

In 1892, the Browns moved to a new park (Union Park) and later switched to Robison Field, where they remained until 1920. Those Browns fell into new ownership and were renamed the Cardinals.

In 1902, a new American League entry called the Browns returned to Grand and Dodier in the facility to be called Sportsman's Park. With the Browns as owners and Cardinals as tenants beginning in 1920, Sportsman's Park hosted major league baseball through 1965. In 1953, when Anheuser-Busch purchased the Cardinals and the Browns moved to Baltimore, the facility was renamed Busch Stadium (although Busch reportedly originally favored the name Budweiser Stadium).

When the Cardinals moved into new Busch Stadium in 1966, Busch donated the site to the Herbert Hoover Boys Club. The park's stands and infrastructure are gone, but the field site remains intact.

First game: April 23, 1902. The Browns beat Cleveland, 5-2.

Final game: May 8, 1966. The Cardinals lost to the Giants, 10-5.

■ Site of 10 World Series (1926, '28, '30, '31, '34, '42, '43, '44, '46, and '64)

■ Site of three All-Star Games (1940, '48 and '57)

Sportswriters and broadcasters got a bird's-eye view of game action from their pressbox perch high on the second-deck roof behind home plate.

Located at the intersection of Grand and Dodier, this was the third version of Sportsman's Park at the famous St. Louis corner, which had served the city's baseball needs dating all the way back to 1871. Built for the Browns after the 1908 season — although the Browns played at the site as early as 1902 — while the Cardinals still were playing at tiny Robison Field, the reconstructed steel-and-concrete structure stood as a sports monument into the 1966 season in a thriving area near Gaslight Square, the Fabulous Fox theater and upscale residential neighborhoods.

That 1909 Sportsman's Park featured a roofed double-deck grandstand that wrapped behind home plate from first base to third, a covered single-deck grandstand that extended down the left field line and single-deck bleachers that bordered the entire outfield, with lines that measured 353 feet (left) and 320 (right) and a center field distance of 430. A renovation after the 1925 season nearly doubled the capacity to 34,000 and gave the park what sportswriter Red Smith called "a garish, county fair sort of layout"— a look it would retain over the next four decades.

The covered double-deck grandstand was extended down both lines to the foul poles, the wooden bleachers were replaced by concrete and the right field stands were roofed, creating a pavilion that would become the park's signature feature. Because the right field line was reduced to 310 feet, the 11½-foot fence was topped by a 33-foot screen that extended 156 feet toward center — a Green Monster-like barrier that would stand from mid-1929 through the life of the park, with only a one-year respite in 1955.

"The screen made it much more interesting," said former Cardinals right fielder Stan Musial, who saw many of his potential home runs get sucked back into play by the imposing barrier. "The ball would fly out there and the runner didn't know if it was going to hit the screen, go over it or how it would bounce. It was hard to score (because outfielders played so shallow) on a single to right in that park."

The pavilion, with its screened view, was the last vestige of segregation in major league baseball—the area to which blacks were restricted into the 1944 season. Overall, fans not obstructed by steel support beams were close to the field and interaction was encouraged. The players' clubhouse walkway traveled through the home dugout and an inside corridor that was open to the fans—at first with no restriction, later with only a chain-link fence providing seclusion.

St. Louisans measure their baseball memories by landmarks and Sportsman's Park had its share—Wally Post hit the Longines clock, perched high on a light standard above the right-center field wall; Mike Shannon's 1964 World Series blast smacked the huge left field scoreboard that screened prodigious clouts from reaching Sullivan Avenue; the right field screen and pavilion roof; the shrubs beyond the center field fence; the Griesedieck Beer sign in right; Grand Avenue home runs; and, of course, the scoreboard eagle, which arrived after August A. Busch purchased the facility from Browns owner Bill Veeck in 1953, renovated its badly neglected infrastructure and renamed the park Busch Stadium.

A year later, the Browns moved to Baltimore, leaving the Cardinals to reign for 12 more seasons over the St. Louis kingdom they had technically ruled

since 1926, when they won the first of Sportsman's Park's 10 National League pennants and seven World Series championships. The Browns were gone, but not the memories of George Sisler's .420 season, Pete Gray's one-armed outfield play, Satchel Paige's bullpen rocking chair and all the crazy Veeck promotions, from midget Eddie Gaedel to the Grandstand Managers and Good Old Joe Earley Night.

Cardinals fans take equal delight with their memories—Mary Ott, the renowned 1930s-era Horse Lady who would tug at her ear and release ear-splitting neighs that could reportedly cause stampedes across the state in Kansas City's stockyards; a 1940s striptease club located under the stands in center field; the rock-hard infield, Pepper Martin's Mud-Cat band, Knothole kids in the left field bleachers, the penthouse pressbox, perched on top of the grandstand behind home plate, where Harry Caray delivered his colorful play-by-play, and a shattered window at the Wells Motor Company on Grand Avenue, courtesy of a 1926 Babe Ruth World Series home run.

But the most precious memory belongs to those fans lucky enough to witness the Cardinals' 1944 all-St. Louis "Streetcar World Series" victory—the only fall classic in which the lowly Browns would ever compete. For one glorious postseason, the baseball spotlight fell exclusively on Sportsman's Park—the house that Sisler, Hornsby, Frisch, Medwick, Musial, Slaughter, Schoendienst and Gibson built.

Life inside Sportsman's early manual scoreboard (top photo, right) could be hot and confining; the later scoreboard was topped by a Budweiser eagle that flapped its wings in excitement (above). The park's signature feature was a right field pavilion fronted by a fence with a 33-foot screen (below).

Exhibition Stadium

Memorable pitching duel: Detroit's Pat Underwood, making big-league debut, beats brother Tommy 1-0, May 31, 1979

I t was an impromptu baseball field, a football facility incapable of doing a quality impersonation. Exhibition Stadium's greatest sin was that it never really looked, felt or smelled like a ballpark, a personality flaw that generated unfair criticism, ridicule and contempt ("Excruciation Stadium") over much of its 12-plus-year major league existence. Its greatest qualities were perseverance and grace under fire—as a Canadian interloper to America's national pastime.

In retrospect, Exhibition might have been a perfect fit for the 1977 expansion Blue Jays and baseball's second venture onto foreign soil (the Montreal Expos had started play in 1969). Because of the facility's exaggerated horseshoe shape, the

Where Tony Fernandez performed with Gold Glove efficiency from 1983-90

Minnesota's Randy Bush gets broken-bat single leading off ninth inning, ruining Jim Clancy's bid for perfect game, Sept. 28, 1982

Blue Jays get 24 hits, batter Orioles 24-10, June 26, 19?

DAVE STIEB, Blue Jays career leader with 175 wins

First A.L. game in Canada: Expansion Blue Jays
urvive cold and snow flurries to beat White Sox
-5 as Doug Ault hits two home runs, April 7, 1977

Angels slugger Willie
Aikens hits grand slams in
consecutive 1979 games
vs. Blue Jays

Catcher Ernie Whitt hits
three homers and Blue Jays
hit major league-record 10
in 18-3 rout of Orioles,
Sept. 14, 1987

Where a warmup throw from Yankees
center fielder Dave Winfield killed a
snoozing seagull, resulting in his postgame
arrest, Aug. 4, 1983

Where fly ball by Jim Sundberg struck top
of fence—a bases-loaded triple that helped
Royals complete comeback from three-
games-to-one deficit in 1985 ALCS

Stieb pitches five-hitter and Blue
Jays record 6-1 win over Royals—
first postseason victory in franchise
history, Oct. 8, 1985

Otto Velez becomes fan favorite
after crashing four home runs in
doubleheader, May 4, 1980

George Bell won A.L. MVP with
47 homers, 134 RBIs in 1987

ankees veteran Phil Niekro, refusing to use his
knuckleball on final day of season, shuts out
Blue Jays for career win No. 300, Oct. 6, 1985

Good line of first basemen in
Toronto: John Mayberry, Willie
Upshaw, Fred McGriff, John
Olerud, Carlos Delgado

For second time in six days, hard-luck
Stieb loses no-hit bid with two out in
ninth as Orioles' Jim Traber bloops hit
over first base, Sept. 30, 1988

Jerry Garvin
picks off
22 runners
in 1977

Blue Jays win 9-0 forfeit
when Earl Weaver pulls his
Orioles off field because
umpires refuse to remove
tarp in Blue Jays' bullpen,
Sept. 15, 1977

LLOYD MOSEBY:
Centerpiece for hard-hitting
outfield that included George
Bell and Jesse Barfield

EXHIBITION STADIUM (1977-1989)

After enduring temporary homes for more than four decades, Toronto's first "permanent" baseball facility opened in 1926—Maple Leaf Stadium, home of the minor league Leafs. It would remain the centerpiece for Toronto baseball for 42 years, until the Leafs were dissolved.

In the 1950s and '60s, with an eye toward major league baseball, Toronto officials discussed appropriate playing facilities. Numerous proposals were recommended—enlarging the Canadian National Exhibition facility, building of a domed stadium—but it took until 1974 for anything to be approved. In '74, the expansion of Canadian National Exhibition became a reality.

In 1976, Toronto appeared ready to become new home for the Giants, who were trying to relocate from San Francisco. That move, however, was turned down by N.L. owners. Shortly thereafter, an expansion team was awarded—baseball's second Canadian franchise—and Exhibition's short major league history began.

And it began in the true spirit of Canada: with snow on the ground. Snow covered the infield and outfield for the first several innings of Exhibition's opener.

Exhibition Stadium remained standing for 10 years after SkyDome opened in 1989, just to the northeast. In 1999, Exhibition Stadium finally was razed.

First game: April 7, 1977. First baseman Doug Ault christened the stadium with two home runs and a run-scoring single as the Jays posted a 9-5 comeback victory over the White Sox.

Final game: May 28, 1989. The Blue Jays' George Bell sent it out with a home run, the stadium's final hit, and the Blue Jays beat the White Sox, 7-5.

■ Site of no World Series
■ Site of no All-Star Game

The mood was festive when the Jays opened the 1988 season vs. the Yankees.

playing field and grandstands were makeshift and unsophisticated, much like the young team that lost 318 games during the franchise's first three years and the enthusiastic fans who struggled to learn the American game. Exhibition Stadium was a first house—no-frills, basic and comfortable as its young Blue Jays matured into a contender; outdated, overmatched and underequipped when they sprouted their championship wings.

The simple fact is major league baseball might never have embraced Toronto without Exhibition Stadium, a pre-1900 facility that expanded over the decades while serving as the showcase for events at the Toronto Fairgrounds. The 350-acre fairgrounds site, a complex of buildings, landscaped gardens, an amusement park, restaurants and concert facilities, still thrives in downtown Toronto as home of the Canadian National Exhibition, an annual three-week fair that attracts millions of world visitors.

The fairgrounds—a stroll through the park, literally—provided a favorable first impression of Exhibition (alias CNE Stadium) while the distant Toronto skyline, CN Tower and nearby Lake Ontario offered a scenic backdrop that few ballparks can match. The clean, landscaped walkways and a modern glass-and-concrete facade suggested life—and baseball—might be good inside. But first you had to get over the shock.

Exhibition Stadium was a long, college football-style facility that was converted for baseball use—much like the Los Angeles Coliseum was transformed into a temporary home for the Dodgers in 1958. The Canadian Football League's Argonauts had played at Exhibition Stadium since 1959 and baseball was an awkward fit, no matter how you tried to twist, turn or manipulate the basic diamond. Facing single-deck stands extended the length of the field, dictating the construction of an elbow that connected one sideline with end zone seats—forming the home plate backstop as well as first and third base stands.

As a result, the main football grandstand, the only covered seats in the stadium, became a left field general admission pavilion. The seats behind the plate and down both lines were really glorified bleachers. A temporary 12-foot chain-link fence (the lower 8 feet padded) formed the perimeter of the outfield, a fence that followed the left field grandstand into deep left-center before curving away and crossing the field at about the football 35-yard line. The symmetrical result (330-400-330) left a large dead area beyond the right field fence and rendered useless the seats that extended beyond the fences to the distant end zone—except for binocular-wielding diehards.

It took several minutes to get a grip on exactly what you were seeing. The playing surface was artificial, seats on the first base side were aluminum benches. There were no multi-decked stands and the only luxury boxes were on top of the left field "bleachers," obviously constructed for football use. One of the strangest sights was the location of the 41-foot-high scoreboard, far away from everything in the opposite end zone.

Once you got past its peculiar appearance, Exhibition Stadium (baseball capacity 43,737) could be a fun place to visit. It was always clean and its bright green and blue coloring lifted spirits. Winds whipping off the lake made for some interesting highlights as well as cold night games, ice and snow were early spring givens and there were always the sea gulls—hundreds and hundreds of scavengers that would wait patiently for games to end and their feast to begin. If you didn't run for the exits when the game ended, you faced the possibility of a scene straight from Alfred Hitchcock's "The Birds."

Unlike many other high-tech parks, baseball was always front and center here and all seats within the playing field area were close to the action. There was always something to appreciate as the Blue Jays grew steadily from a baseball infant into an American League power—a rise fueled by such players as Dave Stieb, George Bell, Fred McGriff, Lloyd Moseby, Jesse Barfield, Jim Clancy, Jimmy Key, Roberto Alomar, Joe Carter and Tony Fernandez.

Exhibition Stadium took on a festive atmosphere in 1985 when the Jays captured their first A.L. East Division title and extended the Royals to the seventh game of the ALCS. A 1989 midseason move to the grand and glorious SkyDome presaged the team's rise to even greater heights—the beginning of another era in a baseball palace that would play host to World Series championships in 1992 and 1993.

Exhibition Stadium, with the CN Tower and Toronto skyline providing a scenic backdrop, was a football field with a baseball diamond fitted inside. Notice the dead area behind the right field fence and the distant scoreboard at the open end of the facility.

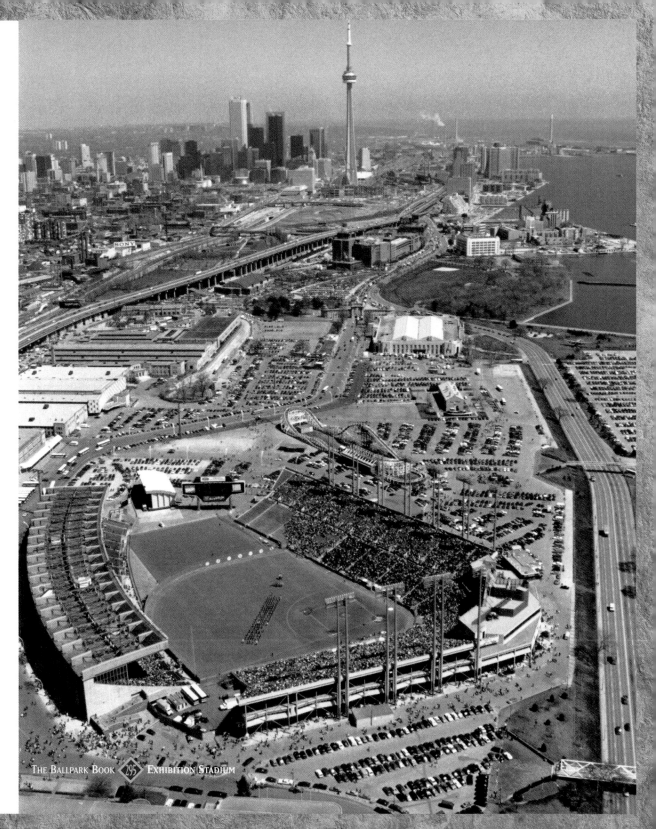

Griffith Stadium

Also known as American League Park (1903-1910); National Park (1911-1920)

Landing point of Mickey Mantle's 565-foot home run off Chuck Stobbs in 1953

Indians' 43-year-old Cy Young wins 500th game, July 19, 1910

Highs and lows: Goose Goslin hit six home runs in the 1924 and '25 World Series . . . Shortstop Roger Peckinpaugh committed Series-record eight errors in 1925

Johnson, pitching his 14th opening day game, defeats Eddie Rommel and A's 1-0 in 15 innings, April 13, 1926

Its tenants were Senators and the President of the United States was an influential neighbor. Through its gates passed key decision-makers and men of power who shaped the political direction of the nation from their offices only a few blocks away. For the best-connected facility in baseball history, Griffith Stadium sure was a major underachiever— a plain, surprisingly unpretentious and championship-starved ballpark of the people.

To appreciate Griffith Stadium you first have to understand the Washington Senators, a franchise that spent more than half a century living up to the old Vaudeville joke, "First in war, first in peace and last in the

BUCKY HARRIS: Boy manager led Senators to only championship as player-manager in 1924; managed team to 1,336 wins overall

Where Giants catcher Hank Gowdy (right) tripped over his mask and missed foul pop, setting stage for winning rally in Game 7 of 1924 World Series . . .

Where Earl McNeely's (left) 12th-inning grounder bounced high over head of Fred Lindstrom, giving Senators their only championship

Detroit's Walt Dropo gets record-tying 12th straight hit in second game of doubleheader, July 15, 1952

Center field indent provided
backyard space for five duplexes

Babe Ruth hit homer into trees over
center field indent . . . Lou Gehrig hit
ball out of stadium in '37 All-Star Game

A's slugger Jimmie Foxx hits
58th home run, Sept. 25, 1932

Tigers rookie Schoolboy Rowe drives in
deciding run, gains record-tying 16th
straight win, Aug. 25, 1934

Mel Ott's 10th-inning homer off Fred
Schulte's glove ends Game 5, gives Giants
1933 World Series title

Cardinals' Ken Boyer leads N.L. to 1956 All-Star
win with three hits, three defensive gems

Where Sam Rice
tumbled into temporary
stands while making
sensational Game 3-
saving catch vs. Pirates
in 1925 World Series

Johnson: 36-7, 1.09 ERA, 243 strikeouts,
11 shutouts in remarkable 1913 season

Johnson beats Detroit
for 300th win, May 14, 1920

Where Earl Averill smashed Dizzy Dean's
toe in 1937 All-Star Game

Home of two-time A.L. batting
champion Mickey Vernon

Where President William Howard Taft set
precedent by throwing out first ball in 1910
season opener, then watched Johnson
throw a one-hit shutout

WALTER JOHNSON:
Fireballing Big Train,
won 416 games
and compiled 2.17 career ERA

William Howard Taft started a Washington tradition in 1910 (left) when he became the first U.S. President to throw an opening day first pitch. The view from upper-grandstand seats down the right field line at Griffith were covered and generally good, if you didn't mind an occasional post.

GRIFFITH STADIUM (1903-1961)

Also known as American League Park (1903-1910); National Park (1911-1920)

The history of Griffith Stadium is a confusing one. The site of the stadium was known officially and unofficially by a number of names, beginning as far back as 1892.

It began as National Park, a 6,500-seat venue at Florida Avenue and Seventh Street NW. In 1901, the American League was formed and its Senators played elsewhere. But they moved back in 1903 and renamed the park National Park.

From 1903 to 1911, it was referred to as League Park, American League Park and National Park interchangeably. In 1911, when fire destroyed the park, it was rebuilt and named National Park.

In 1920, it was renamed Griffith Stadium, in honor of former manager and owner/president/manager Clark Griffith.

Statues to honor Clark Griffith and Senators great Walter Johnson stood outside the main entrance to the stadium. The stadium was demolished in 1965, but the Johnson memorial stands at Walter Johnson High School in Bethesda, Maryland, and the Griffith Memorial stands outside RFK Stadium.

First game: April 22, 1903. The Senators beat the New York Highlanders, 3-1, at then National Park.

Final game: September 21, 1961. Washington's former team — the Minnesota Twins — beat the new Senators, 6-3.

■ Site of three World Series (1924, '25 and '33)
■ Site of two All-Star Games (1937 and '56)

American League." While the Yankees, Red Sox, Tigers and A's dominated the A.L. standings, the Senators plodded through life, sometimes lovable, only occasionally talented enough to challenge for a pennant. This was a team that fit its ballpark—a patchwork structure built on the fly during baseball's steel-and-concrete era; a park that lacked a championship aura but made up for it with charm and character.

Griffith Stadium was a ballpark where you could hit a home run into a center field tree, bounce a ball off a 30-foot (make that 31) right field wall, watch pitchers warm up in a fair-territory bullpen, ricochet a shot off a right-angle fence, marvel at misconstructed grandstands or see a President throw out a season-opening pitch. It was a misshapen, rickety old pitcher's park, constructed under the direction of a former 240-game winner and in the image of the greatest righthander in baseball history.

Clark Griffith was a fading former pitcher in 1911 when National Park, home of the A.L. Senators since their 1903 relocation from American League Park, burned to the ground while the team was in spring training. Remarkably, enough of the facility was rebuilt (with steel and concrete) over the next three weeks to open the season on time and construction would continue gradually over the next decade, eventually producing a ballpark that would undergo only minor changes from 1920 until its 1961 demise.

As manager (1912-20), president and eventual team owner, Griffith molded the ballpark that would eventually carry his name around a big Kansas farmboy named Walter Johnson—an overpowering righthander who would win 416 games over a 21-year career. It was no coincidence that reconstructed Griffith measured 407 feet down the left field line, 421 to center and 328 down the right field line—with the imposing concrete wall to slap down deep line drives.

The original roofed double-deck grandstand wrapped behind home plate, extended just past the infield and gave way to covered single-deck stands that stretched to the foul poles. The 1920 renovation added second decks to the single-deck stands, but the new roof was about 15 feet higher than the original, giving the park a strange, patchwork look. The higher roof was necessary because the foul pole stands had been graded more steeply than those behind home plate.

Such oddities were plentiful at Griffith, where the field-level fences seemed to jut, turn and twist without reason as they snaked around the park's perimeter. Right field foul territory was more expansive than left field and the stands were notched behind the plate to form a backstop. The grandstands arced to a point at the foul lines—about 15 feet before reaching the poles. Thus there was a gap between the left field grandstand and long left field bleachers that stretched all the way from the foul pole to the center field indent.

Everybody remembers Griffith for that infamous indent, a spot in center field where the fence detoured around five duplexes (the owner wouldn't sell) and a huge tree, jutting to a point in the field of play and creating right angles on both sides. An American flag rose proudly from the point and a loudspeaker horn was mounted on top of the 30-foot barrier, which connected to the right field wall at the deepest point of the park.

A right-center field scoreboard was the same height as

The double-deck grandstands added in 1920 were about 15 feet higher than the original grandstands (above), which wrapped behind home plate. The outside of Griffith Stadium (left) was not ornate or stately, like the facades of its stadium counterparts in Philadelphia and Pittsburgh.

the wall and for most of the stadium's existence it was topped by advertisements featuring, at different times, National Bohemian Beer, Old Georgetown Beer, Chesterfield cigarettes and Coca-Cola. The National Bohemian sign had a three-dimensional beer bottle that protruded from the top, 56 feet above the ground. For a while, the home bullpen was a boxed-off area connecting the indent and wall in right-center field.

Griffith's color was not limited to physical oddities. This was the home of baseball's original megaphone man, E. Lawrence Phillips, and the site where, in 1910, William Howard Taft began a tradition that would continue throughout the park's Washington history—U.S. Presidents officially opening a season with a ceremonial first pitch from the box next to the first base dugout. This also was the home of the NFL's Redskins and a part-time home for several Negro League teams, including the Homestead Grays and power-hitting catcher Josh Gibson, who reportedly belted two moonshots over the left field bleachers.

When Griffith died in 1955, his nephew and adopted son Calvin took over the team and built an outfield bleacher addition, raising the park's peak capacity to 27,410. He also relocated the bullpen behind a 6-foot fence in the corner, reducing the left field distance to 350 feet and providing an inviting target for sluggers Harmon Killebrew, Bob Allison and Jim Lemon. That configuration remained intact until Calvin relocated his team to Minneapolis in 1960 and the expansion Washington Senators played their only Griffith Stadium season in 1961.

It was during the 1950s renovation that team officials discovered the right field foul line, which had always been marked at 328 feet, was really 320, and that the 30-foot right field wall was really 31 feet high. Such is the crazy mystique of Griffith Stadium,

where the Senators failed to post winning records in 40 of their 58 A.L. seasons. Three of their winning marks did produce A.L. pennants, however, and one, in 1924, gave Washington its only World Series championship.

Early Griffith featured a manual scoreboard perched atop its outer bleacher wall in left field—and topped by that popular Longines clock.